REG CHRISTENSEN

# FEAR NOT

## Messages of Hope, Healing, and Peace in the
## Book of Revelation

Cover image: *Misty Pine Grove* © Peter Zelei. Courtesy of istockphoto.com.
Cover design © 2010 by Covenant Communications, Inc.

Published by Covenant Communications, Inc.
American Fork, Utah

Printed in Canada
First Printing: October 2010

16 15 14 13 12 11 10    10 9 8 7 6 5 4 3 2 1

ISBN-13 978-1-59811-995-4

REG CHRISTENSEN

# FEAR NOT

Messages of Hope, Healing, and Peace in the
## Book of Revelation

Covenant Communications, Inc.

# Contents

# Preface

I HAVE COME TO APPRECIATE the book of Revelation as a message of hope, healing, peace, and triumph. In my gratitude for this knowledge and understanding of the book of Revelation, I have desired to write and share my thoughts with others. My hope is that you may read the book of Revelation and be enabled in plainness and simplicity to see the wonderful gems and jewels of inspired doctrine that are found therein.

About the time I was preparing for my mission and during the Vietnam War, I heard a little joke about the book of Revelation. The story goes that a soldier in the war was shot in the chest but had his life miraculously preserved. As the medics examined him, they found a pocket-sized Bible in his chest pocket and, upon closer examination, discovered that the bullet was not able to get through the book of Revelation. I think I laughed at the joke, but have also felt over the years that I could relate to the story much better than I cared to admit. In my first attempts to *get through* the book of Revelation, I seemed unable to penetrate the symbolism and strange language used by John the Revelator. My initial attempts to make any sense of it seemed futile.

You have perhaps heard the statement by the Prophet Joseph Smith wherein he referred to the Revelation of John as one of the *plainest* revelations ever given. A common response I have heard to this statement is, "That's easy for him to say—he has seen the movie." I have also been able to relate to *that* sentiment. I have wondered over the years if the vision would ever be plain to me.

As taught in the Book of Mormon, the prophet Nephi was able to see the things that John the Revelator later saw, but Nephi was not permitted to write the full account of his vision. "Behold, he shall see and write the remainder of these things. . . . And behold the things which this apostle of the Lamb shall write are many things which thou hast seen; and behold, the remainder shalt thou see" (1 Ne. 14:21, 24). Once again I confess that I have shared with some of my students the wish that Nephi had been permitted to just keep on writing in his plain and easy style.

During recent years, however, an interesting thing has happened. Even though I have much more to learn and understand about this wonderful vision, I have come to the realization that I have now been able to get through the book several times. It is becoming plain to me. And although I continue to enjoy the writings of Nephi and would still be interested at some eternal date in his edition of the continued vision of latter days, I have gained a deep sense of gratitude for the writings of John the Revelator. I am grateful that he was called by the Lord to write the remainder of the vision.

A few years ago, I decided to conduct a more in-depth study of the book of Revelation than I previously had. I examined the King James Version of the Bible, the Joseph Smith Translation of the Bible, the other standard works, the official published manuals of the Church Educational System, and a few other writings from some respected scholars. After a time of personal study, I organized some classes at our institute so we could study and discuss the book together. Our study has been an inspiring and enlightening experience. Why is this so and what have I learned?

I have learned that the Revelation of John is a revelation of peace, healing, triumph, power, hope, charity, faith—and, really, a revelation of the true and guiding principles of the gospel that help us through our mortal probation. It is so beautifully written and so wonderfully inspiring. In our present world where so many write about the times in which we live—and even specifically interpret the book of Revelation with a focus on the grotesque, the bizarre, the sensational, the doom and gloom, the scary, and the discouraging—John writes to uplift and to inspire and to invite all to come unto Christ and enjoy eternal life with him.

My purpose in writing is not to provide a verse-by-verse analytical commentary on the book of Revelation—there are inspiring and informative works already written that do this quite well. I am not attempting to offer an interpretation of every beast and symbol. I believe that there are many things in the Revelation that are not yet made known to mortals. I have no desire to speculate on some of the controversial symbols for which the meaning has not been revealed to us. Nor am I attempting to catalog or chronicle the book.

What I desire to do is present some questions for your consideration and to share some insights about the book of Revelation. Although I will not have the blessing of hearing your responses to my questions, I trust that *you* will hear your responses as well as the response from the Spirit and that you will be encouraged, motivated, and inspired by what you hear.

As you read this book, I hope:
- To offer you a comfortable and simple perspective of the book of Revelation. I hope that you may then continue to study the vision, having gained some helpful hints for future thought and reference.
- That you will find this book to be a fairly easy read, and that the experiences and insights shared will make sense.
- To assist you in looking beyond the symbolism to spiritual meanings, principles, and doctrines. I hope you will be prompted by the connections I have made to my personal life to make your own helpful connections to your personal life.
- To help you gain a greater sense of appreciation for our latter-day revelation and how much our lives are blessed by the ministry and mission of our living prophets.
- To help you discover a few basic, hopeful messages from each chapter. I hope that these messages will become more clear to you than they may have been in the past.
- That you will be guided by the sustaining influence of the Holy Ghost—who is the true teacher of gospel truth.

There is one question I will suggest at the outset that I hope will serve as a constant guide for you throughout this book: *How can I find hope, healing, peace, and triumph in the Revelation of John?* At the end of your reading and pondering, if you have successfully answered that question many times over and have found multiple examples of these inspiring themes, I will be very grateful.

As life has tossed me around, I have sought for peace and for healing. Years ago, I would not have guessed that I would have found such peace and healing in such a strange place as the Revelation of John—but that is exactly what has happened. I have come to know that the book of Revelation is really an invitation from our Lord and Savior to "Come . . . and take the water of life freely" (Rev. 22:17). I invite you to accept this profound invitation from our Savior. The messages of hope, healing, peace, and triumph are there if we will diligently and humbly seek them out.

# An Invitation

# "Ye Ought to Search the Scriptures"

WHAT ARE SOME OF THE *greatest invitations you have ever received?* Let's review a great invitation offered by the prophet Alma. As he was diligently teaching and ministering to the poor Zoramites who had been cast from their synagogues, he challenged them to search the scriptures. To them he said, "Behold, ye have said that ye could not worship your God because ye are cast out of your synagogues. But behold, I say unto you, if ye suppose that ye cannot worship God, ye do greatly err, and *ye ought to search the scriptures*" (Alma 33:2; emphasis added). Yes, we really "ought to search the scriptures." I invite you to personally search your own scriptures as you read this book.

During my years of teaching seminary, I sometimes used a simple little mind exercise at the beginning of the year to try to help motivate and remind my students to actually have their scriptures in hand and use them in both our class and their personal study time. I asked them to pretend that they were flying in an airplane that was well stocked with every imaginable type of survival equipment and provision. Within their reach they would find tools, radios, protective clothing of many varieties, food, water, shelter, first-aid supplies, medicine, global positioning equipment, fishing gear, and most anything else they could imagine.

I then asked the students to pretend that they just learned that the airplane is going to crash momentarily, and they have time to choose only one item to take with them. I then invited them to share which one item they would choose and why. Some said the radio system would be the best choice so they could call for help. Others said water would be the most essential—and so forth. Usually within moments, one alert student would declare the obvious that others had apparently taken for granted: "I would choose a parachute." How profound! How basic! How essential! I would then explain that our scriptures are like *spiritual parachutes* and that they serve us only when they are opened and used properly. Occasionally when a student forgot to get his scriptures from the shelf, I reminded, "We are ready to study—you will need your parachute." I believe, and I tried to teach them to believe, that strength and power come to us from carrying and using our scriptures.

In getting acquainted through the *Church News* with Elder David A. Bednar of the Quorum of the Twelve Apostles, I was pleased to read of a tradition at BYU—Idaho. During the weekly devotional, the students there hold their scriptures in the air to show that they are ready to be taught from the scriptures. As Elder Bednar spoke to the students shortly after his call to the Quorum of the Twelve, he reminisced about the tradition and reminded them that the reason for it was to demonstrate that they were ready to be taught from their scriptures by the power of the Holy Ghost.

As you read the verses I quote in my writing, I invite you to turn to your own scriptures. By my writing, I hope to simply help guide and inspire you to ponder the words of the scriptures and to seek and find the personalized peace and healing contained in the book of Revelation. I want the book to taste good to you—not to be a bitter herb of frightful sorrow and despair.

The Prophet Joseph Smith, in his discourse known as the King Follett Sermon, taught the *sweetness* of the doctrines of eternal life. Just as we can taste honey and recognize its sweetness, we can know of the sweetness of true gospel doctrine. My sincere hope is that as you traverse the pages of the book of Revelation, it will taste good to you and offer you much peace, hope, and healing. I invite you to open up your own spiritual parachutes as we jump into our study of the Revelation of John.

# Introduction of the Revelator

*WHEN YOU PREPARE TO READ a book, what is the first thing you want to know, and why is this knowledge important for you?* Personally, I want to know the qualifications of the author. Does he write with knowledge, experience, and authority? Is he qualified to present his intended message? What is his purpose in writing? I recently read a great biography of an American president; the book was recommended by one of our institute students whom I love and respect for his scholarship, spiritual depth, and searching and analytical mind. His recommendation alone would have been sufficient to whet my appetite for the book he was recommending. He then told me that one of his professors at the university commended the author of the biography as probably the nation's foremost historian about that particular president. I now had a double recommendation, and I went into the book with great anticipation of learning an accurate and enlightening account of a great man. I was not disappointed—my study was as expected.

*Who is the author of the book of Revelation, and how is he qualified to write such a vision?* Let's examine what I believe to be the most profound qualification of John's authorship. In Nephi's vision, the angel tells him, "But the things which thou shalt see hereafter thou shalt not write; for the Lord God hath ordained the apostle of the Lamb of God that he should write them" (1 Ne. 14:25). In other words, John, the Apostle of the Lamb, has been ordained or appointed by *the Lamb—even Jesus Christ*—to be the official historian of the events of the latter days as shown him in vision. There is no higher qualification or endorsement than that. The Creator of heaven and earth has commissioned an ordained Apostle to write. This verse alone should greatly increase our confidence in John as an official historian of the events that precede and include the winding-up scenes of the temporal world.

We learn more about John from the seventh section of the Doctrine and Covenants. The Prophet Joseph Smith and Oliver Cowdery were wondering about the status of John—had he died, or was he still on the earth? Section 7 is a translated version of an actual record John had made. The main message of the record is that the Prophet learned that John was granted the blessing of the Lord to tarry until the Second Coming and that he would "prophesy before nations, kindreds, tongues and people." He was to be "a ministering angel . . . for those who shall be heirs of salvation who dwell on the earth" (D&C 7:3, 6).

We have the blessed assurance of the protection of the priesthood on the earth. Even through the long centuries of apostasy and darkness when the organized Church of God was absent from the earth, it is comforting to remember that the Apostles who did not die—John the Beloved and the Three Nephites—held the priesthood and remained on the earth to keep Satan in proper bounds.

We sometimes refer to John as a member of the First Presidency. As I think of the personal love and respect I have for our current First Presidency and the collective love and respect we have as a church for them, it is not too difficult to transfer that love and respect to the Apostle John. John, along with Peter and James, was appointed by the Savior to hold the keys of presidency. These three men received their endowment of eternal life while on the Mount of Transfiguration and were visited and ministered to by angelic beings in their preparation to serve as the First Presidency of their day.

We thus have an ordained and endowed Apostle, a member of the First Presidency, and a man of faith and courage who has been specifically appointed and ordained to be the author of one of the greatest revelations ever given to mankind. Authors just do not get higher recommendation than that! We can read and study the book of Revelation with great confidence that it is the true word of God, revealed to His true messenger.

# Introduction of the Revelation

*NOW THAT WE BETTER KNOW the Revelator, how can we better know the Revelation and its purpose?* I believe that the place to begin to understand the Revelation of John is with another revelator—actually a pair of them: the prophet Lehi and his son Nephi. The visions and revelations experienced by Lehi and Nephi can help guide our understanding of the Revelation of John. Chapters 8 through 14 of 1 Nephi serve well as introductory chapters to the book of Revelation and help establish a framework, context, and timeline for the Revelation of John. The plain and precious doctrines taught in these chapters become, in essence, the plain and precious doctrines taught in the book of Revelation. The message is the same. The message is inviting and beautiful. The message is a great invitation for all to come unto Christ and in Him find peace, joy, and salvation.

Lehi, like John, had the privilege of looking to the future. For both, this future was undoubtedly a vision of high adventure— mingled with some uncertainty and a great dose of sadness for those who would not follow the gospel path. The vision of Lehi becomes a profound roadmap for us here and now in plotting our course through our mortal probation. For me personally, Nephi's expanded and interpretive commentary of his father's vision is very motivating and has prompted in me much contemplation of the peace and divine assistance our Lord offers us. Let's sample a few of Nephi's teachings.

In the eleventh chapter of Nephi, we learn that he had a strong desire to "know the things that my father had seen." Being "caught away in the Spirit of the Lord" he was able to see and understand his father's inspired vision. I love the profound and simple logic of the Holy Ghost in conversing with Nephi: "And the Spirit said unto me: Believest thou that thy father saw the tree of which he hath spoken? And I said: Yea, thou knowest that I believe all the words of my father." This "believing heart" response of Nephi caused the Spirit to shout, "Hosanna" and to proclaim, "blessed art thou, Nephi, because thou believest in the Son of the most high God" (1 Ne. 11:1, 4–6).

For emphasis, let's restate this message in a simplistic paraphrase:

THE HOLY GHOST: Nephi, do you believe in the tree?
NEPHI: Yes.
THE HOLY GHOST: How wonderful—you believe in Christ!

As Nephi's vision continues, he actually sees the tree his father saw: "And I looked and beheld a tree; and it was like unto the tree which my father had seen; and the beauty thereof was far beyond, yea exceeding of all beauty" (1 Ne. 11:8). The Holy Ghost then asked Nephi, "What desirest thou?" (v. 10). Nephi replied, "To know the interpretation thereof" (v. 11). To this, the Holy Ghost invited him to "look" (v. 12). As Nephi did so, he saw a wonderful vision of the condescension of God the Father and Christ. He saw Mary, the mother of Jesus, and saw that she became "the mother of the Son of God, after the manner of the flesh" (v. 18). He then saw the "Lamb of God, yea, even the Son of the Eternal Father" and was subsequently asked, "Knowest thou the meaning of the tree which thy father saw?" (v. 21). To this question, Nephi replies, "Yea, it is the love of God, which sheddeth itself abroad in the hearts of the children of men; wherefore, it is the most desirable above all things" (v. 22).

*What "is the most desirable above all things?" If you could get to the very depth and core of your heart and soul, what is it that you most desire above all else?* I believe that if we fully and truthfully answer these questions, we will conclude that to obtain eternal life through the grace and mercy of our Lord and Savior would be the *very* most desirable thing we could ever hope to obtain. The Lord sustains this conclusion: "And, if you keep my commandments and endure to the end you shall have eternal life, which gift is the greatest of all the gifts of God" (D&C 14:7).

As Nephi's vision continues, he begins to appreciate and understand the life and ministry of the Savior and the beautiful plan of salvation by which this great gift of eternal life is brought about in the lives of the human family. He sees the great Redeemer and His baptism, ministry, Judgment, Crucifixion, and ultimate triumph over evil. He tastes the sweetness of the plan of redemption. He envisions the "greatest of all the gifts of God." He sees the Lord assisting and enabling us to overcome evil and partake of this greatest gift.

The vision of Nephi is thus also the vision of John. By studying and understanding these beautiful visions of Lehi and Nephi, we are *previewing* and *overviewing* the book of Revelation. The message is that our Father in Heaven and our Savior live and that They love us. Father in Heaven has provided a plan whereby we can return to live with Him. Our Savior holds the power and the authority to carry out the Father's plan. The path of our return is sure, and all are invited to follow it.

As we follow the path, there will be many distractions and enticements to tempt and persuade us to wander from the path. The lure of the "great and spacious building" (1 Ne. 8:26) will be powerful and compelling. Many will wander. Many will be lost. Many will die—physically and spiritually. Life will be scary. Our Father and our Savior stand firm and invite us to come safely unto Them. We can come safely unto Them if we are willing and faithful.

The grand theme of the book of Revelation is of the permanent and eternal triumph of good over evil—of Christ over Satan. Try as we might, humankind will not, with our own strength, solve the problems of the world. For salvation, we must put our trust not in the arm of flesh, but in the redeeming power of our Savior. All of the symbolism and imagery of the book of Revelation lead us to this one conclusion—that through the Atonement of Jesus Christ, eternal victory over death and hell is achieved.

Nephi now passes the torch to a new author—even John the Revelator. What a beautiful vision he offers us! What a wonderful plan Father in Heaven gives us!

# Chapter One
# The Power and Glory of the Risen Lord

*IF YOU WERE SHOPPING FOR a service to be performed—to have your house painted or your car tuned up—what would you want to know about the qualifications of the painter or the technician? How would you gain your desired information?* You might ask trusted friends to refer you to someone well qualified—someone with whom they have had personal experience. I was recently interested in a particular service and learned from an advertisement in the phone directory that the technician had thirty years of experience in his trade. This knowledge gave me greater confidence in the man's abilities. I correctly supposed that in thirty years of work, he would have encountered most, if not all, of the challenges he would likely encounter in my project. His experience would insure that he would know how to do what I wanted done.

Chapter 1 of the Revelation of John speaks confidence to us of the position of our Savior. It tells us who He is and what He does and what qualifies Him to do His work. What assuring knowledge could be more essential and appropriate than this as we begin our study of the Revelation?

## READ, HEAR, KEEP, AND UNDERSTAND . . . BY GRACE
*What is the role of the Lord's grace in helping us to know and understand the doctrines of eternal life?* Recall that the Savior told Nephi that John the Beloved would write the remainder of the Revelation. The very first verse now confirms this appointment and informs us that this is truly "The Revelation of Jesus Christ, which God gave unto him . . . sent and signified . . . by his angel unto his servant John" (Rev. 1:1). John

has received his commission and begins the writing of his revelation with a charge to us who read the vision. The Lord does not want us to grope in darkness but rather wants us to be informed—to know the signs of His coming and what we must do to prepare.

From verse 3 we learn that we are to read, hear, and keep the words and message of the prophecy. From the Joseph Smith Translation of the same verse, we can also add the charge to "understand." The wonderful message of peace, hope, and joy available from the Revelation can come to us only if we are willing to pay the price of reading and pondering and praying for enlightenment to understand. As we come to understand the message, we need to be willing to keep—in other words, *do*—what we are charged to do. This charge is the same as given us by the prophet Moroni in the Book of Mormon—that we should be willing to "ask with a sincere heart, with real intent, having faith in Christ" (Moroni 10:4).

*Do we have this "real intent"? What could enable and motivate us to have such resolve?* John does not leave us to wonder for long as he bids us "grace" and "peace from him which is, and which was, and which is to come" (Rev. 1:4). Grace is divine assistance from God and Christ. Grace is a power of enabling us to have the strength, courage, and wisdom to know what we must know and to do what we must do to gain eternal life. As we do all that we can personally do in faith and humility, the Lord, through His divine grace, assists us in going the extra mile to achieve the victory. (As we will discover at the conclusion of the book of Revelation, this beautiful doctrine of grace stands as bookends, appearing at both the beginning and the end of the book.)

Let's illustrate this thought of grace and enabling power using the words of the Lord to the prophet Abraham. The Lord taught Abraham that "if two things exist, and there be one above the other, there shall be greater things above them" (Abr. 3:16). Following this statement is a discussion of the stars and planets of the heavens. The discussion then shifts to spirits, and we learn that "if there be two spirits, and one shall be more intelligent than the other; there shall be another more intelligent than they; I am the Lord thy God, and I am more intelligent than they all" (Abr. 3:19).

As I have pondered this passage, I have sought to understand why the Lord would make such a point of telling us that He is more intelligent than everyone else. Is this an idle boast? Certainly that cannot be, since He is of perfect motive and character, and such would not include idle boasting. Is it pride? Unrighteous pride could simply not come from one who is perfect in all things. I am left to conclude that the statement *I am more intelligent than they all* must be a statement of humility, grace, love, and reaching out to help us all. I can imagine the Lord saying, *Do not get caught up with comparing yourselves to others. If you do, you will be setting yourselves up for frustration and disappointment because you will always be able to find someone smarter or richer or more eloquent.*

The only comparison we ever need to make is not with our neighbor, but with our own past. Our guiding questions become, *How am I doing now compared with how I have done before? Am I steadily and faithfully moving in the right direction? Do I have sufficient faith and trust in the Lord to know that He can and will help me obtain eternal life?*

We might imagine the Lord saying to us, "Just humbly trust that I, your Savior, have the power and the ability to enable you to overcome the world and to someday gain eternal life. I love you with a perfect love and I know how to exalt you."

Our Savior's desire to exalt us is affirmed by John: "And hath made us kings and priests unto God and his Father; to him be glory and dominion for ever and ever" (Rev. 1:6).

To better understand the message that the Savior desires eternal life for us, let's look at a few scriptural passages. The first is the statement of the Lord to Moses: "For behold, this is my work and my glory—to bring to pass the immortality and eternal life of man" (Moses 1:39). In this statement is revealed the true and pure motive of our God—He loves us and wants to save us. He enables us to attain immortality and eternal life. That is why He reminds us that He is "more intelligent than they all."

The next passage is from the Book of Mormon. Speaking of our progression along the path to eternal life, Nephi reminds us how salvation and eternal life will come to us with these words: "for ye have not come thus far save it were by the word of Christ with unshaken faith in him, relying wholly upon the merits of him who is mighty to save" (2 Ne. 31:19). He is "mighty to save" and has the intelligence, power, humility, love, and charity to help us gain exaltation. His greatest desire for us all is that we will reach out and accept of His offering of grace and thereby gain exaltation in celestial glory.

### Ten Thousand Saints—Washed in Blood

*How may we be forgiven of our sins? How may we become qualified for exaltation?* John speaks of Christ as "him that loved us, and washed us from our sins in his own blood" (Rev. 1:5). This presents to us an interesting metaphor of being washed clean in blood. During his mighty wrestle before God, Enos hungered for peace, hope, and forgiveness. In response to his pleadings, the Lord answered, "Enos, thy sins are forgiven thee, and thou shalt be blessed. And I, Enos, knew that God could not lie; wherefore, my guilt was swept away. And I said: Lord, how is it done? And he said unto me: Because of thy faith in Christ, whom thou hast never before heard nor seen. And many years pass away before he shall manifest himself in the flesh; wherefore, go to, thy faith hath made thee whole" (Enos 1:5–8).

As the Savior ministered to the Nephites, He taught them, "And no unclean thing can enter into his kingdom; therefore nothing entereth into his rest save it be those who have washed their garments in my blood, because of their faith, and the repentance of all their sins, and their faithfulness unto the end" (3 Ne. 27:19). This blessing of being washed from our sins in His blood becomes available to us from our constant prayer, our unshakable faith, our continuing repentance, and our enduring faithfulness.

*But given all the people who seem so good and so valiant, do I really have a chance of gaining exaltation?* Yes, you really *do* have a chance of gaining exaltation. The granting of eternal life is not restricted by caps or quotas. Not only do we have a chance—we have the absolute assurance that we may gain exaltation if we come unto Christ and live as He asks us to live. It concerns me that in our limited mortal view, we may contemplate the imposing task of washing from us our sins and may then develop a false notion of the capacity of the Atonement. The infinite and eternal nature of the perfect Atonement is that there is provision for all.

It also concerns me that sometimes we may wonder if the celestial kingdom of God is not just a place reserved for those who may attain a high status in the leadership of the Church. This concern is answered in the Joseph Smith Translation of Revelation 1:7, which states, "For behold, he cometh in the clouds *with ten thousands of his saints in the kingdom, clothed with the glory of his Father"* (emphasis added).

The number *ten thousand* should be testament enough to teach us that there seems to be adequate provision for all in eternal glory, but some understanding of number symbolism can further enhance our hope and perception. The number *ten* simply means "fullness" or "completeness." As an example, the parable of the ten virgins is not a parable about only ten virgins but is rather a representative parable about those who are valiant and prepare themselves and those who do not. The five wise virgins are simply representative of the myriads of Saints who prepare themselves for exaltation.

As we ponder these verses, let's feel the magnitude of the glory and power of Christ. He really can wash us from our sins and can qualify us to be kings unto God, which glory will last forever and ever. His grace really is sufficient for all who are willing to be humble and to keep the commandments. There really is no maximum seating capacity in the celestial kingdom.

## ALPHA AND OMEGA—THE FINISHER

*It seems that so much has gone wrong in my life—how can it all be made right?* The prophet Nephi taught, "For we labor diligently to write, to persuade our children, and also our brethren, to believe in Christ, and to be reconciled to God; for we know that it is by grace that we are saved, after all we can do" (2 Ne. 25:23). The doctrine that we are saved by the grace of Christ after all we can do prompts the question, *How does He do it—how does Christ take all of the successes, trials, failures, and joys of our life and blend them into a soul qualified for exaltation?* We read in the Revelation, "I am Alpha and Omega, the beginning and the ending, saith the Lord, which is, and which was, and which is to come, the Almighty" (Rev. 1:8). My ponderings of this verse have led me to consider two key words that have become very useful in helping me understand and appreciate the saving roles of Christ in my life. The words are *Finisher* and *Orchestrator.*

Let's begin with the concept of Christ as *Finisher,* something I will illustrate with a personal and practical example. I have spent a fair amount of my life doing handyman things—carpentry, roofing, floor covering, tree removal, and so on. I own many tools, but since I do not engage in any one trade on a full-time basis, it is impractical for me to own every tool I might need to perform all of the tasks that come my way. I have grown very appreciative of the tool and equipment rental businesses in our area, especially A to Z Rentals. It did not take long for me to figure out that, as their title suggests, they would pretty well be able to supply any tool or piece of equipment needed for most tasks I would need to perform. Over the years, I have rented from them chain saws, stump grinders, log splitters, pneumatic nailers, power washers, and cherry pickers. I have learned that they really are A-to-Z people—they really can supply most everything I need to *finish* my work.

Alpha and Omega are the first and last letters of the Greek alphabet. Using the analogy of the A-to-Z folks, it is not too difficult for me to think of Christ not just as Alpha and Omega—but also as Gamma, Delta, Iota, Sigma, Upsilon—and all other letters of the alphabet. He is not just the "first and the last" and the Finisher, but He is everything in between. As we learn from latter-day scripture, "Thus saith the Lord your God, even Jesus Christ, the Great I Am, Alpha and Omega, the beginning and the end, the same which looked upon the wide expanse of eternity, and all the seraphic hosts of heaven, before the world was made; The same *which knoweth all things, for all things are present before mine eyes*" (D&C 38:1–2; emphasis added). Christ is omniscient, omnipresent, and omnipotent. He has the tools, the ability, and the power to see and to know all that we deal with, and He has the power to help us bring our lives into harmony with the will of God through His eternal plan of happiness for us.

Recently as I began the task of removing a large, dying tree from our yard, I did not want to simply cut it down—I wanted to cut it up, clean up the limbs and debris, remove the stump, haul in new soil, and plant new lawn where the tree once stood. I did not just need a chain saw—I needed a variety of tools to help me finish my work. Such is the case with our Lord and Savior. He does not want to simply *begin* the process of our salvation—he wants to *finish* the process. It is not enough for us to just hear and accept the gospel and be baptized—He wants to help us finish our upward quest for exaltation by continuing on the gospel path.

As the prophet Moroni taught, "And after they had been received unto baptism, and were wrought upon and cleansed by the power of the Holy Ghost, they were numbered among the people of the church of Christ; and their names were taken, that they might be remembered and nourished by the good word of God, to keep them in the right way, to keep them continually watchful unto prayer, relying alone upon the merits of Christ, who was the author and the *finisher* of their faith" (Moroni 6:4; emphasis added). The great "Alpha and Omega" is a finisher. He sees the end from the beginning and has all of the needed tools to help us *finish* our course to eternal life.

## THE ALMIGHTY—THE ORCHESTRATOR

My second key word in understanding Alpha and Omega is *Orchestrator*. I think of a conductor of a great musical performance who organizes and directs the performers and helps correlate a wide range of talent into a polished and inspiring performance. To *orchestrate* is "to arrange or control the elements of, as to achieve a desired overall effect"[1] or to "combine in a harmonious way."[2]

The Greek word for the title *Almighty* is *pantokrator* and means basically one who has might, power, and dominion and who organizes, regulates, and holds all things together. For me, that definition seems to fit comfortably with my concept of *orchestrator*. Christ has the power and the might to orchestrate and direct our lives to our desired outcome of eternal life. He is capable of orchestrating all of the elements of our lives into the great finished product of an exalted being. As we come unto Him, our lives come into sweet harmony with His divine purpose for us.

I will illustrate the concept of Christ as the Orchestrator with a Christmas season performance of *Music and the Spoken Word* that my wife and I attended in the LDS Conference Center. The center was beautifully decorated with all of the color and light of the season. It was evident that many people had worked many hours to get everything just right. We always like to arrive early and enjoy the rehearsal of the performance. This affords us the double benefit of hearing the beautiful music and the inspiring message two times. We also enjoy watching the many behind-the-scenes activities. There are sound, light, and camera technicians busily performing their varied tasks. The narrator practices his presentation. The members of the orchestra and the members of the choir use this time to adjust and rehearse their parts under direction of the gifted conductor—truly a master of his trade.

To my untrained musical ear that day, the practice session already seemed perfect, but it was apparently not yet up to the standard of the master. After a complete rehearsal of the full program, he continued an intense fine-tuning of the performance. He had the choir sing one part over several times. He directed the narrator to repeat the introduction a few times as he better coordinated this spoken word with the music. After he seemed satisfied, he dismissed the musicians for a short break, during which time we as the congregation were instructed on what was expected of us during the actual performance.

Finally came the great moment. I watched the technician signing a final countdown and then the performance commenced. It was thirty minutes of perfection and inspiration. Everything was done just right and was evidence not just of the morning rehearsal but of many lifetimes of dedication in the development of so many varied talents. It was awe inspiring! It was a portrayal of the true spirit and feeling of Christmas. For me, it was also a metaphor of the role and mission of Christ. As spoken to the Prophet Joseph, Christ has "descended below" all things (D&C 122:8). There is no joy, sorrow, heartache, betrayal, disappointment, success, or emotion that He does not understand. If we are willing to come unto Him in humility and with real intent, He can orchestrate every aspect of our being into a well-blended and perfected eternal life.

*How does the knowledge of Christ as Alpha and Omega and as the Almighty increase your personal confidence in His ability to help you overcome your trials and to exalt you?* I love these inspiring words of Christ: "And if men come unto me I will show unto them their weakness. I give unto men weakness that they may be humble; and my grace is sufficient for all men that humble themselves before me; for if they humble themselves before me, and have faith in me, then will I make weak things become strong unto them" (Ether 12:27). The great Alpha and Omega, the Lord Almighty, can help orchestrate all the elements of our lives to achieve the desired overall effect of our immortality and eternal life.

## THE LIGHT OF THE SEVEN GOLDEN CANDLESTICKS

*How do we find testimony of Christ in a lamp stand burning with olive oil?* John is now instructed to write what he sees in a book and distribute it to the seven churches: "What thou seest, write in a book, and send it unto the seven churches which are in Asia; unto Ephesus, and unto Smyrna, and unto Pergamos, and unto Thyatira, and unto Sardis, and unto Philadelphia, and unto Laodicea" (Rev. 1:11). The balance of the first chapter is mostly a depiction of how the Savior deals with and supports the members and leaders of the seven churches. Since He is unchanging in His principles, these ideas certainly have application to us in our day, regardless of which branch or ward of the Church we may make our residence. It is inspiring to contemplate how He leads those whom He loves and serves.

We learn that the seven churches are represented in the vision by seven candlesticks centered on Christ as their leader and master: "And I turned to see the voice that spake with me. And being turned, I saw seven golden candlesticks; And in the midst of the seven candlesticks one like unto the Son of man, clothed with a garment down to the foot, and girt about the paps with a golden girdle. His head and his hairs were white like wool, as white as snow; and his eyes were as a flame of fire. And his feet like unto fine brass, as if they burned in a furnace; and his voice as the sound of many waters" (Rev. 1:12–15).

Our first impulse may be to think of a modern candelabra holding wax candles, but it is more natural and instructive to think of the seven-branched menorah of ancient times. We can now envision seven oil lamps full of olive oil and lighted at the wick placed in each lamp. We are taught in the book of Moses that "all things have their likeness, and all things are created and made to bear record of [the Savior]" (Moses 6:63). In other words, if we seek for Christ, we can find Him throughout all of His creation.

Let's first discuss the light of the lamp stand. It is helpful to remember that candlesticks, or lamps, simply carry light but do not *create* it. Light is created and disseminated by the Light of the World, even Christ. The Light of Christ is a universal, divine influence that guides all of God's children in their earthly course. This light or divine power, if heeded, is what inspires and enables all of mankind to goodness. Our lives are constantly blessed and uplifted by the Light of the World—even Jesus Christ.

*How does Christ, the Light of the World, deal with the members of the seven churches and, therefore, with you and with me?* The number *seven* is symbolic of perfection and completeness. Think, for example, of how many times we are to forgive. Seven times? Seventy times seven times? No—we are to *perfectly* and *completely* forgive (see Matt. 18:22). Christ deals completely with all people of all wards and branches by standing in their midst and uplifting them and enabling them.

As I contemplate this image of Christ uplifting His saints, I consider the central message of the classic film, *Mr. Krueger's Christmas.* In the film, Mr. Krueger is a widowed apartment custodian who finds escape from his lonely life through several daydreams. In one daydream, he finds himself visiting and worshipping the newborn baby Jesus in the manger. He expresses his gratitude to his Savior for uplifting and strengthening him throughout his trials—particularly at the time of the death of his beloved wife. So it is with us—Christ does stand firm in our midst and uplifts us through our trials.

The Book of Mormon helps us clarify the relationship between us as Latter-day Saints striving to be "*a* light unto the world" and our Savior as "*the* light of the world." In His ministry to the Nephites, the Savior taught, "Behold, I am the law, and the light. Look unto me, and endure to the end, and ye shall live; for unto him that endureth to the end will I give eternal life." A few verses later, He says, "Ye are my disciples; and ye are *a* light unto this people, who are a remnant of the house of Joseph." And a few chapters after that He goes on to say, "Therefore, hold up your light that it may shine unto the world. Behold I am the light which ye shall hold up—that which ye have seen me do" (3 Ne. 15:9, 12; 18:24; emphasis added). From my study of the Revelation, I now have fixed in my mind an image of my Savior standing—not far away, but close at hand. He is even in our midst and is ready and willing and able to sustain and support us in our lives. Our charge is to hold Him up to all in the world so that all may come and receive of His gifts.

## THE OIL OF PEACE AND HEALING
*How can an understanding of the oil of the candlestick serve as a lesson to us about the peace and healing available from our Savior?* We gain

inspiration from considering the olive oil used to fuel the lamps and the symbolism and the meaning thereof. Olive oil is representative of healing. Think of the parable of the man who was robbed and beaten by thieves. The "certain Samaritan . . . went to him and bound up his wounds, pouring in oil and wine" (Luke 10:30–34).

The oil also represents peace. It is significant that the dove, itself a symbol of peace, returned to Noah with an olive leaf (see Gen. 8:11). The Prophet Joseph Smith received a wonderful revelation of hope and peace that he designated the "olive leaf . . . plucked from the Tree of Paradise, the Lord's message of peace to us" (D&C 88, section heading).

The oil also represents the atoning blood of our Savior. The word *Gethsemane* means "olive press." Olives that are pressed in an olive press give up precious oil. In Gethsemane, when our Savior was pressed upon for the sins of the world, He gave up His precious blood.

The light, healing, and peace we have described are also attributes of the Holy Ghost. In ancient Israel, the leaders were anointed with olive oil, reminding them that they were to rule by the direction of the Spirit.

As we blend all of this imagery together, we have in our focus the Savior of the world—the very Light of the World, standing in the midst of His spiritual children proffering them peace, light, healing, and redemption through His atoning, sinless sacrifice. His very appearance bespeaks His purity and virtue. If we were to seek out the common thread woven through His "golden girdle," "his head and his hairs . . . white like wool, as white as snow," "his eyes . . . as a flame of fire," "his feet like unto fine brass, as if they burned in a furnace" (Rev. 1:13–15), we would have a living symbol of the purity for which we all strive and to which we may all attain by acceptance of His gospel. Such whiteness and virtue also stand symbolic of His victory over sin and death. Here we have a formula for moral victory—being moral brings victory. If we are willing to "let virtue garnish [our] thoughts unceasingly," we can have the peace and healing of the Spirit to guide us to "an everlasting dominion" (D&C 121:45–46) of eternal life.

## SERVANTS IN THE HAND OF CHRIST

*When have you felt the sustaining power of the Savior in your life?* It is inspiring to observe that as Christ stands amidst His churches, He holds in His right hand the servants of those churches. "And he had in his right hand seven stars" (Rev. 1:16). (Note that in verse 20, the "stars" are described as "angels." In the Joseph Smith Translation of Rev. 1:20 found in the footnote, the word *angels* is changed to *servants*.) We can be assured that servants of the kingdom who diligently try to serve in the manner Christ prescribes experience His upholding power and influence.

As a personal example of this sustaining power, I remember the time I served as bishop of my ward. I lived just across the street from our meetinghouse, and the bishop's office was on the opposite side of the building from my home. In order to get to my office, I often walked through the chapel. At the hours I came and went, it was usually unoccupied, peaceful, and quiet. Often I approached my tasks as bishop with a feeling of wonder and inadequacy. How could I, a layman in such matters, offer counsel on how to save a marriage? What could I do or say to help motivate a hardened sinner to seek a softened heart? Where did I get my station, as a sinner myself, to call another soul to repentance? And so went the endless barrage of questions through my mind and heart. But I had been called and I was the Lord's *star* or *servant,* and I knew that I was entitled to His *upholding.*

I always tried to arrive early enough to ponder and pray and prepare. Then the people came, the challenges surfaced, and the questions arose. I responded with counsel and scriptures and doctrines and priesthood blessings and sometimes laughter and tears and happiness and heartache. Then the evening of service concluded and I started for home, back through the quiet chapel. I often stopped there and just sat alone in the dim light for a while. I recalled the many sermons I had heard preached from the pulpit—and the many I had preached. My mind flooded with the many testimonies I had heard borne—and had borne myself. I recalled the countless times I had partaken of the sacrament there. The accumulated inspiration of years of hearing inspiring music enveloped my soul.

After a while, I went home with a grateful heart and a sure witness that the so-called *mantle of a bishop* is very real indeed. I felt the love of my Savior who, in a sense, was upholding me in His right hand, and I arrived home so grateful for His love of me and of those I was called to serve. I was profoundly grateful that my Savior had lived and died and was "alive forevermore," and that He held the "keys of hell of and death" (Rev. 1:18).

And thus we have the first chapter—an introduction to us of the Savior of the world. We have the absolute assurance that even though the devil may seem to have a never-ending stranglehold on planet earth, he will not prevail over true Saints. We are all invited to come unto Christ and become true Saints. In due time our Savior, exercising His keys of death and hell, will lock Satan away in the place prepared for him and we will go forward in our quest in a world of peace, hope, healing, and triumph. What joy comes to us as we realize the power and majesty of our Savior! What a great preface we are given in Chapter 1 to the inspiring Revelation of John the Beloved!

# Chapter Two
# Overcome Evil with Good— Gain Eternal Life

*WHY DO YOU READ THE SCRIPTURES? When you read, what are you looking for?* Many years ago as I was just beginning my seminary teaching career, the Church Educational System produced a modern and motivating filmstrip series entitled "Like Unto Us" for use in the seminary Book of Mormon course. The filmstrip episodes depicted the principles and doctrines of the Book of Mormon applied in the lives of modern teenagers. An integral part of the program was an LP record album containing a series of songs especially written for the course. I still recall the album cover portraying two teens—one from the Book of Mormon era and one from our modern era. My students used to delight in playing the songs on our old record player and singing along with the music. (My, how quickly fly the years! I wonder if I were to show the old album to my grandchildren if they would even have any idea what it might be.)

The "Like Unto Us" theme came from the Book of Mormon where Nephi is explaining why he emphasized the teachings of the prophet Isaiah. He says, "but that I might more fully persuade them to believe in the Lord their Redeemer I did read unto them that which was written by the prophet Isaiah; for I did liken all scriptures unto us, that it might be for our profit and learning" (1 Ne. 19:23). Although the old record albums and the songs they contained are long gone, the principle of striving to liken the scriptures unto ourselves still remains with me as my daily quest in all of my personal study and teaching.

In the Revelation of John, the second and third chapters contain the Lord's counsel to the seven churches in Asia. (Since the number *seven* is symbolic of completeness or wholeness or perfection, it is likely that the Lord chose seven churches as representative or illustrative of all Saints of all churches). Repeatedly, the Lord speaks collectively to the members of these churches: "the Spirit saith unto the churches" (Rev. 2:7). (Note that this message is repeated in verses 11, 17, and 29 of chapter 2 and in verses 6, 13, and 22 of chapter 3.) Although I have deep respect for these ancient Saints, they are long gone from our mortal view—just as are the old albums and record player. Of more relevance is to learn how the doctrines and principles taught to these ancient Saints specifically apply in my own life and in the lives of those I teach.

I recognize that some things are meant for specific people in specific times, but when we find eternal truth, it can be applied throughout the ages. Repeatedly, the Lord said to the early Saints of this dispensation, "What I say unto one I say unto all" (D&C 82:5; 92:1; 93:49). That is what I am seeking in the Revelation of John— those eternal truths applicable across the ages. I believe that Nephi's charge to liken the scriptures unto ourselves applies every whit to the Revelation of John as it does to the writings of Isaiah. My hope and prayer for you is that as you study the counsel to the churches of John's vision of long ago, you will find personal application of these enduring principles in your life. My hope and prayer is that an examination of these principles will speak peace, hope, and joy to your soul.

## THOU CANST NOT BEAR THEM WHICH ARE EVIL

The Saints of the churches in Asia in John's day were much like us—they were doing many things right and were thus deserving of the Lord's commendation. They lived in the same fallen world as do we, and many, like us, were succumbing to temptation and were thus in need of the Lord's warning, chastisement, and correction. Beginning with the Church in Ephesus, the Lord offers them the comforting reminder that he "holdeth the seven stars in his right hand" and that he "walketh in the midst of the seven golden candlesticks" (Rev. 2:1). Hopefully this knowledge that Christ walks with us and holds us in His hands brings us comfort and peace. The knowledge that Christ is ever constant through all ages with His grace and sustenance is an anchor to our souls. Personally, I feel great hope and peace as I contemplate the enduring mercy of the Lord as it spans the dispensations.

Occasionally in our modern society a bank or other business will strive to elicit confidence in customers by reassuring them that the business has been operating for *one hundred years*. Compared to the length of time our Lord and Savior has been at His mission of sustaining us, one hundred years seems but a blink of the eye. What a glorious comfort we have to know that we can always lean on His ample arm and that He will always be there for us.

*How do we feel when we are confronted with sin and corruption? Do we have a proper aversion to evil?* The Lord commends the Saints for working hard, being diligent, and being patient. He also commends them for their aversion to evil—"I know thy works, and thy labor, and thy patience, and how thou canst not bear them which are evil" (Rev. 2:2). I have come to appreciate the plea of Nephi in his psalm: "O Lord . . . wilt thou make me that I may shake at the appearance of sin?" (2 Ne. 4:31). On one occasion I observed a fellow instructor teach this passage to his class with an example of how he had counseled his daughter that "he hoped she would just get sick every time she witnessed evil." I had a feeling of concern and compassion for the daughter, because in our world, if that hope of her father were to literally come to be, she would be ill pretty much all of the time. And yet I share the concern of this righteous parent. I am sure he did not intend a literal application of his statement—but how many of us as parents have sometimes wished that the consequences of partaking of evil were just a bit more immediate and dramatic in the lives of our loved ones in order to motivate them to avoid the terrible plagues of evil in our world? How much better a brief and dramatic aversion illness may be than the lingering and debilitating disease of being deeply infected, for example, by pornography or substance abuse.

The real question remains for us—Can we or can we not bear them that are evil? My hope and prayer for myself and for those I love and care about is that we cannot—that we may have an aversion to evil and that we act appropriately in dealing with this aversion. My hope and prayer for myself and for those I love and care about is that we can learn to have zero tolerance for sin and evil and yet have unlimited tolerance for the Lord's allowance for change and repentance in the lives of all who do succumb to evil. Our Savior said, "For I the Lord cannot look upon sin with the least degree of allowance; Nevertheless, he that repents and does the commandments of the Lord shall be forgiven" (D&C 1:31–32).

## THE LORD'S LAW OF THE HYPOCRITE

*Does hypocrisy in others cause us to self-examine, as with the ancient Apostles who queried, "Lord, is it I?" (Matt. 26:22) when told by the Savior that one of them would betray Him? How can we protect ourselves and our loved ones from hypocrisy?* The Ephesians were commended for their detection of hypocrisy: "and thou hast tried them which say they are apostles, and are not, and hast found them liars" (Rev. 2:2). We have been taught that one of the signs of our dispensation will be the presence of false prophets and even false Christs. I confess that I have not had much personal angst from false prophets (those who profess themselves as prophets). Although I have been aware of some, generally their claims have been so bizarre to me that I have been able to brush them aside without much consideration. I have had more personal awareness of and heartache from the false elder or high priest who may occasionally creep in among us. Recently, for example, I became aware of a man who portrayed himself as a good and faithful member of the Church and, while so doing, defrauded many good, honest, hard-working people of their life savings. The man, gratefully, is now in prison.

*How can we detect hypocrisy? Once detected, how should we deal with hypocrites?* We would be blessed to generally give them no audience, and we should not let them shake our faith in the true and living God and in His Church and kingdom. The Lord Himself counsels us in this matter in what could be referred to as the "Lord's Law of the Hypocrite": "But wo unto them that are deceivers and hypocrites, for, thus saith the Lord, I will bring them to judgment. Behold, verily I say unto you, there are hypocrites among you, who have deceived some, which has given the adversary power; but behold such shall be reclaimed; But the hypocrites shall be detected and shall be cut off, either in life or in death, even as I will; and wo unto them who are cut off from my church, for the same are overcome of the world. Wherefore, let every man beware lest he do that which is not in truth and righteousness before me" (D&C 50:6–9). After we have done what is prudent in informing authorized leaders, we would be well served to leave the matter in the Lord's hands and then continue in a personal course of truth and righteousness.

John's vision of the Lord's counsel to the Church of Ephesus is a good pattern for us to follow: "And [thou] hast borne, and hast patience, and for my name's sake hast laboured, and hast not fainted" (Rev. 2:3). As we keep our focus on building the kingdom, we will be less likely to be derailed by our detractors. I have personally found great peace from letting go of troubling matters that lie beyond my stewardship. I believe that this "Law of the Hypocrite" is very closely tied to the Lord's "Law of Forgiveness." He said, "I, the Lord, will forgive whom I will forgive, but of you it is required to forgive all men" (D&C 64:10).

## THY FIRST LOVE

*What really matters to you in your life—what do you love most and value most above all else?* It has been said that if you want to know what really matters to a person, observe what he *does* with his time. Hopefully what he *says* will be congruent with what he *does,* but to really know, we must observe what he *does.* For example, if a man were to say that he really believes in bettering the plight of the homeless in his community, but he has never offered any contribution of his time, money, or influence for their betterment, it would be obvious that his words were just words and nothing more. He doesn't really value the plight of the homeless.

Have you ever observed a young couple in "first love" who seem to have undeterred focus and attention on each other? They seem to always speak kindly and act respectfully and charitably toward each other. They constantly serve one another. And then months and years pass, and the exuberant show of love and respect sometimes seems to pale and take a second priority to the grind and struggle of daily life. Their joyful attention to one another seems to give way to indifference and distraction.

In contrast, have you ever observed a senior couple, married for many decades, who seem to have constantly preserved their love and affection? Their lives are a living testament to the priority of their sacred union. It seems as though they have never left their first feelings of love for each other. Their very nature is to always interact with charity and compassion and respect.

The Lord now chastises the Saints for a serious shortcoming: "Nevertheless I have somewhat against thee, because thou hast left thy first love" (Rev. 2:4). Although still faithful in many things, their zeal for their conversion to Christ seemed to be diminishing.

*Are there some things for which you would and should give up all else?* The Lord answered this query to the conniving Pharisees when they asked Him, "Master, which is the great commandment in the law?" He answered them, "Thou shalt love the Lord thy God with all thy heart, and with all thy soul, and with all thy mind. This is the first and great commandment. And the second is like unto it, Thou shalt love thy neighbour as thyself. On these two commandments hang all the law and the prophets" (Matt. 22:36–40). Yes, we can and should focus all of our priorities on one great principle—we are to love the Lord and love our neighbor. If we do so, all else—including our marriage and family relationships—will have proper balance and success.

We may all have deep desire to arrange this priority as our number-one quest, but then we may get choked by the tares and cares of the world to the point that we sometimes let our allegiance slip to other, less important things. That seems to have been the challenge of the Saints at Ephesus—they had left their first love. They were commanded to "Remember therefore from whence thou art fallen, and repent, and do the first works" (Rev. 2:5).

*How can we evaluate our lives to see if we are truly remembering and giving proper service to our first love?* The temple recommend interview serves as an essential key. This interview can cause us to honestly self-examine whether we are being true to our first love—whether we are firm in our testimony of the Godhead and of the Atonement of Christ. We can reaffirm that our family relationships are proper, that we are striving to follow and sustain the prophet, that we are living a chaste and moral life, that we are being honest, and so on.

We need not wait for our temple recommend interview to conduct this self-examination. Our weekly sacrament meeting serves the same purpose. Our daily prayer and pondering of the scriptures also serve the same purpose. Through quiet and personal reflection, we can look at ourselves and see how we are doing in being true to our first love. As we are true to our first love, we are more naturally true to all of the other loves of our life—particularly our families and our fellow servants in the kingdom.

## THE NICOLAITANS, WHICH THING I HATE

*What do you hate most? If you could magically eliminate some hateful things from the world, what would you eliminate and why?* The usage of the word *hate* in the scriptures is an enlightening study. The Lord's constant doctrine is to *love* Him and to *love* people but to *hate* evil. The Psalmist said, "Ye that love the Lord, hate evil: he preserveth the souls of his saints; he delivereth them out of the hand of the wicked" (Ps. 97:10). From Proverbs, we learn what the Lord hates: "These six things doth the Lord hate: yea, seven are an abomination unto him:  A proud look, a lying tongue, and hands that shed innocent blood. An heart that deviseth wicked imaginations, feet that be swift in running to mischief, A false witness that speaketh lies, and he that soweth discord among brethren" (Prov. 6:16–19).

In the book of Revelation, this doctrine of the Lord's hatred of evil is again taught by his condemnation of the Nicolaitans. Even though the Saints had faltered somewhat in their commitment to their first love, they were commended for hating gross evil: "But this thou hast, that thou hatest the deeds of the Nicolaitans, which I also hate" (Rev. 2:6).

*Who are the Nicolaitans and what are their hateful deeds?* The Nicolaitans were a religious group who sought to justify themselves in sin. They kept up the pretense of being righteous but were evil in their hearts and secret deeds. They could not let go of Babylon for the cause of Zion. The Savior's condemnation of them is made a bit more modern by the command to Newel K. Whitney to "be ashamed of the Nicolaitane band and of all their secret abominations" (D&C 117:11).

Years ago as I participated with my military unit in our annual training exercise, I witnessed an example of modern-day Nicolaitans as I observed a few "active" members of the Church who looked at this time as a "vacation" from their gospel covenants. Although this experience was somewhat of a trial of faith to my young mind, it was a vivid lesson to me of the hazards posed by modern-day Nicolaitans. This experience has caused me much thought about our Savior's example and teaching to hate the false and deceptive deeds and doctrines of the Nicolaitans while striving to forgive and love those who are deceived. If we have been deceived by the example of the Nicolaitans—ancient or modern—our charge is to triumph over evil through our repentance. "So hast thou also them that hold the doctrine of the Nicolaitans, which thing I hate. Repent; or else I will come unto thee quickly, and will fight against them with the sword of my mouth" (Rev. 2:15–16).

## Tribulation Ten Days

*Are you ever burdened with what seems like a load of care? Are we trusting the Lord to help and guide us through our trials?* The Lord taught, "He that hath an ear, let him hear what the Spirit saith unto the churches; To him that overcometh will I give to eat of the tree of life, which is in the midst of the paradise of God" (Rev. 2:7). As previously discussed, we come unto the tree of life by coming unto Christ and accepting His gospel. Receiving the tree of life means to receive eternal life through the Atonement and mission of Christ.

The Lord then goes on to instruct the Saints of Smyrna that part of this overcoming is the true enduring of trials and tribulation: "Fear none of those things which thou shalt suffer: behold, the devil shall cast some of you into prison, that ye may be tried; and *ye shall have tribulation ten days:* be thou faithful unto death, and I will give thee a crown of life" (Rev. 2:10; emphasis added).

*What is the significance of having "tribulation ten days?" How do our trials relate to receiving the crown of eternal life?* Let's consider the Lord's counsel to the Prophet Joseph Smith: "If thou art called to pass through tribulation. . . . And if thou shouldst be cast into the pit, or into the hands of murderers . . . if the billowing surge conspire against thee . . . if the very jaws of hell shall gape open the mouth wide after thee, know thou, my son, that all these things shall give thee experience, and shall be for thy good. The Son of Man hath descended below them all. Art thou greater than he?" Therefore, hold on thy way, and the priesthood shall remain with thee . . . fear not what man can do, for God shall be with you forever and ever" (D&C 122:5, 7–9).

On several occasions I have visited the site of the old Liberty Jail where this revelation was given and have pondered the severe trial of the Prophet and his friends, who were confined while their families and fellow Saints so needed their love and leadership. So it is with us—our personal, family, and professional lives are so often held prisoner by the distractions of this fallen and polluted world. A serious and lingering illness may prevent us from working to our desired capacity. A child's plan for mission or education may be sidetracked by a drug addiction. Our desires to live a happy and productive life may be thrown off balance by discouragement and depression.

*How are we to cope with the trials of life?* We are to hold on and be faithful for "ten days." The number *ten* can mean "completeness." Think of the ten plagues on Pharoah of Egypt—it was a *complete* breaking down of his determination to continue to hold the Israelites captive. Think again of the parable of the ten virgins—it was a *complete* parable taught to teach all of the necessity of *complete* gospel preparation. Think of the parable of the ten lepers—it was a parable taught to demonstrate the need for *complete* gratitude for our Savior's healing. When only one leper returned to express gratitude, "Jesus answering said, Were there not ten cleansed? but where are the nine?" (Luke 17:17). When trials come into our lives, we must learn to respond by being faithful for "ten days"—in other words, by being *completely* faithful unto death. Then we shall be awarded the crown of life or eternal life in God's celestial kingdom.

The Lord continues this theme of properly enduring to the end to the Saints in Thyatira. They are told, "But that which ye have already hold fast till I come. And he that overcometh, and keepeth my works unto the end, to him will I give power over the nations" (Rev. 2:25–26). It is instructive that the Lord never seems to allow us a respite from our commitment to keep our covenants. His consistent message for us to be faithful *unto death* and to keep His works unto the end offer a great challenge for us—a challenge accompanied by great hope. Alma, at the waters of Mormon, taught that we, as children of the covenant, must be willing "to stand as witnesses of

God at all times and in all things, and in all places . . . until you are dead as to the mortal body; and may the Spirit of the Lord be poured out upon you; and may he grant unto you eternal life, through the redemption of Christ, whom he has prepared from the foundation of the world" (Mosiah 18:9, 13). When we put our hand to the gospel plow, we must be willing stay the course forever, and by so doing, we are granted *forever* or *eternal* life.

Our Savior, the great Alpha and Omega, expects us to endure all things; though His grace, He will enable us to so endure. This is profound doctrine. Just as the great Alpha and Omega suffered all things for us, we must be willing to endure all things as part of our true enduring and preparing for exaltation. Yes, we will be completely tried for *ten days*—but the glorious reward for valiantly enduring will far outweigh our sufferings and will serve to put them into proper perspective in our lives. Joyous, peaceful, triumphant eternal life will forever eclipse the trials and torments of our present state.

## HIDDEN MANNA AND A WHITE STONE

*Are you rich? How so?* We are blessed as we learn to recognize the guiding hand of the Lord in all things and as we keep an eternal perspective of the grandeur of His promised reward to those who remain faithful. We must not be distracted by the lesser reward that comes in the form of the fleeting riches and treasures of the earth. The Lord reminded the Smyrna Saints, "I know thy works, and tribulation, and poverty, (but thou art rich) and I know the blasphemy of them which say they are Jews, and are not, but are the synagogue of Satan" (Rev. 2:9).

I recall a fun little dialogue I once had with a seminary student that has caused me much reflection over the years. One day, right in the middle of a class discussion, he raised his hand and asked, "Brother Christensen, are you rich?" After a brief pause, I simply replied "Yes!" and went on with the discussion. I could tell that my affirmative response had prompted him to further thought. A few moments later, he raised his hand again and said, "Oh, I get it—you are rich in blessings." I replied, "Yes, I am rich in blessings and in money." Once again, I continued with the class discussion.

I could tell that he was now perplexed, and after letting him digest this new thought for a while, I told him that I was of the opinion that he and all others in the class were also rich in blessings and in money. I said I could prove it with a few questions. I asked how many had slept in a bed the previous night and how many had eaten a meal in the last twenty-four hours. Everyone answered yes to both questions. I told the students that compared to much of the world's population, their positive responses to my questions had placed them in a "rich" category. In the disparity of economic wealth among nations, it is easy to get confused about the meaning of riches.

The counsel to the ancient Saints that "thou art rich" may be a double reminder of both their temporal and spiritual blessings, but the greatest doctrine is of the spiritual and eternal rewards that await the righteous. By making and keeping covenants with Christ, we have potential to become joint heirs with Him in receiving the promised blessing that "he that receiveth my Father receiveth my Father's kingdom; therefore all that my Father hath shall be given unto him" (D&C 84:38). Those who keep their allegiance and focus on their "first love" will be rich beyond imagining. As promised, "To him that overcometh will I give to eat of the *hidden manna,* and will give him a *white stone*, and in the stone a new name written, which no man knoweth saving he that receiveth it" (Rev. 2:17; emphasis added).

If we were to truly comprehend the significance of our potential rewards for overcoming the world, I believe we would do all in our power to obtain the "hidden manna" and the "white stone." Their value is far greater than any earthly treasure, as evidenced by the Savior's command in the Sermon on the Mount to "lay not up for yourselves treasures upon earth, where moth and rust doth corrupt, and where thieves break through and steal: But lay up for yourselves treasures in heaven, where neither moth nor rust doth corrupt, and where thieves do not break through nor steal: For where your treasure is, there will your heart be also" (Matt. 6:19–21).

*What is the meaning of receiving hidden manna?* The meaning is the same as that of eating the "Bread of Life." In the gospel of John, we read the great "Bread of Life" message. The Lord said, "Verily, verily, I say unto you, He that believeth on me hath everlasting life. I am that bread of life. Your fathers did eat manna in the wilderness, and are dead. This is the bread which cometh down from heaven, that a man may eat thereof, and not die. I am the living bread which came down from heaven: if any man eat of this bread, he shall live for ever; and the bread that I will give is my flesh, which I will give for the life of the world" (John 6:47–51).

How significant that the Bread of Life, even Jesus Christ, the Savior of the world, came to earth in humble circumstance and was born in the *House of Bread*, the Hebrew meaning of "Bethlehem." He did so, according to the great plan of happiness of our Eternal Father, so that he could offer each of us who is willing to overcome the world the great reward of hidden manna or eternal life—a gift that will remain hidden to those who reject this great invitation but that will nourish forever those who worthily seek to partake of it.

*How do we receive the hidden manna, or the Bread of Life?* We eat the Bread of Life by living in such a manner that we receive the full blessing of the Atonement of Christ in our lives. Our reminding symbol of receiving this blessing is our partaking of the sacrament—we are saved by figuratively eating the flesh and drinking the blood of Christ. In other words, we accept Him as the divine Son of God who came here to do the will of the Father. By partaking of the sacrament, we symbolize that we are willing to accept His gospel, keep His commandments, and endure to the end. The reward of doing so is that we will be exalted and gain eternal life.

*What is the meaning of the "white stone" and how will receiving this "white stone" bless our lives?* The Lord answered these questions for us in modern revelation to the Prophet Joseph Smith: "The angels do not reside on a planet like this earth; But they reside in the presence of God, on a globe like a sea of glass and fire, where all things for their glory are manifest, past, present, and future, and are continually before the Lord. The place where God resides is a great Urim and Thummim. This earth, in its sanctified and immortal state, will be made like unto crystal and will be a Urim and Thummim to the inhabitants who dwell thereon, whereby all things pertaining to an inferior kingdom, or all kingdoms of a lower order, will be manifest to those who dwell on it; and this earth will be Christ's. Then the white stone mentioned in Revelation 2:17 will become a Urim and Thummim to each individual who receives one, whereby things pertaining to a higher order of kingdoms will be made known; and a white stone is given to each of those who come into the celestial kingdom, whereon is a new name written, which no man knoweth save he that receiveth it. The new name is the key word" (D&C 130:6–11).

*Do you ever wish for the blessing of having the tapestry of your life fully unfurled before your eyes with perfect comprehension of why and how all things happened as they did?* One of the most hopeful and peaceful thoughts of my life is to look forward to eternal glory with the assurance that all of these blessings will have perfect fulfillment for us. We have the potential of having a personal white stone or Urim and Thummim. *Urim* and *Thummim* are Hebrew terms meaning "lights" and "perfections." Let's imagine the beauty of living with perfect light—of having all things revealed to us and of experiencing a fullness of joy. All our questions will be answered. All our life mysteries will be solved. All the blessings of enduring our trials will be granted.

One of the great blessings of understanding the gospel is the encouragement we have from our doctrine to continually make progress each and every day toward our eternal goals. Although the process of learning in this mortal world can be a real challenge and may even seem like a losing battle as our memory fades and diminishes, we must have hope that our efforts to broaden our minds will pay current and future dividends. We are told that, "Whatever principle of intelligence we attain unto in this life, it will rise with us in the resurrection. And if a person gains more knowledge and intelligence in this life through his diligence and obedience than another, he will have so much the advantage in the world to come" (D&C 130:18–19). Our prophets have consistently taught us that our education and striving for knowledge and wisdom is not for this world only but to prepare us for eternal life.

### RULE WITH A ROD OF IRON

*If you had the power to change one thing about the world, what would you change and why?* In summary of chapter 2, if we avoid evil, keep our gospel covenants, love and serve the Lord, repent of our sins, and faithfully endure our trials, we will be blessed with great power. The scripture states, "And he that overcometh, and keepeth my works unto the end, to him will I give power over the nations: And he shall rule them with a rod of iron; as the vessels of a potter shall they be broken to shivers; even as I received of my Father" (Rev. 2:26–27). Does that promise appeal to you—to beat the nations with a rod and break the people to shivers? If we take this King James translation at face value, it certainly is a challenge to understand. We have countless examples of despots and tyrants who have taken a brutal and evil approach to administering their acquired power—who have literally beaten their subjects into submission and broken them to shivers.

Within the leadership structure of the Church we have also "learned by sad experience" that some are prone to misuse power and authority. Of such evil the Lord warned, "Behold, there are many called, but few are chosen. And why are they not chosen? Because their hearts are set so much upon the things of this world, and aspire to the honors of men, that they do not learn this one lesson—That the rights of the priesthood are inseparably connected with the powers of heaven, and that the powers of heaven cannot be controlled nor handled only upon the principles of righteousness. . . . We have learned by sad experience that it is the nature and disposition of almost all men, as soon as they get a little authority, as they suppose, they will immediately begin to exercise unrighteous dominion" (D&C 121:35–36, 39).

*How do we find true application of God's power granted to mankind?* Let me share a personal example of how, through a call to serve, I was tutored in the proper application of power and authority. I was called by my stake president to serve as bishop of my ward. I was also told that he could not sustain or ordain me for six weeks due to his hectic travel schedule. During this interval, I was permitted to counsel with the outgoing bishop. This was a great time of training and preparation.

I knew we had many youth in our ward, but I was surprised to learn that the number was greater than I had imagined; there were about sixty youth ages twelve to seventeen and about sixty young single adults ages eighteen to thirty. The Spirit worked on me concerning these precious souls who would soon be under my stewardship, or in my power. Through counseling with the soon-to-be former bishop, through prayer and scripture study, and through much thought and meditation, I soon had a plan in mind of how I would approach this awesome challenge.

As soon as I was sustained by the ward and ordained by the stake president, I trained my counselors and priesthood leaders in their roles and basically delegated the administration of the ward to them. I then held a meeting with the parents of the youth and took them through a scriptural discussion on the basic principles of eternal life. I then informed them that I would like to meet with their sons and daughters individually and have basically the same discussion with them. My request was that they help their youth keep their appointments and come prepared with scriptures in hand to individually counsel with the bishop during a one-hour appointment. We then went to work. My executive secretary did a marvelous job—he was very tenacious and got every single youth and young adult except one in to see me that first year.

During those many interviews, I got to know the hearts and minds of these precious souls. We laughed and cried and counseled together. We searched the scriptures together and discussed how holding to the iron rod would bless their lives and keep them safely on the path. Often I felt prompted to give them blessings of peace and comfort and encouragement by the power of the holy priesthood that I held. In the spirit of love and prayer and fasting, I often witnessed the Spirit cleansing and changing their hearts. For example, I recall how the mother of one young man came to me with genuine concern about some improper behaviors of her young son. I moved him to the front of the interview list. In my time with him, we were able to use the scriptures and frankly discuss why the course he was flirting with was not a proper course. He humbled himself. He repented. He charted a good and true life course that took him on a mission and on to a temple marriage.

This year of personally meeting individually with every youth and young adult was one of the greatest experiences of my life. I felt so good about it that we repeated the process each year of my service. I felt the power of the Lord's love and concern for His children. I was humbled by my call to serve and felt so grateful to have the power of the priesthood to help shape and mold the lives of these valiant souls. I developed a great personal love for them and always felt, as I entered their hearts and souls, that I was treading on very sacred ground. I was joyful that I was able to help nurture their testimonies—it seemed as though I were a "potter" and they were as "soft clay in my hands." Not every experience was an immediate success, of course, but for the most part, I felt that I was able to use the power and authority I had been given to bless their lives.

Let's now take a second look at this doctrine of "power over the nations and ruling with an iron rod." In the Joseph Smith Translation of these verses we read, "And to him who overcometh, and keepeth my commandments unto the end will I give power over many kingdoms. And he shall rule them with the word of God; and they shall be in his hands as the vessels of clay in the hands of a potter; and he shall govern them by faith, with equity and justice, even as I received of my father" (JST, Rev. 2:26–27). These inspired verses give us proper direction and understanding to power and leadership in the Lord's kingdom. Do righteous Saints seek for power? Yes, righteous Saints seek for the proper application of power so they can teach, persuade, and influence lives for good. That is true power. Having such power is a true blessing.

In summary, we live in a fallen and corrupt world, but we have the constant reminder that Christ rules over Satan and the constant promise that we, as individuals and families, may triumph over evil. We will be blessed to always remember the admonition of Paul: "Be not overcome of evil, but overcome evil with good" (Rom. 12:21).

# Chapter Three
# True Conversion—
# The Book of Life

*HOW MAY WE GAIN CONFIDENCE in resisting evil and protecting ourselves from the constant grind of temptation in our lives?* Once when I was a young and somewhat inexperienced seminary teacher, I was in a parent-teacher conference with the father of one of my students. The father was of rough and stocky build and was mature and seasoned by life. In our conversation about the state of the world and the challenges faced by the youth, I said something that implied that he and I—because we were active, faithful Church members—seemed to have perhaps transcended being tempted in a particular area. I vividly remember the lesson he taught me. He leaned toward me and doubled both of his fists as though he were preparing to hit me. He then said to me, with his fists still doubled and with a gruff and commanding voice, "Young man, you would do well to always keep your guard up!" I have thought much about this lesson over the years and have concluded that we all, no matter our age or station in life, would do well to always keep our guard up.

## THOU LIVEST, AND ART DEAD

*What specific actions are we taking to always keep our guard up?* The Lord continues His guiding counsel to the seven churches, beginning with the Church in Sardis: "And unto the angel of the church in Sardis write; These things saith he that hath the Spirits of God, and the seven stars; I know thy works, that thou hast a name that thou livest, and art dead. Be watchful, and strengthen the things which remain, that are ready to die: for I have not found thy works perfect before God" (Rev. 3:1–2). Many are doing many things right, but all are in need of repentance.

A very real hazard of all ages is when Saints, sometimes enmeshed in a religious culture that may differ from the actual gospel, make the error of mistaking *active* for *righteous*. How subtle is the adversary who can sometimes persuade people to believe that because they are wrapped in the cultural pretense of being active and righteous Saints, they are thus alive spiritually—even though the more weighty matters may be left undone. In a sense, they have *let down their guard*. Some in Sardis seemed to have groomed a public reputation for righteousness but were inwardly spiritually dead. Apparently this hypocrisy was also of concern in the Church at Philadelphia, as the Lord said to them, "Behold, I will make them of the synagogue of Satan, which say they are Jews, and are not, but do lie" (Rev. 3:9).

There are some in the Church today who have convinced themselves that they are spiritually alive, but they are actually dead to spiritual matters. *Does this doctrine offend us? Or does it humble us and prompt in us an attitude of repentance? How are we to deal with this malady of spiritual hypocrisy?* In response, let me share a little proverb from my farm-boy youth. I call it the "proverb of the manure pile." As anyone who has had firsthand experience with the care and keeping of cattle would know, try as you may to avoid it, you will experience *manure* on a personal basis. As I recall my own personal unpleasant encounters with this hazard, I remember having stepped in it and fallen in it. I have had my face swatted with a dirty cow tail. I have been splashed by the soupy variety and pelted by the more solid-texture strain. From my experiences, I have concocted this proverb: "If a man falls into a manure pile, he is left with basically two options: A) he can clean himself up, or B) he can go through life trying to convince himself and others that he does not stink."

The Lord, of course, would have us clean ourselves up, as He further counsels, "Remember therefore how thou hast received and heard, and hold fast, and repent" (Rev. 3:3). Our proper course as Saints must be to continually look deep into our souls and search out anything that may be amiss.

*Are we going to follow the Lord's admonition to the Saints of Sardis to hold fast and repent, or are "we undertaking to cover our sins, or to gratify our pride, our vain ambition" (D&C 121:37)? Do we merely have a testimony of the gospel, or are we coupling that testimony with true conversion by a gospel-in-action life?* These must be our guiding questions to enable us to keep our feet securely planted in the gospel path. If we choose not to clean up and "watch [ourselves], and [our] thoughts, and [our] deeds" (Mosiah 4:30) we run the risk of being blindsided by the coming of the Lord, who further said, "If therefore thou shalt not watch, I will come on thee as a thief, and thou shalt not know what hour I will come upon thee" (Rev. 3:3). However, if we will be diligent and not "sleep . . . but . . . watch and be sober," then we will not be "in darkness, that that day should overtake you as a thief" (1 Thess. 5:6, 4). May we all stay clean—speedily repent when we fall—and always keep our guard up.

## THE BOOK OF LIFE

*What is your understanding of the book of life?* Following the chastisement for hypocrisy, the Lord is now quick to point out that not all are spiritually dead: "Thou hast a few names even in Sardis which have not defiled their garments; and they shall walk with me in white: for they are worthy" (Rev. 3:4). We are then introduced to one of the greatest messages and themes of the book of Revelation—that of the "book of life": "He that overcometh, the same shall be clothed in white raiment; and I will not blot out his name out of the book of life, but I will confess his name before my Father, and before his angels" (Rev. 3:5).

To get and keep our name written in the book of life must be our life quest. *What does it mean to have our name written in the book of life? Is our self-perception always congruent with the account in our book of life?* As an illustration, let's consider George Bailey, the leading character of the classic Christmas movie, *It's a Wonderful Life.* George, in his self-perception, was living a mediocre life of unfulfilled dreams. He felt trapped by tradition and expectation as he took over the management of his deceased father's savings-and-loan business. He struggled with the pernicious danger of comparative thinking and felt that his life was just not of as much worth as the lives of others who seemed more successful or prosperous.

Then George was given a great gift. He was able to view his life in the panorama of God's eternal perspective. He learned that his *true life* was far greater than his self-perception—and much greater than the warped perception of Mr. Potter, a wicked man who had unjustly judged and abused him. George learned that a person's success in life can't be measured by the entries in an account book or by the size of his financial portfolio. He saw that his true book of life was much more than all of that—it was not just what he had *done,* it was what he had *become* through years of service and compassion to others.

So also it is with us. Our book of life is not merely an accounting ledger—it is a view of what and who we become through our lifetime of choices. It is possible to gain a testimony of the truth and not be fully converted to the truth. We may *know* in our hearts and minds that the gospel is true—but true conversion is when we *do* something about our testimony. As we continually *do* what we are prompted to do, the cumulative product of our doing is what we *become.*

To have our names written in the Lord's book of life is much more than just a ledger listing of our good and charitable deeds. It involves a mighty change of heart. It involves *becoming* a charitable person. It is the process, really, of having our souls transformed by application of the principles of the gospel until we really do become like Christ. We all know people who have been consistently true to their gospel covenants. They have a spiritual countenance about them. Their very bodies bespeak their soul. We can, in a sense, *read* their lives from their countenance as we would read a book. Their righteous lives become their book of life.

The book of life cannot be altered by mortal man. This helps explain why the five wise virgins in the parable did not share their oil with the five who were foolish. It was not that the wise were stingy and uncaring—it is simply that the entry in our personal book of life is not something that we can give to others. It is *our* life. We can share our testimony by telling others about it, but we cannot implant it into another person. We can't give someone else our spiritual experience. We can offer guidance and counsel. We can share our example. But we cannot cause another to become what we have become. We cannot give them what we have obtained. It is not like simply writing someone a check from our bank account. The wise virgins shared not because they could not—it is impossible to impart to another what one has become over a lifetime of consistent gospel living. This book of life is a writing project that must be completed personally and individually. This book of life cannot be plagiarized. This book of life is, in the very real sense, who we really and truly are!

## THE KEY OF DAVID

*How do you secure your valuables?* If you had something extremely precious that you wanted to preserve and safeguard—like rare jewels or valuable coins—you would perhaps want to store them in a more secure location than your own home, since your home might be susceptible to fire or theft. You might seek out a reputable bank vault and put them on deposit with a trusted official. You would want and expect that only specially authorized and trusted representatives of the bank be given the key to access your treasure.

*In a spiritual sense, to whom would we entrust our own souls and the souls of our loved ones?* We would naturally seek out the One who would be the most trustworthy—the One who has invested the most into our care and keeping. We, as sheep of the fold, would desire the watch care of the true Shepherd—even Christ. To the Saints in Philadelphia, the Lord said, "These things saith he that is holy, he that is true, he that hath the key of David, he that openeth, and no man shutteth; and shutteth, and no man openeth; I know thy works: behold, I have set before thee an open door, and no man can shut it: for thou hast a little strength, and hast kept my word, and hast not denied my name" (Rev. 3:7–8).

Being holy and true, Christ is the most trusted representative in whom we could entrust the key to our lives. He holds the "key of David." In a messianic prophecy of Isaiah we learn, "And the key of the house of David will I lay upon his shoulder; so he shall open, and none shall shut; and he shall shut, and none shall open" (Isa. 22:22). (See also the chapter heading of Isaiah 22: "Messiah shall hold the key of the house of David.") David, while serving as king, wielded absolute power over his subjects. What he decreed was the law. Christ, who descended from David, thus rightly inherited the key of mortal rule. He, being the divine Son of God, also has all of the spiritual and temporal power and authority of His Father.

Our Savior has the power to open and shut all doors. He can lock Satan away. He can unlock the windows of heaven for our benefit. He can lock our hearts against temptation, if we will so allow: "because thou hast kept the word of my patience, I also will keep thee from the hour of temptation, which shall come upon all the world, to try them that dwell upon the earth" (Rev. 3:10). He can unlock the influence of the Holy Ghost in our lives. He can lock us, His sheep, securely in a safe fold. In essence, He has the power and authority to unlock for us the very path and entrance to eternal life if we are willing to accept Him and His Atonement. We can trust Him with our own souls and with the souls of those we love. What peace, joy, and comfort this gives us to know that our Savior is always there and that we can place our unqualified trust in Him!

The prophet Nephi was well aware of this key of David concept as he prayed, "May the gates of hell be shut continually before me, because that my heart is broken and my spirit is contrite! O Lord, with thou not shut the gates of thy righteousness before me, that I may walk in the path of the low valley, that I may be strict in the plain road!" (2 Ne. 4:32).

Even as Christ is willing to lock and unlock the needed doors to move us along our path, we must be willing to do our part by accepting Him and heeding His counsel. As we do so, we have potential to gain a sure place in His kingdom. As we do so, we have privilege to gain a crown of glory that cannot be stolen or damaged by another. "Behold, I come quickly; hold that fast which thou hast, that no man take thy crown" (Rev. 3:11). This crown of eternal life represents the supreme goal and desire of righteous Saints.

*How much time, energy, and effort do we spend procuring and securing spiritual treasures—even the crown of eternal life?* The Savior guides us in this matter with His inspired counsel: "Lay not up for yourselves treasures upon earth, where moth and rust doth corrupt, and where thieves break through and steal: But lay up for yourselves treasures in heaven, where neither moth nor rust doth corrupt, and where thieves do not break through nor steal: For where your treasure is, there will your heart be also" (Matt. 6:19–21).

## A PILLAR IN THE TEMPLE OF MY GOD

*Is there someone you have considered to be a pillar of righteousness or a pillar of the community?* As we allow Christ to use His "key" to guide our lives, He sets our feet on the path to becoming "a pillar in the temple of God." "Him that overcometh will I make a pillar in the temple of my God, and he shall go no more out: and I will write upon him the name of my God, and the name of the city of my God, which is new Jerusalem, which cometh down out of heaven from my God: and I will write upon him my new name" (Rev. 3:12).

I have gazed in awe at some of the grand pillars of the world. Those of the Luxor Temple in ancient Egypt or of the Parthenon of ancient Greece have caused me great wonder as I have contemplated the centuries through which these pillars have so long endured. Many of our government and church buildings are constructed on and arrayed with beautiful pillars—symbolic of strength, endurance, majesty, and responsibility.

A few years ago we witnessed, via satellite transmission, the Joseph Smith Commemorative Broadcast from Sharon, Vermont, in celebration of the two hundredth birthday of the Prophet. In his message, President Gordon B. Hinckley told of the great granite pillar that was erected under the direction of Junius Wells. This impressive pillar stands thirty-eight and one-half feet tall, symbolic of the years of the life span of the martyred Prophet. President Hinckley described the creation and erection of the monument as symbolic of the life of the Prophet Joseph Smith. Joseph characterized his own life by stating, "I am like a huge, rough stone rolling down from a high mountain; and the only polishing I get is when some corner gets rubbed off by . . . striking with accelerated force against . . . mobs, blasphemers, licentious and corrupt men and women—all hell knocking off a corner here and a corner there. Thus I will become a smooth and polished shaft in the quiver of the Almighty.'"3

As impressive as manmade pillars may be, they are prone to eventual destruction. Even though they have outlasted any mortal lifespan, the pillars of Luxor and Athens are showing the stress of their age. *Is it possible to seek out pillars that will endure forever and never fall?* Yes, it certainly is. As in President Hinckley's example of the Prophet Joseph, the pillars of strength in the form and design of exalted men and women, made by God, will never fall—not ever! We have the absolute assurance in the gospel plan that those who use this mortal life to prepare to meet God by overcoming the world will "sit down in his kingdom, *to go no more out*" (Alma 34:36; emphasis added). What blessed assurance it offers us to know that an eternal and forever-enduring state of glory will be ours if we prepare ourselves to become pillars in the Lord's kingdom.

*Have you ever daydreamed of having a particular name/title?* To become a pillar in the Lord's kingdom is to have His very name placed upon us: "and I will write upon him my new name" (Rev. 3:12). Consider for a moment the striving of mankind to acquire a "new name." During the Vietnam War, there were songs written about the prestige and status of gaining the name/title *Green Beret.* Years of effort at a university are required to earn the privilege of being called a full professor. Many expend much time and energy to be addressed as *Doctor* or *Senator.* Consider the incessant wrangling in our country to gain the honor of being addressed as *President.* And yet, all of these names pale when compared to the ultimate name of *God.* The worthy prospect of having our Lord and Savior write upon us "the name of my God" is the ultimate quest of mankind and connotes that we have opportunity to become like Him.

In speaking of those who gain eternal life, the Lord said, "Then shall they be gods, because they have no end; therefore shall they be from everlasting to everlasting, because they continue; then shall they be above all, because all things are subject unto them. Then shall they be gods, because they have all power, and the angels are subject unto them" (D&C 132:20).

If ever we should grow melancholy at the loss of a promotion with a new name on our office door or at not making the cut to be able to be called a member of a particular team or group, we may gain hope and direction in pondering the sure promise the Lord has offered all of His children, regardless of race, physique, intellectual prowess, or economic status. This sure promise is to be called by the name of *God.* This is a worthy aspiration.

*How is it possible for me, a mere mortal, to ever gain such a magnificent blessing?* All of this is made possible by the grand pillar Himself—even Jesus Christ, the great "Amen." It is instructive that our Savior applies this name/title, *the Amen,* to Himself: "These things saith the Amen, the faithful and true witness, the beginning of the creation of God" (Rev. 3:14). *Amen* derives from a Hebrew verb meaning to "prop or make firm." In our modern usage of *amen* at the end of a prayer, it means "to validate" or "to bind." Think of this meaning when we close our prayers and ordinances, "In the name of Jesus Christ, amen." Could we not paraphrase and say, "I, your Savior, will bind and validate your prayer and ordinance. I will support and sustain you. I will prop you up through your times of trial—I will support you as a strong pillar. I will help you stand firm in the face of temptation and adversity. I will make of you an enduring pillar of eternity!" What hope, peace, and joy this promise offers to the weary who struggle through mortality.

### HOT, COLD, OR LUKEWARM?

*How do you maintain your faith and hope through the trials of life? What is the key to keeping your testimony alive and burning brightly within your soul?* As I have taught the book of Revelation, I have often found myself saying something like, "Through all the happenings and trials of life, and throughout the book of Revelation, there is always woven a *golden thread of testimony* and hope in our Savior to carry us through."

One morning I went to visit the seminary class of a particular teacher who had been in a discussion with me when I had used this "golden thread of testimony" example. She had constructed on her wall a large visual to help motivate her students to examine the book of Revelation. On her visual were these words, which I feel captured the intent of my heart in our discussion: "In the Revelation of John, Look for the Golden Thread of the Testimony, Power, and Grace of Christ. Good over Evil. Love over Hate. Christ over Satan."

That is how I see the Revelation of John. It portrays the golden thread of the enabling grace of our Savior running throughout the lifetimes of all His creations. He will prop us up and uphold us and validate us and bind us to Him through His love and Atonement.

To receive the full extent of this enabling grace and support, we must cast our lot with and give our all to Him. We must accept Him as our Lord and Savior and be willing to do what He asks of us. We cannot be fence-sitters—we must decide. We cannot approach His gospel as we would our local smorgasbord/buffet, picking and choosing what we will eat and what we will pass by. His law of justice and mercy does not provide for His *full* support and protection of us if we lend only *half* of our heart and commitment to Him.

The branch of Laodicea was a short distance south of Hierapolis, where some hot springs were located. By the time the water from these hot springs reached Laodicea, it was "neither cold nor hot" but merely "lukewarm." Using this profound and natural visual object lesson, the Lord taught the Laodiceans, "I know thy works, that thou art neither cold nor hot: I would thou wert cold or hot. So then because thou are lukewarm, and neither cold nor hot, I will spue thee out of my mouth" (Rev. 3:15–16).

The Lord then offers a chastisement of those who say, "I am rich, and increased with goods, and have need of nothing"; He reminds them that in their pride and arrogance, they are really "wretched, and miserable, and poor and blind and naked" (Rev. 3:17). He then offers a great antidote for those with this terrible sickness of lukewarmness. He counsels them "to buy of me gold tried in the fire, that thou mayest be rich" (Rev. 3:18). From these images of hot water and hot, refining fire we are better able to understand the charge, also recorded by John the Revelator, that we must "be born of water and of the Spirit" [or "fire"] in order to "enter into the kingdom of God" (John 3:5).

*What, then, must we do to inherit eternal life?* We must be willing to choose to be hot, rather than cold or lukewarm, in the gospel. We must be willing to let the refining fire burn all dross and evil out of our souls. We must be willing to allow the Lord to mold and shape our hearts, for "as many as I love, I rebuke and chasten: be zealous therefore, and repent" (Rev. 3:19).

Just as Abraham was tested with the instruction to offer up his son, Isaac, we will each have our Abrahamic tests in life. Our tests will be heart-wrenching and will often seem more than we can bear. The Lord said, "we will take of these materials, and we will make an earth whereon these may dwell; And we will prove them herewith, to see if they will do all things whatsoever the Lord their God shall command them" (Abr. 3:24–25). To "do all things" is to be hot, rather than lukewarm. To be hot in the gospel is to keep our personal testimony always alive and vibrant.

*Do you know someone who is hot in his or her commitment to the gospel?* In the early days of my employment with the Church Educational System, we were often blessed to have Brother William

E. Barrett—one of the great, early leaders of Church education—as a special guest at our conferences. He occasionally spoke to us. I recall him telling of an old Danish brother who was his Sunday School teacher. The brother spoke with a heavy accent and his demeanor seemed strange to the students. At first glance, he didn't seem like a teacher who would connect with the more modern students. And yet the power of his faith and testimony had lasting influence in their lives.

*In summary, then, how may we be hot in living the gospel?* We need not be popular, articulate, rich, or famous. We simply need to keep our testimony of the true gospel alive and well and forever burning in our hearts. We do this by daily exercise in matters of spirituality. We live our lives so that those around us could feel the warmth of our faith As we so live, the Lord offers us a promise and blessing: "To him that overcometh will I grant to sit with me in my throne, even as I also overcame, and am set down with my Father in his throne" (Rev. 3:21).

## I STAND AT THE DOOR AND KNOCK

*How do we overcome the world so we can sit with God on His throne? How do we feel about the Savior's charge, "Be ye therefore perfect" (Matt. 5:48)? Do we view it as a personal invitation to us?* We have a delightful invitation from our Savior: "Behold, I stand at the door, and knock: if any man hear my voice, and open the door, I will come in to him, and will sup with him, and he with me" (Rev. 3:20).

We are likely all familiar with the famous painting by artist Holman Hunt,  inspired from this verse in the Revelation, depicting Christ knocking at a door. A friend of the artist once questioned him as to why the door had no outside handle. Holman replied that the painting was intended to portray the human heart. The human heart, like the door, could only be opened from the inside. We must personally open the door and invite the Savior into our lives. As we do, He will come in and sup with us and minister to us.

The message of the Savior to the seven churches of Asia can certainly be likened to us of the modern Church and to all Saints of all dispensations. The message is a great invitation to come unto Him and to accept of His gospel. This same message is well portrayed by the prophet Moroni as he offered his concluding testimony: "Yea, come unto Christ, and be perfected in him, and deny yourselves of all ungodliness; and if ye shall deny yourselves of all ungodliness, and love God with all your might, mind and strength, then is his grace sufficient for you, that by his grace ye may be perfect in Christ; and if by the grace of God ye are perfect in Christ, ye can in nowise deny the power of God. And again, if ye by the grace of God are perfect in Christ, and deny not his power, then are ye sanctified in Christ by the grace of God, through the shedding of the blood of Christ, which is in the covenant of the Father unto the remission of your sins, that ye become holy, without spot" (Moroni 10:32–33).

Sadly, those who reject this invitation of the Savior will lament and regret the choice, as so poignantly expressed by the prophet Mormon, "O ye fair ones, how could ye have departed from the ways of the Lord! O ye fair ones, how could ye have rejected that Jesus, who stood with open arms to receive you!" (Morm. 6:17).

*Can we imagine the joy of being accepted into the arms of the Savior and of becoming "holy, without spot" (Moroni 10:33)? "Can ye look up to God at that day with a pure heart and clean hands . . . having the image of God engraven upon your countenances" (Alma 5:19)?* I am constantly humbled to think of the awesome power and grace of our Savior. His love and promise of salvation for us really does shine as a golden thread, spanning the dispensations. He really does stand with open arms to receive us into His kingdom. And what a glorious kingdom that is for Him and can be for us.

# Chapter Four

# Worship the Lord with Crowns of Glory

*DO YOU EVER MARVEL AT how quickly our world seems to be spiraling downward in wickedness? Do you look forward with encouragement and hope to life in celestial glory?* At the time of this writing, my wife and I have been interested in a story on our local news. We were drawn to this particular news broadcast because of the current investigation of a horrific murder in our community and the fact that we are acquainted with the roommates of the man being investigated for the crime. As I thought about the situation, my mind went back to the time of my return from my mission some three-plus decades ago and a murder in a neighboring community of the small town where I lived. There seems to be a stark contrast between that time and this time. The crime then was major news for a very long time—it was a rare occurrence in that time and place. The current crime in our community seems to be almost commonplace and representative of an almost daily occurrence in our more modern society.

Our fallen world seems to continue on a downward spiral, causing us to gasp in wonder at how things could get much worse—and yet they seem to do just that. Such deteriorating conditions certainly sweeten the prospect of the ultimate cleansing of the earth and the longing to achieve a better day.

John, of course, will see and report on the horrible happenings of the history of our temporal earth. But for now, he has the marvelous experience of seeing the end from the beginning. The downward spiral of wickedness on earth seems to have been put on pause as John is permitted to see the ultimate glory of the Father and the Son with Their exalted children and all of creation praising Them for the saving plan They have effected in the lives of all who would accept thereof. Indeed, John looked and, "behold, a door was opened *into* heaven" (JST, Rev. 4:1; emphasis added), and he was invited to "come up hither, and I will shew thee things which must be hereafter" (Rev. 4:1). He experiences the reality of what celestial glory is all about. His vision of eternal splendor and the triumph of good over evil undoubtedly prepared him for his long mortal ministry in a fallen world. Just as a soldier's vision of eventual peace and reuniting with loved ones motivates him to endure the horror of warfare in our fallen world, so we may gain the strength to endure the continuing battle for the souls of mankind if we can but gain a vision of the nature of celestial glory. Chapters 4 and 5 of the book of Revelation help us gain that vision.

### A Rainbow Encircling the Throne Of God

*To what would you compare God's glory? How do you envision His life in celestial splendor?* In John's visit to the celestial realm, he is taken to the very throne of God, whom he beholds in bright and eternal splendor, symbolized by precious stones: "And he that sat was to look upon like a jasper and a sardine stone: and there was a rainbow round about the throne, in sight like unto an emerald" (Rev. 4:3).

In the Revelation of John, colors, like numbers, are symbolic. The sardine stone is of blood-red color and could thus symbolize death. The jasper is generally of green hue, and could thus symbolize life. So to look upon God, the "one [seated] on the throne" (Rev. 4:2) is to look upon one who has power over life and death and who has orchestrated both into a perfection of ultimate glory.

We can comprehend much about the celestial state and nature of God by considering the eternal significance of the rainbow. The perplexity of my youthful efforts to capture that proverbial pot of gold at the end of the rainbow was much relieved when I learned that the rainbow is not a two-ended arch, as we perceive it, but is actually a full and complete circle, "round about the throne" (Rev. 4:4). (One of my intelligent doctoral students explained scientifically to our class why this is so, but in my more simple view, I understand that we see an arch because we are looking at the bow on the horizon of the earth. If we were flying above the earth and looking down, we could view the complete circle.) So John is now seeing as God sees—in complete circle—the past, present, and the future all in one eternal round. "But they reside in the presence of God, on a globe like a sea of glass and fire, where all things for their glory are manifest, past, present, and future, and are continually before the Lord" (D&C 130:7).

For me, one of the many appealing aspects of gaining eternal life is the anticipated joy and excitement of being able to experience the past, present, and future all in perfect perspective and view. I would like to visit and understand with fullness of knowledge the motives and designs of the great historical events of time. I would like to visit the camp of General George Washington and be permitted to comprehend his fears and inspirations. I would like to sail with Columbus and correlate that journey with the lines I learned as a youth about him—"Sail on, Sail on, Sail on!" I look forward to experiencing an eternal view of the Sacred Grove and of feeling the peace and beauty of that lovely spring morning. I want to get better acquainted with my wife and children and come to understand and feel what my relationship was like with them in premortal life. My wish list could go on and on—indeed, it could go on forever. I believe it will be a great blessing to have all things—past, present, and future—encircled around us as a rainbow.

By coupling our view of the rainbow round about the throne of God with the great gems and jewels of doctrine and inspiration given us by the Prophet Joseph in his inspired translation of the Bible, we further learn that the rainbow is not just a symbol that the earth will never again be covered by flood, but that Zion—even that righteous city of Enoch—will return. The rainbow is a symbol of the Lord's covenant that He and the worthy members of His Church of the Firstborn will come and dwell on the earth: "And the bow shall be in the cloud; and I will look upon it, that I may remember the everlasting covenant, which I made unto thy father Enoch; that, when men shall keep all my commandments, Zion should again come on the earth, the city of Enoch which I have caught up unto myself. . . . And the bow shall be in the cloud, and I will establish my covenant unto thee, which I have made between me and thee . . . And God said unto Noah, This is the token of the covenant which I have established between me and thee; for all flesh that shall be upon the earth" (JST, Gen. 9:21, 24–25).

As we contemplate God on His throne encircled by the rainbow, we have the peace, hope, and assurance that everything He has promised will come to pass. We can trust Him with perfect and absolute confidence. His love, compassion, power, and glory do not have an end, but rather are like the rainbow—without ending or beginning.

I have a favorite child's illustrated book entitled *Children's Letters to God,* compiled by Stuart Hample and Eric Marshall. One letter states, "Dear God, I didn't think orange went with purple until I saw the sunset you made on Tuesday. That was _cool!_ Eugene."4 We may trust that God in His wisdom can take all of the colors of the universe and of our lives and meld them into a glorious eternal life for each of His children. Our black sorrows and our blue days can be tempered by the bright and glorious hues of God's plan and the redemptive Atonement of His Son. Remember, *Urim and Thummim* means "lights and perfections." The awesome rainbow around the throne of God can certainly be described as light in perfection. What a beautiful sight is the rainbow when we think of it as representative of God on His throne, in all of His splendor and perfect light and glory, inviting us to come there and, by covenant, join Him. "To him that overcometh will I grant to sit with me in my throne" (Rev. 3:21).

## FOUR AND TWENTY ELDERS

*Of what significance are the number* twelve *and multiples thereof? Who are the twenty-four elders seated around the throne?* John now sees twenty-four elders wearing crowns of gold: "And round about the throne were four and twenty seats: and upon the seats I saw four and twenty elders sitting, clothed in white raiment; and they had on their heads crowns of gold" (Rev. 4:4). The Joseph Smith Translation clarifies for us that the twenty-four elders were seated "in the midst of the throne" (JST, Rev. 4:4).

We now come to one of the greatest blessings we have in striving to understand the Revelation of John. We have the direct and inspired words of the Prophet Joseph Smith, shared with us from his question-and-answer session with the Lord. This Q-and-A session is found in the seventy-seventh section of the Doctrine and Covenants. (We will, in this book, make sure that we look at the entire section in the course of our study.) Joseph asked, "What are we to understand by the four and twenty elders, spoken of by John?" The Lord answered, "We are to understand that these elders whom John saw, were elders who had been faithful in the work of the ministry and were dead; who belonged to the seven churches and were then in the paradise of God" (D&C 77:5).

The number *twelve* represents the priesthood. As members of the Church, we could easily complete a fill-in-the-blank exercise such as, *The _____ Apostles form a governing quorum of the Church* or *A full quorum of deacons consists of _____ members* or *The stake president is assisted in his administration of the stake by _____ high councilors* or *A full quorum of elders consists of _____ members* or *_____ priests form a full quorum.* Each blank should be filled in with *twelve* or a multiple thereof (twelve deacons, forty-eight priests, and ninety-six elders constitute full quorums—see D&C 107:85, 87, and 89, respectively). When we multiply twelve by another number, we are simply portraying the increasing power and magnitude of the priesthood.

The power and magnitude of the priesthood increases in influence and glory as more souls accept the gospel. Could not the twenty-four elders then be representative of all who have lived or will live worthily, accept the gospel, and qualify for eternal life?

From the Doctrine and Covenants, we learn of some specific beings who "have been faithful in the ministry and are now dead" and are well on their way to admission to the seats around the throne of God—"Abraham . . . Isaac also and Jacob did none other things than that which they were commanded; and because they did none other things than that which they were commanded, they have entered into their exaltation, according to the promises, and sit upon thrones, and are not angels but are gods" (D&C 132:37). And whatever their present glorious status may be, the fullness of their glory will not be complete until a later time. The Prophet Joseph Smith taught, "and Adam receiving his Presidency and authority from the Lord, but cannot receive a fullness until Christ shall present the Kingdom to the Father, which shall be at the end of the last dispensation."[5]

## A SEA OF GLASS

*Will exalted beings really live on a big glass ball without all of the natural beauty of the earth we now enjoy?* John now describes what, at first glance, may seem a bit strange. He sees "a sea of glass like unto crystal" and "four beasts full of eyes before and behind. And the first beast was like a lion, and the second beast like a calf, and the third beast had a face as a man, and the fourth beast was like a flying eagle. And the four beasts had each of them six wings about him; and they were full of eyes within" (Rev. 4:6–8). What could all of this possibly mean?

Fortunately Joseph had similar wonderings and inquired of the Lord, "What is the sea of glass spoken of by John, 4th chapter, and 6th verse of Revelation?" The Lord's answer to this question was, "It is the earth, in its sanctified, immortal, and eternal state" (D&C 77:1).

When I consider the earth as a sea of glass I recall the concerns of some of my seminary students over the years as we discussed this concept of our earth someday being celestialized. Their concern was a certain sadness or disappointment that the many "orchards . . . gardens . . . [and] vineyards" created by God "to please the eye and to gladden the heart" (D&C 59:17–18) may need to give way to a stark and bland orb of glass. We found comfort in the words, "And the end shall come, and the heaven and the earth shall be consumed and pass away, and there shall be a new heaven and a new earth. For all old things shall pass away, and all things shall become new, even the heaven and the earth, and all the fulness thereof, both men and beasts, the fowls of the air, and the fishes of the sea; *and not one hair, neither mote, shall be lost, for it is the workmanship of mine hand*" (D&C 29:23–25; emphasis added).

Even without this passage, a common-sense approach would suggest that the beauty of the earth would certainly not be lost in the eternal realm. The things that are to "be consumed and pass away" are the corruptions and pollutions that have so often strangled and disgraced the workmanship of the Lord's hands. From the analogy of the sea of glass we conclude that just as glass is clear, is free of impurities, and allows us unobstructed vision, so we may imagine clear and pure rivers, flowing without toxins, amidst an Eden-like flora and fauna. At that day we will have unobstructed vision of

God's creation and the purposes thereof. Just as the sea is broad, deep, and well beyond what mortal man can now envision and comprehend, so earth will reveal the breadth and depth of its beauty and enlightenment. Spiritually, we may envision the very best of music, art, laughter, and joy without the degrading and deprecating vices of profanity and pornography that dominate our cultural world at present. What will pass away is the workmanship of Satan's dark and evil hands, as well as the workmanship of those mortal men who uphold his work.

### FOUR BEASTS

*How will the Lord's plan of salvation apply to the animal kingdom? (Or, as so often asked by my students over the years, "Will I see my dog or cat in heaven?")* Joseph's next question about chapter 4 of Revelation was, "What are we to understand by the four beasts, spoken of in the same verse?" The Lord answers, "They are figurative expressions, used by the Revelator, John, in describing heaven, the paradise of God, the happiness of man, and of beasts, and of creeping things, and of the fowls of the air; that which is spiritual being in the likeness of that which is temporal; and that which is temporal in the likeness of that which is spiritual; the spirit of man in the likeness of his person, as also the spirit of the beast, and every other creature which God has created" (D&C 77:2).

We often speak of the happiness and felicity of mankind—but not as much of the destiny of animals. Let's share a few doctrines and thoughts about them.

In 1909, the First Presidency taught, "Nevertheless, the whole animal creation will be perfected and perpetuated in the Hereafter, each class in its 'distinct order or sphere,' and will enjoy 'eternal felicity.' That fact has been made plain in this dispensation" (D&C 77:3).[6]

I have been impressed by the teaching of the Prophet Joseph Smith to the marchers of Zion's Camp. As the brethren were preparing to camp for the evening, they encountered three prairie rattlesnakes, which they were about to kill. The Prophet taught them, "Let them alone—don't hurt them! How will the serpent ever lose his venom, while the servants of God possess the same disposition, and continue to make war upon it? Men must become harmless, before the brute creation; and when men lose their vicious dispositions and cease to destroy the animal race, the lion and the lamb can dwell together, and the sucking child can play with the serpent in safety."7

I have appreciated stories and examples of tenderness toward animals and the lessons we can learn from them. Of the many such stories I have heard, one of my favorites is told by a friend of mine, Ron, as he was a supervising some workmen in the Tabernacle at Temple Square. There had been a choir concert on an especially warm night, so the workman had opened the doors to cool the building in preparation for the events of the next day, which included a repeat of the concert the next evening. While the doors were open, a sparrow flew into the Tabernacle and was not discovered until the next morning. The workmen tried everything they could think of to get the sparrow out of the building. Animal control officials were called in to assist and even suggested shooting the tiny guest, but my friend didn't think Church leaders would appreciate them shooting holes in the Tabernacle. Also, like me, Ron has a tender spot in his heart for animal life and creation.

In his quandary, Ron separated himself from the others and offered a simple and heartfelt prayer: "Heavenly Father, if this sparrow is important to you, could you please let us know how to safely remove it?"8 Almost immediately the answer came. Ron directed that all of the window blinds and all of the doors except one be closed and that all the lights be turned off. As soon as they had accomplished this, the frightened sparrow, now perched on top of the organ, followed the light of the open doorway and immediately flew to freedom. This story is not only a story about the tenderness and caring that converted souls have for God's creation, but is a great object lesson that God cares for His creatures and desires to lead all to the light of His love and glory.

Joseph now asks, "Are the four beasts limited to individual beasts, or do they represent classes or orders?" The Lord answers, "They are limited to four individual beasts, which were shown to John, to *represent* the glory of the *classes* of beings in their destined order or sphere of creation, in the enjoyment of their eternal felicity" (D&C 77:3; emphasis added). With this key, we can read Revelation 4:7 with a greater understanding by simply considering various "classes" of beasts—wild, domestic, flying, and human. The wild beast "like a lion" is representative of the tigers and bears and wolverines. The domestic beast "like a calf" could be a delegate for the goat and the horse and the pig. The beast with the "face as a man" is our representative. The beast "like a flying eagle" could also portray the goldfinch and the hawk and the pigeon.

It is instructive that only one face is mentioned, and that is the "face as a man." *Man* is distinguished or set apart from the animal kingdom. All of the animals have faces too, of course. But our face is different. From our face (from our mouth) we speak and exercise our God-given moral agency. Animals, in their quest for their realm of eternal felicity, need not and cannot exercise moral agency.

I recall an incident many years ago when my daughter was very young. I arrived home to find that she had secured her pet cat in a cardboard box. When I asked what she was doing, she informed me that the "cat had been bad and was in 'time-out.'" When I asked what the cat had done, she informed me that the cat had killed a bird in the backyard. I'm not sure how impressed she was at her young age with my proclaiming the innocence of the cat with a doctrinal exposition on the moral agency of man, but I enjoyed the lesson. (I have had occasion to discuss this with her now that she is older and have better made my point.)

Animals do not have moral agency. Nephi taught, "Where there is not law given there is no punishment; and where there is no punishment there is no condemnation" (2 Ne. 9:25). By nature, my daughter's cat was not guilty. We, as humans, differ from the animal kingdom. We exercise agency, and with it we have moral responsibility. We declare our allegiance to God "with our face" and by our actions.

## The Eyes and Wings of the Beasts

*How do you imagine the omniscience, the omnipotence, and the omnipresence of God?* John next sees that "the four beasts had each of them six wings about him; and they were full of eyes within: and they rest not day and night, saying Holy, holy, holy, Lord God Almighty, which was, and is, and is to come" (Rev. 4:8). Joseph asked the meaning of this: "What are we to understand by the eyes and wings, which the beasts had?" He was told, "Their eyes are a representation of light and knowledge, that is, they are full of knowledge: and their wings are a representation of power, to move, to act, etc." (D&C 77:4).

As I visit the seminary classes under my stewardship, I sometimes ask the students to imagine their upcoming birthday, Christmas, or other occasion on which they might receive a gift. I then ask them to share with the class what their dream or fantasy gift would be—and I suggest that money or other temporal restraints are of no object or condition on the gift they want. I can predict most of the responses. Some wish for a dream mansion in the Pacific Islands. Some imagine an expensive car—a Ferrari or a Lamborghini. I have heard expressed desires for time machines and goldmines—and much more.

I then talk to them about a potential gift they could all have—one that would be far greater than any they could ever imagine. This great gift is eternal life: "And, if you keep my commandments and endure to the end you shall have eternal life, which gift is the greatest of all the gifts of God" (D&C 14:7). We discuss how archaic and useless a Ferrari would be to someone who, with "six wings" (the power to move), could hie to Kolob in little more time than the twinkling of an eye. Even the most elaborate time machine imagined by science fiction would offer nothing to a being "full of eyes" who had the past, present, and future always present. The power of a magic wand would pale in comparison to the ability to speak and have mountains move. Of what value would a goldmine be to someone who held the resources of "worlds without number" (Moses 1:33)?

The capstone of our discussion is always the requirement for obtaining this great and marvelous gift. We are required to keep the commandments and endure to the end (see 2 Ne. 31:18–20). Or, to put it another way, we are to "rest not day and night" in living the gospel and in praising our "Holy . . . Lord God, Almighty" (Rev. 4:8). By our consistent, daily keeping of our covenants, we demonstrate our giving "glory and honour and thanks to him that sat on the throne, who liveth for ever and ever" (Rev. 4:9).

## CROWNS BEFORE THE THRONE OF GOD

*What is the greatest tribute someone could give you?* Sometimes I try to remember my life as a young teenager and try to remember how

I thought and lived back then. Perhaps I too would have wished for a fancy car or a time machine. But I am very certain of my present desire—which is the same as the desire of Lehi upon tasting eternal life. He simply wished the same eternal life for his family: "And as I partook of the fruit thereof it filled my soul with exceedingly great joy; wherefore, I began to be desirous that my family should partake of it also; for I knew that it was desirable above all other fruit" (1 Ne. 8:12). If I were asked the finest gift my children could give me, my answer would be an absolute no-brainer. It would simply be for them to present to me their lives—worthy and fully qualified for eternal life. I could not possibly wish for anything more.

Herein is the key to understanding why our Father in Heaven lives in perfect and complete joy—it is because of His children presenting to Him their perfected lives. They present to Him their crowns of eternal life and thank and praise Him forever for His love and for His great plan of happiness. "The four and twenty elders fall down before him that sat on the throne, and worship him that liveth for ever and ever, and cast their crowns before the throne, saying, Thou art worthy, O Lord, to receive glory and honour and power: for thou hast created all things, and for thy pleasure they are and were created" (Rev. 4:10–11).

This doctrine of the family has been profoundly and beautifully proclaimed by living prophets to all people of the world. From the inspired proclamation on the family and other teachings in scriptures and modern revelation, we learn that we lived in the premortal heavens as sons and daughters of God and that we there exercised our agency to follow the plan of our Father in Heaven. By this righteous choice, we received the blessing to come to earth and live and grow as families. Through sacred temple ordinances, we seal and unite our families forever and as such, return to the presence of God to abide in His glory forever.

This explains the concept of the power and knowledge of God expanding. It is not that He needs to obtain more power—He is omnipotent. It is not that He needs to gain more knowledge—He is omniscient. It is that He has invited all of His children to come unto Him and gain eternal life. It is that He delights in giving total freedom to His creations. It is that He has been successful in His "work and glory" of providing "immortality and eternal life" (Moses 1:39) for His children. Is it any wonder that all of creation—including beasts and humans—continue in their praise of Him forever and ever?

# Chapter Five
# Worthy Is the Lamb

DO YOU EVER FEEL CHALLENGED *to make sense of our troubled and fallen world?* I spend much time in my car as I administer the Church Educational System programs for which I have responsibility. I have been able to travel not only the highways and byways of Wisconsin, but through the blessing of audio books, to also travel the geography and history of the world. As a sample of my readings, I have listened to *The Story of Civilization,* the classic series by Will and Ariel Durant. These gifted authors chronicle the history of the world in a most vivid portrayal of countless scenes of war, torture, oppression, revenge, famine, rape, plunder, and of all human suffering.

To contemplate the wicked panorama of history is often depressing and heart-wrenching. In my mind, it seems that the more I learn, the *higher and deeper has become the pile of dead bodies.* For me as a mere mortal to attempt to make sense of the vista of the temporal history of this fallen world has caused me to weep—often in my heart and sometimes with real tears. My study and my emotional reaction to what I have learned have helped me to better understand the experience of John the Revelator as he viewed the great scroll of the earth unfurled, wherein was depicted all of the misery and heartache of the ages. Such visions of the trials of God's children serve to accentuate the necessity of the redeeming plan of salvation and perfect Atonement as pillars of faith, hope, and salvation in a troubled world.

## A BOOK SEALED WITH SEVEN SEALS

As John's vision continues, we learn of our Father in Heaven seated in His throne of glory and power and holding a book in His right hand:

"And I saw in the right hand of him that sat on the throne a book written within and on the backside, sealed with seven seals" (Rev. 5: 1). The fact that the book was written "within and on the backside" suggests that the book is full—that it contains the complete picture of the world. Nothing of good or evil has been omitted.

John's vision is focused on a period of about seven thousand years, beginning at some point after the Fall was effected in the lives of our first parents. This book seen by John prompted the next set of questions from the Prophet Joseph Smith: "Q. What are we to understand by the book which John saw, which was sealed on the back with seven seals? A. We are to understand that it contains the revealed will, mysteries, and the works of God; the hidden things of his economy concerning this earth during the seven thousand years of its continuance, or its temporal existence" (D&C 77:6). *Temporal* is defined as "lasting only for a time; transitory, temporary, not eternal."9 Thus, the book is a recording of the temporary stage of the earth—or the existence of the earth during its fallen state. The world is not destined to remain in this fallen condition any more than are we, as children of God, to be stuck in this stage of our existence forever. We are just in a transitory or temporary time in our forward progress to eternal life. Similarly, our earthly home is also in a transitory and temporary state, which is approaching an end as it is being prepared to be "renewed and receive its paradisiacal glory" (A of F 1:10).

When contemplating the temporal existence of the earth, I find it helpful to remind myself of what I *do not know*. For example, I do not know the age of the earth. I do not know the length of the days of creation. I do not know if all of the days of creation were of equal length. I do not know if there was a time of respite between each of the days of creation. I am content to leave these questions to further study by science and further revelation from God. What I *do know* is that God created the earth and all things therein and that He also created Adam and Eve and all flesh, human and animal.

I do not know the exact timeline of the Fall of Adam and Eve—I do not know how long the process of the Fall took. I just know that it happened and that, as a condition of the Fall, Adam and Eve began their new adventure in a lonesome and challenging world—a world that itself was to be in a temporary fallen condition.

Joseph's next question was, "Q. What are we to understand by the seven seals with which [the book] was sealed? A. We are to understand that the first seal contains the things of the first thousand years, and the second also of the second thousand years, and so on until the seventh" (D&C 77:7). As we examine the seven thousand-year period of the earth's temporal existence, it's possible to get distracted by the unknowns; instead, we could seek out the higher and more valuable doctrine of *why* our earth exists. John's focus is on the latter.

## John Wept Much

*Where can we turn for peace? Can anyone help us in our trouble?* How could John endure witnessing the entire depressing scene of the history of the world in the relatively brief moment of his Sabbath vision? The condition of being "in the Spirit" (Rev. 1:10), of course, was key to his enduring this experience. Sometimes it is difficult for us to make any sense of our fallen world. Who can reconcile the evil of humanity with the goodness of God? Who can help lift us from our wretched, temporal condition?

I occasionally seek out a competent attorney to help me understand the complicated wrangling and legal jargon of the business of life. For example, in my recent quest to bless and protect the life of my mother, who has Alzheimer's disease, I was trying to become her legal guardian. I sat with a specialized attorney, who needed to examine some medical and financial documents. The first thing the attorney did was *open* and read the documents. He then used his knowledge and experience to help me take the proper course of action to best help my mother. At the appropriate time, he went with me to court, where he represented me and advocated for the best interest of my mother. In a sense, he helped me *save* her from some rather serious potential pitfalls. It could be said that in a very real way, he made sense of her difficult circumstance and reconciled the disparity between the reality of her life situation and the further help that she needed. His comprehension of the matters at hand enabled a judgment that was a right and just decision in the case.

As John viewed the events that would take place in the world, his first reaction was that the plight of man seemed quite hopeless. It seemed to him that no one would be able to make sense of the evil, save the people, and reconcile reality to potential. John records, "And I saw a strong angel proclaiming with a loud voice, Who is worthy to open the book, and to loose the seals thereof? And no man in heaven, nor in earth, neither under the earth, was able to open the book, neither to look thereon" (Rev. 5:2–3).

If the vision were to stop here, it would end in darkness and despair. Even the experience of merely viewing in revelation this seemingly unsolvable condition of the world caused John great sorrow. What mortal on earth, or even angel in heaven, could possibly make sense of the cumulative chaos of the earth's history? And even if one could understand, how could all that has gone wrong possibly be put right? Of his feeling of helpless sorrow, John writes, "And I wept much, because no man was found worthy to open and to read the book, neither to look thereon" (Rev. 5:4).

## THE LION OF JUDA PREVAILS

*Can you imagine the joy and peace John would have felt to have his vision transform from the dark and hopeless to the light and glory of the mission of the Savior of the world?* We know that Heavenly Father does not forget His children, and that He has provided a way to fix all that has gone wrong throughout all time. We read in modern revelation, "And the redemption of the soul is through him that quickeneth all things, in whose bosom it is decreed that the poor and the meek of the earth shall inherit it. Therefore, it must needs be sanctified from all unrighteousness that it may be prepared for the celestial glory; For after it hath filled the measure of its creation, it shall be crowned with glory, even with the presence of God the Father; That bodies who are of the celestial kingdom may possess it forever and ever; for, for this intent was it made and created, and for this intent are they sanctified" (D&C 88:17–20). This plan of the Father to sanctify the earth and fulfill the measure of creation requires that someone execute His will. The plan requires a Savior—someone to save us from the downward spiral of this temporary and terrible condition of our fallen world.

John now sees the execution of the will of the Father: "And one of the elders saith unto me, Weep not: behold, the Lion of the tribe of Juda, the Root of David, hath prevailed to open the book, and to loose the seven seals thereof. And I beheld, and, lo, in the midst of the throne and of the four beasts, and in the midst of the elders, stood a Lamb as it had been slain, having seven horns and seven eyes, which are the seven Spirits of God sent forth into all the earth. And he came and took the book out of the right hand of him that sat upon the throne" (Rev. 5:5–7).

John is brought from his sorrow and weeping to the knowledge and testimony of the redeeming mission of Christ. What great joy and comfort is John's and ours as we contemplate that a Savior was provided to open the book, make sense of it, and right all that goes wrong in the lives of all who have ever lived. What peace we have at the thought of Christ lifting or opening the seals of spiritual and physical death and of Him relieving the pain and suffering of all humanity. The dark thread of suffering, heartache, misery, and death through the span of the seven seals can be tempered and transformed into a bright and golden thread of joy, peace, comfort, and light through the Atonement and Resurrection of our Savior. He, the "Lamb"—even though He "had been slain"—lives again and prevails over death and hell.

### Twelve Servants Proclaim Redemption into All the Earth

*How does Christ administer His salvation to all the world?* The inspired translation of the Bible provides significant clarification to John's vision of the ministry of the Savior: "And I beheld . . . a Lamb as it had been slain, having *twelve* horns and *twelve* eyes, which are the *twelve servants* of God, sent forth to all the earth" (JST, Rev. 5:6; emphasis added).

*Horns* represent power. *Eyes* represent knowledge. *Twelve* represents the priesthood. The cleansing *power* and saving *knowledge* of the priesthood is appropriately centered in and administered by Jesus Christ. He is the *head* of the Church. (It is instructive to think how the head of an animal, for example, controls and gives direction and power to the horns.)

Christ, in perfection and purity, emanates His grace and mercy throughout the earth with the assistance of His *twelve servants*—even the anointed Apostles. Paul taught, "Seeing then that we have a great high priest, that is passed into the heavens, Jesus the Son of God, let us hold fast *our profession.* For we have not an high priest which cannot be touched with the feeling of our infirmities; but was in all points tempted like as we are, yet without sin. Let us therefore come boldly unto the throne of grace, that we may obtain mercy, and find grace to help in time of need" (Heb. 4:14–16; emphasis added). The profession of Paul and of all Apostles is to witness of Christ to the world.

A few years ago on a late-night drive I was listening to a preacher on the radio. He quoted a verse that I have long believed to be a great definition of the role and mission of an Apostle: "Beginning from the baptism of John, unto that same day that he was taken up from us, must one be ordained to be a witness with us of his resurrection" (Acts 1:22). The preacher then commented, "An Apostle must be a personal witness of Christ." I perked up and thought, *Wow, he sure got that right!* He then went on to say, "Therefore, there are no Apostles today." Wow, he sure got that wrong! When I consider all that I have learned and felt about the atoning sacrifice of the Lamb of God, it is with gratitude that I acknowledge the work of the twelve servants of the Lamb as the ministers of spiritual truth. I am grateful for all of the sermons spoken and testimonies borne by these powerful and humble servants, "sent forth into all the earth" (Rev. 5:6) by our Savior.

## CHRIST ON THE RIGHT HAND OF GOD—MYRIADS SAVED

*How significant is it to you to know that you can have implicit faith and trust in your Savior?* A common phrase used to describe a responsible and worthy person is *right-hand man*. In light of that phrase, it is interesting to consider Christ and His role at the right hand of the Father. In his dying testimony, Stephen said, "Behold, I see the heavens opened, and the Son of man standing on the right hand of God" (Acts 7:56).

Consistent with our earlier discussion that Christ holds the keys of death and hell (see Rev. 1:18) is the understanding that the Father has personally given Him charge of the book with seven seals: "And he came and took the book out of the right hand of him that sat upon the throne" (Rev. 5:7). The Father has implicit trust in the Son to carry out His will. Imagine a struggling corporation seeking a new chief executive officer. As they searched, the board of directors would seek someone who had the qualifications and experience to *save* the company. The successful candidate would need to be *worthy* of the responsibility such a position entailed. Once the board found the right leader, they would naturally *empower* that person with all available resources and authority to remedy errors and move the company successfully forward. Here is where the analogy falls short: in the temporal, corporate world, there is no divine guarantee up front that the leader will be successful. (Wouldn't *that* be an amazing thing?)

In the economy and plan of God, however, there *is* a proven and sure leader: His Only Begotten Son. The Savior is completely trustworthy because of His sinless life and His divine mission. With total confidence, the Father divinely invests His authority in His Son. There is no doubting of the Son's qualifications. There is no questioning of His worthiness. There is no second-guessing His leadership abilities. There is absolute confidence that Christ stands in perfect unity with the Father in the mission of saving the Father's children. There is peace knowing that He is divinely appointed to be the Father of our salvation. The vision of John offers us hope in the prospect of eternal life for *all* who choose to follow the "strait and narrow path which leads to eternal life" (2 Ne. 31:18).

There is comfort in knowing that our Father in Heaven has calculated sufficient provision for the salvation of all of His children. John records, "And hast made us unto our God kings and priests: and we shall reign on the earth. And I beheld, and I heard the voice of many angels round about the throne and the beasts and the elders: and the number of them was ten thousand times ten thousand, and thousands of thousands" (Rev. 5:10–11). As broad and inclusive as the multiplication of tens of thousands may be, these are merely figurative numeric expressions of a divine truth: God has made provision for the salvation of *all* His children. Indeed, that is what He dearly wants. There is great rejoicing that a leader capable of carrying out the salvation of the world has been given charge of the world! *Rejoicing* is the inspiring theme of the rest of this chapter.

## A NEW SONG: WORTHY IS THE LAMB

*Have you ever been so happy and encouraged by an event or condition that you felt like singing out with praise and joy?* As we think about some of the classic examples of this kind of joy, we visualize musical outbursts like, "Oh, what a beautiful morning!" and "The hills are alive with the sound of music!" With the knowledge that Christ has charge of the earth and that the work and glory of the Father will continue, John may now cease his weeping, dry his tears, and look with joy to the salvation of the world.

All creatures (represented by the four beasts) and all who seek eternal life (represented by the four and twenty elders) sing out their songs of joy and praise at this glorious hope for salvation: "And when he had taken the book, the four beasts and the four and twenty elders fell down before the Lamb, having every one of them harps, and golden vials full of odours, which are the prayers of saints. And they sung a new song, saying, Thou art worthy to take the book, and to open the seals thereof: for thou wast slain, and hast redeemed us to God by thy blood out of every kindred, and tongue, and people, and nation" (Rev. 5:8–9).

How fitting that the praise of the Lord is portrayed through a "new song." Although I claim no personal musical talent, my soul is comforted and my heart is lifted by worthy and inspiring music. Occasionally as we sing a particular hymn in sacrament meeting, I find myself wondering why I have never before "heard" the words of the song. It becomes as a new song to me—a song of beauty, praise, worship, and gratitude to my Savior. The inspired lines of many of our hymns help give me courage to dry my tears of sorrow and to go forward with hope and faith in Christ.

How inspiring it would be to someday sit in sacrament meeting and sing the new song of John's vision with the accurate and appropriate mix of words and music he envisioned. In the meantime, God has inspired gifted artists to inspire us by the same message—if not the exact composition. One such artist is George Frederick Handel, who, under inspiration from God, so beautifully portrayed the message of the new song of John's vision. His work, the *Messiah* is described in this way:

> On the right day in London of the 1740s you could see him walking down Brook Street in the vicinity of Grosvenor Square. An elderly gentlemen, neatly dressed in his lace coat, ruffles and three-cornered

hat, he would proceed at full steam, talking to himself as if the problems of the nation were on his shoulders, and then pause abruptly to contemplate his surroundings. The people he passed often noticed that he spoke a mixture of two languages. He was the greatest composer England ever had, though he was an adopted one from Germany. If you had followed this curious cosmopolitan gentleman along Brook Street to his home on August 22, 1741, you might have seen him sit at his desk in the front room and start to put notes on paper with remarkable speed. For the next 23 days he wouldn't leave the house; his manservant would bring his meals to the room. Then on September 14, after a little over three weeks of feverish work on the manuscript, he would shut the completed "Messiah" in his drawer where it would remain practically untouched for the next seven weeks! Whatever the case, we know that Handel was deeply moved during the 23 days. At one point, after having written down the Hallelujah Chorus, he called to his manservant and with eyes filled with tears exclaimed, "I did think I did see all heaven before me, and the great God Himself."[10]

I attribute the greatness of Handel's work to several factors: the greatness of his subject matter, his marvelous talent, and the profound vision and expression of John—as well as those of other prophets whose words became a part of his masterpiece. What a glorious message is composed from the words of John: "Worthy is the Lamb that was slain to receive power, and riches, and wisdom, and strength, and honour, and glory, and blessing. And every creature which is in heaven, and on the earth, and under the earth, and such as are in the sea, and all that are in them, heard I saying, Blessing, and honour, and glory, and power, be unto him that sitteth upon the throne, and unto the Lamb for ever and ever" (Rev. 5:12–13).

As John explains, the response to the new song inspired awesome worship in all of creation: "And the four beasts said, Amen. And the four and twenty elders fell down and worshipped him that liveth for ever and ever" (Rev. 5:14). Hopefully, we may all feel to rejoice with the four beasts and the four and twenty elders as they speak "Amen" to the Great Amen, even the Savior of the world. By so doing we proclaim the truth, surety, and validity of His station as the Messiah and Redeemer. We also proclaim His worthiness and power to open the book and perform an infinite and eternal Atonement for all that happens in our temporal world. If we can so rejoice and proclaim, we will be better prepared to come off conqueror in the pending battle with Satan, the great dragon.

# Chapter Six

# The Opening of the Seals

*WHAT DIFFERENCE WOULD IT MAKE in your life if you could see the complete view of the world—to know the end from the beginning?* I occasionally daydream about living in a future day when the earth will be full of the knowledge of the Lord—when all things will be made known. There are so many curious and mysterious things to discover—so many dots to connect. How exciting will be our history class in the Millennium when we have a complete and unbiased account of the story of civilization.

As exciting as that day will be, today is not that day, and we must content ourselves with a partial view. Although John shares much with us in his vision, we still have only a very limited view of all things past and future. For example, as we now begin our study of the opening of the seven seals, we have only a few representative samples of the whole. Within a mere eleven verses, John presents us with a brief summary of the first five seals—the first five thousand years of the earth's temporal existence.

As we learned in the very first verse of the Revelation, the context of John's vision was mostly futuristic for him: "The Revelation of Jesus Christ, which God gave unto him, to shew unto his servants things which must shortly come to pass" (Rev. 1:1). Although John speaks a few words about each of the dispensations, he deals mostly with his future—the latter dispensations. He was able to see through the darkness and with the illuminating light of the Spirit, allowing him to speak and write about the events of the latter days when all things would come together to prepare the earth for the Second Coming of Christ and the completion of the plan of salvation.

## PATIENCE WITH THE PUZZLE

*Do we patiently trust that the Lord will, in His own due time, reveal all things yet unknown? Do we strive to see the big picture of life without being overly distracted by less significant details?* Let's consider what is meant by the "less significant details." We should be cautious about trying to construct geographies and chronologies from the book of Revelation. We should resist the urge to format the vision into an exact, sequential timeline—because constructing such a timeline is unnecessary or even impossible, it would be an absolutely futile exercise. A more practical and edifying approach would be to focus solely on the plan of happiness and our Father's mission to exalt His children. We would be wise to patiently examine the various pieces of the puzzle as they are unveiled to us.

A few times each year as I travel to Salt Lake City, I try to spend some time on Temple Square. In the North Visitors' Center, a beautiful kiosk depicts Jerusalem at the time of Christ. Surrounding the display are helpful descriptions; each is accompanied by a button that activates a brief narration and causes a small light to come on at the appropriate geographic point of interest. Each time I visit the display, I gain a few new insights of the ancient city by walking around, pushing the buttons, looking at the lights, and listening to the commentary. Gaining a comprehensive view of the earth's history is somewhat like visiting the Jerusalem kiosk—the more we find out about the specifics, the greater our understanding of the whole.

There are some important points of chronology we already know. In the life of Christ, for example, it is certainly important to place the events of the Upper Room before the events of the Garden of Gethsemane. In the Revelation of John, we should keep in mind that the "woman fled into the wilderness" (Rev. 12:6) before John "saw another angel fly in the midst of heaven" (Rev. 14:6). But we don't need to worry too much about whether the great earthquake will still be quaking as the moon turns to blood. The approach I take with my study of the Revelation is to keep walking around, pushing the buttons and looking at the lights. There is still much I need to piece together, and I am fairly confident that I will not understand some pieces at all during mortality—but the view of the grand design is increasing in clarity for me.

## LITERAL VERSUS FIGURATIVE

*How may we find encouragement when we discover new truths without getting frustrated that we can't discover the meaning of all things?* It's a challenge to determine what in John's vision is literal and what is figurative. We don't always know, and we aren't always told. Sometimes it matters, and sometimes it doesn't. Sometimes a scene may have both a literal and a figurative meaning. The counsel to strive for an understanding of the grand view is of great benefit as we study—and when we are wondering, for example, if John was seeing a modern military tank (and struggling to find the words to describe it) or whether he really was seeing a horse with fire, smoke, and brimstone pouring out of its mouth. If we keep the grand view in mind while seeking true principles and life applications, passages like these should not cause much of a distraction.

We should also remember that a symbol describing a particular event or time may apply to other events and times. For example, even though the horseman on the black horse of death and famine may be seen riding through the third seal, common sense and experience would tell us that this same horseman continues to ride through all of the seals—famine is a plague of every age.

## THE FIRST SEAL

With this background and perspective, let's now view the opening of the first seal—the time from Adam to Enoch. John records, "And I saw when the Lamb opened one of the seals, and I heard, as it were the noise of thunder, one of the four beasts saying, Come and see. And I saw, and behold a white horse: and he that sat on him had a bow; and a crown was given unto him: and he went forth conquering and to conquer" (Rev. 6:1–2). The prophet Enoch certainly fits the description of the rider on the white horse. His strength and stratagem as a commander of both physical and spiritual enemies were unequaled.

As we are introduced to the different conquerors on various colors of horses, we can better understand them by looking at how we conquer today. When the leader of a nation wants to exhibit his country's military might, he stages a parade of soldiers with their weaponry. The soldiers wear the appropriate uniform—with camouflage suiting the current campaign—and are outfitted with the most contemporary protective equipment, such as night vision goggles and global positioning systems. Along with the march of infantrymen comes the tanks, missiles, boats, planes, and guns. The implied message of the parade is *we will conquer* or *we have conquered.*

In ancient times, leaders of various nations had the same motive in displaying their warfare. To understand what was happening, we need only substitute our modern implements of war with theirs— such things as horses, chariots, swords, spears, bows, arrows, and shields. The implied message is the same—*we will conquer* or *we have conquered.*

Everything about the symbol of the horseman on the white horse speaks of victory. White symbolizes victory and purity. The crown represents the wreath or garland of a conqueror. The bow symbolizes an offensive weapon. So when we think of the first thousand-year period of our temporal earth, Enoch is a fitting representative symbol of the time. What an impressive campaign he waged! What modern general with his sophisticated weaponry would not delight in the ability of Enoch to cause the mountains to flee "and the rivers of water [to turn] out of their course" (Moses 7:13)?

As impressive as was Enoch's military might against evil tyrants, there is a much greater and more profound lesson to be learned from him. As we consider his life and mission, we naturally draw application to the battle of good and evil—the battle of God and Satan. As God's children, we are doing daily battle with the hosts of Satan. The word *conquer* also becomes a modern charge given us to "pray always, that you may come off conqueror; yea, that you may conquer Satan, and that you may escape the hands of the servants of Satan that do uphold his work" (D&C 10:5). Enoch was truly this kind of conqueror. It is instructive that as a symbol of the first seal John presents a man of such righteous influence that he was able to lead and motivate his people to be of one heart and mind and to "[dwell] in righteousness" so completely that they truly conquered this fallen world by being "taken up into heaven" (Moses 7:18, 23).

*How do you feel about your ability to conquer evil?* We may gratefully acknowledge the example of Enoch's victory over evil at the *beginning* of the world as a type and shadow of things to come at the *end* of our mortal trial and endurance. The vision of our ability and capacity to conquer Satan, gain eternal life, and be safely taken to the peace and security of heaven rings very consistent with the theme of hope, healing, peace, and triumph from the Revelation of John. Hopefully this vision will motivate us to march diligently and consistently forward with the battle cry etched firmly in our minds and hearts: *We will conquer Satan and triumph over evil.*

## THE SECOND SEAL

John now sees the opening of the second seal: "And when he had opened the second seal, I heard the second beast say, Come and see. And there went out another horse that was red: and power was given to him that sat thereon to take peace from the earth, and that they should kill one another: and there was given unto him a great sword" (Rev. 6:3–4). Red—the color of blood—symbolizes this era. The horseman who was powerful enough to "take peace from the earth" sounds like Lucifer himself; that horseman can also represent countless of Lucifer's followers who murdered and raged through the earth between 3000 and 2000 BC.

As we see this red horse of war and destruction riding through the second seal, we need only look around to see him riding through our day as well. We also live in a day of war that was described being "when peace shall be taken from the earth, and the devil shall have power over his own dominion" (D&C 1:35). Just as this red horse of destruction rode through the days of Noah, when "every man was lifted up in the imagination of the thoughts of his heart, being only evil continually" (Moses 8:22), he continues his ride through our place and time.

*How do we give battle to the red horse of war and destruction—how are we to survive our day of war and bloodshed?* Obviously, we need to seek out and support righteous leaders. We need to be good citizens and fulfill our patriotic duty to defend our freedoms and put down tyranny. But the first part of our patriotic duty is our *personal* preparation to conquer the red horse. And the first step in our personal battle is being honest with ourselves and others by recognizing the status of war and violence in our own lives. Have we ever heard the statement, "Oh, that movie is fine—it just has some violence but no sex." Or how about the comment, "I am mature enough to handle it—it doesn't affect me." Are we personally preparing to battle the red horse, or are we defecting to his cause?

As Alma counseled his wayward son Corianton, he clearly taught us the gravity of murderous violence when he spoke of unchastity as being "an abomination in the sight of the Lord; yea, most abominable above all sins save it be the shedding of innocent blood or denying the Holy Ghost" (Alma 39:5). This passage gives the murdering rampage of the red horse its proper priority.

To be successful in our personal battle with war and violence, we must follow the counsel of King Benjamin when he taught, "watch yourselves, and your thoughts, and your words, and your deeds . . . and perish not" (Mosiah 4:30). We are blessed to have clear standards of moral decency given by prophets. As the world struggles to ascertain what is appropriate for young and old, we are taught to not touch the evil and damning things of the world at any age.

As Captain Moroni was battling the red horse of his era, he encountered what he at first supposed was the apathy of his government and threatened to turn his forces first to the task of housecleaning this inner vessel. He said, "Now I would that ye should remember that God has said that the inward vessel shall be cleansed first, and then shall the outer vessel be cleansed also" (Alma 60:23). Our modern-day prophets have continued this battle cry for the cleansing of the inner vessel. As we cleanse the inner vessel and purge violence and immorality from our personal lives, we are preparing to join with the throngs of other righteous Saints in doing battle with the terrible and frightening red horse—who, in reality, is weak and powerless in the face of true righteousness and gospel preparation.

## THE THIRD SEAL

When the third seal was opened, John "heard the third beast say, Come and see. And I beheld, and lo a black horse; and he that sat on him had a pair of balances in his hand. And I heard a voice in the midst of the four beasts say, A measure of wheat for a penny, and three measures of barley for a penny; and see thou hurt not the oil and the wine" (Rev. 6:5–6). In the economy of that day, a measure of wheat had the price tag of a day's wages—it was all they could do to earn enough to stay alive from one day to the next.

This black horse of famine riding through the third seal has been vividly portrayed by some of the great leaders of that period. Of necessity, Abraham left his homeland because "the famine became very grievous" (Abr. 2:21). Joseph, who was wickedly sold into seeming oblivion by his brothers, became their temporal savior because of his providential rise to power and his prudent storage of food and provision: "Now therefore be not grieved, nor angry with yourselves, that ye sold me hither: for God did send me before you to preserve life" (Gen. 45:5).

*How does this famine apply to us and how may we learn the principles of provident living to guide us through our life of limited resources?* Although it is challenging to find a message of peace and hope in a time when famine hurts so many, we can be grateful for the teachings and resources we have received from our inspired leaders that help us provide for the temporal welfare of our loved ones. Our charge and challenge then become to share these saving truths with all the world.

Specifically, I am grateful for the example and teachings of an elderly couple who were our neighbors for many years. For more than two decades, we lived next door to this couple. He was the stake president and the man I replaced in the seminary; she was hardworking and well-educated. They were true stewards of the earth and lived mostly from the work of their own hands and from the production of their own food.

Because our orchards and gardens bordered each other, I was privileged to spend countless hours through the years talking with them over the fence as we waited for our irrigation water to soak the ground or as we took a break from our labors. They spoke and lived such principles as *Use it up, wear it out, make it do—or do without* and *Debt is like a crying baby—attend to it immediately.* They shared their knowledge throughout the stake and blessed many lives with their example of simplicity, frugality, service, charity, and providence. After many years I presided as bishop at the funeral of this dear sister; my remarks were naturally drawn to pay tribute to her as the "virtuous woman" whose "price is far above rubies," one who "eateth not the bread of idleness" (Prov. 31:10). She and her husband were the epitome of provident living.

John's counsel that we "hurt not the oil and the wine" (Rev. 6:6) implies that we are to protect and preserve our resources and to be valiant in our stewardship. For so doing, the Lord has promised that "it is my purpose to provide for my saints, for all things are mine. But it must needs be done in mine own way; and behold this is the way that I the Lord, have decreed to provide for my saints, that the poor shall be exalted, in that the rich are made low. For the earth is full, and there is enough and to spare" (D&C 104:15–17). If we are provident, obedient, and faithful in keeping the commandments, we can have the peace and assurance that He will "rebuke the devourer for [our] sakes" (Mal. 3:11). If we are willing to do the Lord's work in the Lord's way, we need not fear the black horse and its rider.

## THE FOURTH SEAL

As the fourth seal is opened, John sees "a pale horse: and his name that sat on him was Death, and Hell followed with him. And power was given unto them over the fourth part of the earth, to kill with sword, and with hunger, and with death, and with the beasts of the earth" (Rev. 6:8). (*Pale* refers to a sickly "pale green." When someone looks very ill, we often say he is "pale" or that she looks "green.") The pale horse referred to in this verse is the color of death. Death from war and all of its attending plagues was the overriding theme of this period.

During this time of massive war, death, and destruction, we see excessive blood on the hands of the kings of Israel—even Saul, David, and Solomon. We are horrified by the brutality of the Assyrian and Babylonian captivities—it seems that the inhumanity of mankind has reached a level never before imagined. And so goes the reign of the pale horse.

In the previous chapter, I summarized my readings of wars and destructions with the phrase, "The pile of dead bodies keeps getting higher and deeper." Although this is not a pleasant thought, it is stark reality—a reality that will yet continue for a time. We know from modern revelation that the pale horse of death and destruction will continue to ride until the very end of the earth's temporal timeline—war will continue until it "hath made a full end of all nations" (D&C 87:6). *How can we live in a wicked, warring world and not lose our eternal hope and our true perspective? Where can we look for an example of how to live and how to cope with such overwhelming destruction?* There are many possible examples; one of the most profound is the life of a great man who actually lived near the end of the fourth seal and who, for much of his lifetime, gave battle to the pale horse and his riders: Captain Moroni.

In the Book of Mormon, we learn that "Moroni was a strong and a mighty man . . . of a perfect understanding; yea, a man that did not delight in bloodshed; a man whose soul did joy in the liberty and the freedom of his country . . . a man whose heart did swell with thanksgiving to his God . . . who did labor exceedingly for the welfare and safety of his people . . . a man who was firm in the faith of Christ, and he had sworn with an oath to defend his people, his rights, and his country, and his religion, even to the loss of blood" (Alma 48:11–13). A great tribute is then paid to Captain Moroni with the words, "if all men had been, and were, and ever would be, like unto Moroni, behold, the very powers of hell would have been shaken forever; yea, the devil would never have power over the hearts of the children of men" (Alma 48:17).

From the valiant life and service of Captain Moroni in the day of the pale horse, we discover the keys that will enable us to survive our own day of death and destruction. We need to be thankful for the many patriots who have given life and fortune that we might have our liberty. We need to turn our individual hearts from bloodshed and violence. We need to give whatever means we have to protect the welfare and safety of our people. And above all, we need to stand firm in the faith of Christ by remembering and honoring our gospel covenants.

## THE FIFTH SEAL

With the opening of the fifth seal, John now sees the Christian martyrs and the eternal reward they will receive for sacrificing their lives to the gospel cause: "I saw under the altar the souls of them that were slain for the word of God, and for the testimony which they held: And they cried with a loud voice, saying, How long, O Lord, holy and true, dost thou not judge and avenge our blood on them that dwell on the earth? And white robes were given unto every one of them; and it was said unto them, that they should rest yet for a little season, until their fellowservants also and their brethren, that should be killed as they were, should be fulfilled" (Rev. 6:9–11).

In his eyewitness account of the martyrdom of the Prophet Joseph Smith and his brother Hyrum, Elder John Taylor wrote that "their innocent blood on the banner of liberty and on the magna charta of the United States, is an ambassador for the religion of Jesus Christ, that will touch the hearts of honest men among all nations; and their *innocent blood,* with the innocent blood of all the martyrs under the altar that John saw, will cry unto the Lord of Hosts till he avenges that blood on the earth" (D&C 135:7; emphasis added).

*Have you ever wondered if you would be willing to die for the gospel cause and for your testimony of Christ and of His Church?* A few times each year, I find myself visiting Carthage Jail, where Joseph and Hyrum were martyred. In the upper bedroom, where the martyrdom took place, I usually seat myself on the windowsill from where the Prophet fell to his death. From this vantage point, I can better imagine the events inside and outside the jail as our missionary guide recounts to us the happenings of that fateful day. Sometimes I ask myself, *What would I have done had I been here on that day more than a century and a half ago? Would I have been afraid to die? Would I have been at peace? Would I have remained true to the end?* I was touched recently when I heard one of our modern Apostles testify that he would have been willing to die there. His testimony lifted my spirit and strengthened my soul. And yet, how can I really know how I would feel and react in such a circumstance? It is difficult to imagine.

*Are you willing to live for the gospel cause?* This is a question that might be easier to answer, and one that provides personal relevancy with the example of the Christian martyrs. Years ago I served as a branch president at the Missionary Training Center in Provo, Utah. Elder Russell M. Ballard of the Quorum of the Twelve Apostles came there occasionally in his role as a member of the Missionary Committee and taught the missionaries about their service. He often quoted the Apostle Paul writing to the Romans: "I beseech you therefore, brethren, by the mercies of God, that ye present your bodies a *living* sacrifice, holy, acceptable unto God, which is your reasonable service" (Rom. 12:1; emphasis added). The application is quite clear: in our current time and place, likely not many will be called on to die for the gospel cause—but all are invited to live for it through our reasonable service. As we love and serve our families, serve in our Church callings, and live and serve as good citizens in our communities, we present ourselves as living sacrifices to the Lord. Most often, our quiet acts of service are not applauded by the world as being unusual or heroic—but in the eternal world, a lifetime of presenting ourselves as a living sacrifice gains the same reward of eternal life as is gained by the martyrs of John's vision.

**THE SIXTH SEAL**

The opening of the sixth seal describes a fantastic and awesome display of quaking earth, falling stars and rocks, and fleeing mountains. John records, "And I beheld when he had opened the sixth seal, and, lo, there was a great earthquake; and the sun became black as sackcloth of hair, and the moon became as blood; And the stars of heaven fell unto the earth, even as a fig tree casteth her untimely figs, when she is shaken of a mighty wind. And the heaven departed as a scroll when it is rolled together; and every mountain and island were moved out of their places" (Rev. 6:12–14).

We have many authoritative statements about the increase of earthquakes and other natural disasters in our day. There has also been much speculation about how the events foretold in John's revelation will play out. Personally, I am content to see it all unfold and then to someday better understand how all things have physically transpired in fulfillment of the vision. What has become more helpful to me than the seismology of the signs of the times is a pondering of the figurative aspects of the events and how I might apply the principles learned in my life. What follows is a sample of three of those events and how I have sought for personal life application of the principles learned from each.

**1. A Great Earthquake**

*How unshakable is our testimony of truth?* When I was a young boy—too young to be part of our local Scout troop camping in

Yellowstone National Park—there was a great earthquake there. Later, as a father, I took my family to see the displaced rocks and disfigured mountains that had resulted from this natural disaster so many years earlier. It was an impressive and awe-inspiring sight to see the massive destruction and change brought about by a few moments of a shaking earth. As we visited there, I vividly remembered the earthquake and the fear and commotion in our little town as families worried about whether their sons in the Scout troop had been spared harm. As I recall, all were soon reported safe.

The Greek word for earthquake is *seismos,* and it refers to a literal shaking of the earth. In a figurative sense, we could imagine a commotion or a shaking in the hearts and souls of men, causing them fear and worry. During the Yellowstone earthquake, there was certainly a shaking in the hearts of the parents of the Scouts. What parent has not experienced a sense of emotional shaking and quaking when the physical or spiritual lives of their children are being threatened by the forces of nature or by the temptations of Satan? Seeing a loved one buffeted by Satan can cause the soul to tremble. Modern revelation teaches us that "the earth shall quake" and "there shall be weeping and wailing among the hosts of men" (D&C 29:13, 15).

Concerned about his job, a friend of mine once used an interesting expression to describe the *downsizing* going on in his company. He said the company officials were "shaking the tree to see how many nuts they could get to fall out." I came to better understand this visual image a few years ago as I visited the pecan orchards of the South; the owner of one of the orchards explained to me that they harvest the nuts with a large machine that vigorously shakes the tree. In a spiritual sense, it seems as though Satan has a stranglehold on the world and is vigorously shaking it to see how many people he can get to fall. Job certainly understood this buffeting of Satan as in the midst of his trials he exclaimed, "Fear came upon me, and trembling, which made all my bones to shake" (Job 4:14).

It is certainly proper and prudent to prepare for actual physical earthquakes that may come our way. At the time of this writing, the historic Tabernacle on Temple Square is being remodeled primarily to make it more resilient to earthquake. On a few recent occasions,

I have stopped to view the work and have watched the workmen digging deep into the earth to shore up and reinforce the foundation pillars of this venerable old building. This can serve as a metaphor for the preparation we must make in order to withstand the spiritual earthquakes we encounter. We need to dig deep into our souls to shore up and reinforce our testimonies. We need to develop an *unshakable* testimony of truth if we are to survive the day of the great physical and spiritual earthquakes.

### 2.  A Blackened Sun, a Moon of Blood, and Angry, Falling Stars

*Have you ever felt that some life experiences are just too painful to bear?* (Remember in chapter 5 that John wept much at the evil plight and condition of the world.) A few years ago, my wife and I were concerned for the spiritual and physical well-being of a young married couple whose lives were being ravaged by the damning effects of drug abuse. The young husband was in serious addiction and his wife was making a desperate effort to reach out and help. As we worked and counseled as to how to best offer our help and support, a friend offered what I felt was a profound and very accurate analogy. She said it was as though the young husband had wandered out into a lake, was mired to his chin, and was nearly ready to drown. The young wife was wading out after him, to the fear and consternation of all of us who were trying to help them. We had beckoned her to not endanger her own life, but she had ignored our plea. We felt we had done all we could possibly do and feared their imminent destruction. Our friend offering the analogy then said that "because of the great love we have for them, it is just too painful to watch. Sometimes we just *have to turn our heads and look away!*"

What a desperate and painful proposition! Through the grace and miracle of God, the young couple survived. Before long, we were able to look to them once again with joy and continue in our active support of them. Through it all, we never stopped loving them and praying fervently for them. Today, they are doing fine.

In modern revelation, the Lord speaks of a day of terrible wickedness and warns the Saints to be "clean from the blood of this generation" and to "entangle not yourselves in sin." He then goes on to say that the time will come when "the earth shall tremble and reel to and fro as a drunken man; and the sun shall hide his face, and shall refuse to give light; and the moon shall be bathed in blood; and the stars shall become exceedingly angry, and shall cast themselves down as a fig that falleth from off a fig-tree" (D&C 88:85–87).

The evil and wickedness throughout the earth during the sixth seal will be so horrible and so unpleasant that the very earth itself shall mourn. Paul taught, "For we know that the whole creation groaneth and travaileth in pain" (Rom. 8:22). We are told in modern revelation that because of "murder, tyranny, and oppression, . . . the whole earth groans under the weight of its iniquity" (D&C 123:7). In this troubling time, is it any wonder that the sun itself may look away from the pain and suffering? As the sun beholds the great bloodshed and wickedness, is it any wonder that the moon, which reflects the image of the sun, will be bathed in blood? Blood red is the color and expression of anger. The earth will become so violent and corrupt that even the moon and the stars may be red with anger.

### 3.  Fleeing and Falling Mountains

*Is our trust in God or in the arm of flesh?* At the time of my high-school graduation, we participated in the tradition of a senior trip. Our school officials arranged a one-hundred-mile bus trip for us to Salt Lake City, where we went out to dinner and attended a movie—the new release, *Where Eagles Dare,* about the shooting down of a British aircraft in Nazi-held territory. An American general was the only survivor of the crash. He was subsequently captured by the Germans and taken to the nearest Nazi headquarters—a massive fortress, high atop a mountain—so high and well protected that seemingly *only an eagle could get there.* The plot unfolds with a British rescue operation, and many subplots of various double agents were woven through the complex rescue mission.

I don't know how much of this fictional movie was based on fact. But the prowess and seemingly impenetrable war machine of the Third Reich is well known. For many years it seemed as though the free world would never succeed in breaking the back of this corrupt enemy. It seemed to some as though the *chief captains* of the *mountain where only an eagle would dare go* would oppress the people forever. And yet, eventually the mountain collapsed and the enemy fell from power—both in the movie and in the reality of World War II. The *mountain* of the Nazi war machine was *moved out of its place.*

Such will be the ultimate fate of all manmade mountains that are constructed in opposition to the great plan and purpose of our Father in Heaven. John saw that "the kings of the earth, and the great men, and the rich men, and the chief captains, and the mighty men, and every bondman, and every free man, hid themselves in the dens and in the rocks of the mountains; And said to the mountains and rocks, Fall on us, and hide us from the face of him that sitteth on the throne, and from the wrath of the Lamb" (Rev. 6:15–16). The final fate of Hitler in his bunker and of Saddam Hussein in his spider hole stand as fitting illustrations of how the mountains of man's power ultimately come crashing down on the wicked. Nephi gave us good counsel and warning: "for I know that cursed is he that putteth his trust in the arm of flesh. Yea, cursed is he that putteth his trust in man or maketh flesh his arm" (2 Ne. 4:34).

As he concludes chapter 6, John poses a profound question—a question worthy of our diligent and solemn soul searching. He asks, "For the great day of his wrath is come; and *who shall be able to stand?*" (Rev. 6:17; emphasis added). We will soon find further answer to this query in chapter 7, but by carrying forward our mountain analogy, we already know the answer—we are to flee the unstable and falling mountains of the adversary and take refuge in the Lord's holy mountain. Isaiah taught, "And it shall come to pass in the last days, that the mountain of the Lord's house shall be established in the top of the mountains, and shall be exalted above the hills, and all nations shall flow unto it" (Isa. 2:2). Only in this Mount Zion of the Lord will we be able to stand and find true safety and protection!

# Chapter Seven

# After Great Tribulation, Many Are Exalted!

WE LEARNED IN THE CONCLUSION of the last chapter, as we learn throughout the Revelation of John, that the Lord's justice will come to the wicked. Part of the beauty of the Revelation is the masterful balance that John achieves in blending the justice of God with the encouragement, mercy, hope, and peace offered to the righteous who keep their covenants and remain faithful. Chapter 7 continues this *golden thread of hope* as we learn of the comfort and peace given to the righteous who are willing to abide the day. They will be *sealed up* so that they cannot be lost.

## A DELAY IN THE HARVEST

*Why is it that the justice of God sometimes seems to be slow in coming to the wicked of the earth?* A brief review of the Savior's parable of the wheat and the tares helps us understand the theme and message of chapter 7. In the parable, a man "sowed good seed in his field" and after doing so "his enemy came and sowed tares among the wheat." The servants proposed pulling out the tares to protect the young wheat crop. To this, the Master counseled, "Nay; lest while ye gather up the tares, ye root up also the wheat with them. Let both grow together until the harvest: and in the time of harvest I will say to the reapers, Gather ye together first the tares, and bind them in bundles to burn them; but gather the wheat into my barn" (Matt. 13:25–26, 29–30).

In the Revelation, John sees the reapers coming forth: "And after these things I saw four angels standing on the four corners of the earth, holding the four winds of the earth, that the wind should not blow on the earth, nor on the sea, nor on any tree. And I saw another angel ascending from the east, having the seal of the living God: and he cried with a loud voice to the four angels, to whom it was given to hurt the earth and the sea, Saying, Hurt not the earth, neither the sea, nor the trees, till we have sealed the servants of our God in their foreheads" (Rev. 7:1–3). The final destruction of the wicked is to be put on brief hold while the Lord completes His work of sealing His righteous Saints.

The number *four* represents the geographic fullness of the earth, symbolized by the four winds and the four corners of the earth. The pending harvest by the four angels is not to be a mere gleaning of the corners of the field but is to be a complete and comprehensive harvest of *every* field and *every* corner of the earth, wherein the righteous will be sought out and preserved and the wicked will be destroyed. Of these reapers, represented by the four angels, Joseph Smith inquired, "Q. What are we to understand by the four angels, spoken of in the 7th chapter and 1st verse of Revelation?" He learned, "A. We are to understand that they are four angels sent forth from God, to whom is given power over the four parts of the earth, to save life and to destroy; these are they who have the everlasting gospel to commit to every nation, kindred, tongue, and people; having power to shut up the heavens, to seal up unto life, or to cast down to the regions of darkness" (D&C 77:8). The Prophet also asked when these things would be accomplished: "Q. What time are the things spoken of in this chapter to be accomplished? A. They are to be accomplished in the sixth thousand years, or the opening of the sixth seal" (D&C 77:10).

*How may we gain safety in the granary of the righteous at the time of harvest?* We have been continually counseled—as we are often reminded in the Revelation of John—that righteousness will be our protection. We are to follow those appointed to the priesthood to lead and guide us safely through trying times of reaping as the Lord gathers His wheat into safety and prepares the tares for destruction. At this reaping, the *tares* (wicked) will receive their just reward for their rebellion and the *wheat* (righteous) will, after their patience, be sealed up unto eternal life.

## THE SEAL OF THE LIVING GOD IN THEIR FOREHEADS

Of the angel, "ascending from the east, having the seal of the living God," the Prophet Joseph Smith inquired, "Q. What are we to understand by the angel ascending from the east, Revelation 7$^{\text{th}}$ chapter and 2$^{\text{nd}}$ verse? A. We are to understand that the angel ascending from the east is he to whom is given the seal of the living God over the twelve tribes of Israel; wherefore, he crieth unto the four angels having the everlasting gospel, saying: Hurt not the earth, neither the sea, nor the trees, till we have sealed the servants of our God in their foreheads. And, if you will receive it, this is Elias which was to come to gather together the tribes of Israel and restore all things" (D&C 77:9).

Yes, the day of the destruction of the wicked will surely come, and much will yet be explained in the Revelation of this destruction. But first, we have a respite of hope and assurance in knowing that the Lord in His tender mercy will first seek out the righteous and seal them up unto Himself. This sealing of the righteous in their foreheads is an interesting contrast to the mark of Satan in the foreheads of those who choose to follow his path, as we will learn later in the Revelation.

*What is the significance of being sealed in our foreheads and why is this sealing of such great importance for us?* This sealing in the foreheads has reference to the new and everlasting covenant of the gospel. As we enter into the new and everlasting covenant, we bind and seal our families to us so that they cannot be lost, but will continue forever: "And again, verily I say unto you, if a man marry a wife by my word, which is my law, and by the new and everlasting covenant, and it is sealed unto them by the Holy Spirit of promise . . . they shall pass by the angels, and the gods, which are set there, to their exaltation and glory in all things, as hath been sealed upon their heads, which glory shall be a fullness and a continuation of the seeds forever and ever" (D&C 132:19).

For many years, I have owned an embossing seal that embosses my name and thereby declares my ownership of the books and documents I have *sealed* to be mine. The seal in the forehead of the righteous denotes ownership by God of His children; it declares nothing less than the fact that we can gain divine potential and receive all that God has. In essence, we have potential to become like Him. We are taught in the latter-day revelation referred to as *the Oath and Covenant of the Priesthood,* "And he that receiveth my Father receiveth my Father's kingdom; therefore all that my Father hath shall be given unto him" (D&C 84:38). To receive the ultimate promise of exaltation in the kingdom of God and to gain a sure knowledge that such a reward will be ours is an assurance far greater than all the wealth of the earth.

*How may we obtain this blessing of eternal sealing?* We receive it by presenting ourselves worthy at the temple to receive our endowment—our gift from the Lord of potential exaltation. Our endowment consists of all needed ordinances to gain eternal life. It is no wonder that our greatest life task is to go to the temple and there receive the necessary ordinances for our exaltation and then spend the rest of our days keeping our temple covenants so that we may qualify for that exaltation.

## AN HUNDRED AND FORTY AND FOUR THOUSAND WHO ADMINISTER THE GOSPEL

*How is it that the sealing blessings of the gospel can be administered to so many righteous souls throughout the earth? Who is to administer these blessings?* These questions lead to one of the most wondered-about verses in the Revelation: "And I heard the number of them which were sealed: and there were sealed an hundred and forty and four thousand of all the tribes of the children of Israel" (Rev. 7:4).

Some strange explanations of this verse have been given. One is that the number *144,000* will be some kind of a "cap"—the highest possible number of those who gain salvation. Thankfully we have the tools of interpretation offered by modern revelation and living prophets. Once again, we enjoy the blessing of Joseph Smith's question-and-answer session with the Lord: "Q. What are we to understand by sealing the one hundred and forty-four thousand, out of all the tribes of Israel—twelve thousand out of every tribe? A. We are to understand that those who are sealed are high priests, ordained unto the holy order of God, to *administer* the everlasting gospel; for they are they who are ordained out of every nation, kindred, tongue, and people, by the angels to whom is given power over the nations of the earth" (D&C 77:11; emphasis added).

Note that the 144,000 are not those exclusively designated for salvation; instead, they are those called to *administer* salvation to others throughout the earth. A few simple illustrations may be helpful. Imagine a new family is moving into the ward and needs help unloading furniture and household items. A priesthood leader would likely issue a call for help from ward members. If the family were small with few possessions, only a few members might be asked to help. If the family is large with many possessions, more people would be asked by the priesthood leader to help.

Imagine we had a task—harvesting at a stake welfare farm, for example—that required one hundred laborers. One hundred people could soon be procured through the stake's priesthood organization. Now imagine that the need is much greater; perhaps we need to offer relief to victims of a devastating hurricane. Thousands of helpers could be organized as the priesthood coordinated multiple stakes from across the nation.

In administering the ordinances of salvation to the nations of the earth, the Lord is amassing a vast army of worthy priesthood holders to accomplish the work. More will be called and trained and put into action as the work progresses. Additional quorums of seventy will be organized. More bishops and stake presidents will be called. The number of temple sealers will be increased throughout the world, commensurate with the need of those to be sealed. As the kingdom rolls forward, the Lord provides the laborers—the miraculous organizational chart of His kingdom provides unlimited resources for the leadership needed to accomplish His work and glory.

The number *144,000* is a figurative number symbolizing that as many helpers as needed will be called to the task. The number is a product of multiples of twelve, which symbolizes priesthood, and ten, which signifies wholeness or completeness—thus, the *complete* force of the *priesthood* is at work in the salvation of the nations. To illustrate, imagine a priesthood task involving an official full quorum of forty-eight priests (representing work needed from the Aaronic Priesthood) combined with an official full quorum of ninety-six elders (representing work needed from the Melchizedek Priesthood). (The official numbers of full quorums are listed in D&C 107:87–89.) What an impressive work force these 144 laborers would be. If our task were to grow and we were to multiply our priesthood holders tenfold, and then tenfold again, and then tenfold once again, we would have the impressive sum of 144,000.

## As Many as Will—Countless Are to Be Saved

*How many are to be saved—how many are invited to receive of the everlasting gospel and gain entrance into the Church of the Firstborn?* The Lord continues with this answer to the Prophet Joseph: "to bring *as many as will come* to the church of the Firstborn" (D&C 77:11; emphasis added). Any other notion would make reason stare—in the great plan of happiness designed by our Father in Heaven, all of His children are given full opportunity to hear and accept the gospel. Granted, for some the opportunity may not come in the confusing conditions of our mortal probation, but we can rest assured that all will have a full and complete opportunity for salvation, according to the perfect plan and timetable of our eternal God.

The prophet Nephi taught, "Hath he commanded any that they should not partake of his salvation? Behold I say unto you, Nay; but he hath given it free for all men; and he hath commanded his people that they should persuade all men to repentance. Behold, hath the Lord commanded any that they should not partake of his goodness? Behold I say unto you, Nay; but all men are privileged the one like unto the other, and none are forbidden . . . he inviteth them all to come unto him and partake of his goodness; and he denieth none that come unto him, black and white, bond and free, male and female; and he remembereth the heathen; and all are alike unto God, both Jew and Gentile" (2 Ne. 26:27–28, 33). What a glorious and comprehensive plan our Father in Heaven has constructed and offered to all His children! What gratitude fills our souls as we contemplate His justice, tender mercy, and never-ending love for us!

Another great message of hope from the Revelation of John is that not only are *all* invited to partake of salvation, but *many* will accept the invitation. John beheld, "and lo, a great multitude, which no man could number, of all nations, and kindreds, and people, and tongues, stood before the throne, and before the Lamb, clothed with white robes, and palms in their hands; And cried with a loud voice, saying, Salvation to our God which sitteth upon the throne, and unto the Lamb" (Rev. 7:9–10). We recall from chapter 5 that the exalted Saints were described as myriads of "ten thousand times ten thousand, and thousands of thousands" (Rev. 5:11). Yes, there will be hundreds of thousands administering the gospel to the nations. An innumerable host will accept this salvation and come to God in His kingdom.

## PRAISING GOD WITH PALMS AND WHITE ROBES

*What difference would it make in our lives if we could live so as to someday wear a white robe and to obtain a palm of victory?* The palm branch is a long-held symbol of joy and triumph. John records of Jesus' triumphal entry into Jerusalem, "On the next day much people that were come to the feast, when they heard that Jesus was coming to Jerusalem, Took branches of palm trees, and went forth to meet him, and cried, Hosanna:  Blessed is the King of Israel that cometh in the name of the Lord" (John 12:12–13). This triumphant rejoicing at the end of the Savior's mortal ministry was a type of the salvation to come in latter days: "After this I beheld, and, lo, a great multitude, which no man could number, of all nations, and kindreds, and people, and tongues, stood before the throne, and before the Lamb, clothed with white robes, and palms in their hands; And cried with a loud voice, saying, Salvation to our God which sitteth upon the throne, and unto the Lamb" (Rev. 7:9–10). These saved myriads will wave their palms of triumph as a sign that they have overcome the sins and filth of the world and are now going forth to their glorious exaltation. Their beautiful white robes are a sign that their souls are pure and victorious and that they have been "washed white through the blood of the Lamb" (Alma 13:11).

In response to this triumphal entry of the righteous into their exaltation, "all the angels stood round about the throne, and about the elders and the four beasts, and fell before the throne on their faces, and worshipped God, Saying, Amen: Blessing, and glory, and wisdom, and thanksgiving, and honor, and power, and might be unto our God for ever and ever. Amen" (Rev. 7:11–12). Even the number of the seven specific praises is symbolic of *complete* and *perfect* worship of the Creator.

## WHENCE CAME THEY?

*What is required for us to obtain the white robe of exaltation? Are we willing to pay the price?* One of the elders of the vision now tutors John with a simple but profound question and answer: "And one of the elders answered, saying unto me, What are these which are arrayed in white robes? and whence came they?" (Rev. 7:13). John rightly trusted that the elder knew the answer: "And I said unto him, Sir, thou knowest. And he said to me, These are they which came out of great tribulation, and have washed their robes, and made them white in the blood of the Lamb" (Rev. 7:14).

Must tribulation be prerequisite to our exaltation? The answer is yes—absolutely. Must we go on an active search for tribulation in order to hasten our quest for exaltation? No—nature will take its course and we will all receive sufficient tribulation to try, test, and school us to the necessary degree that we might gain exaltation.

I once interviewed a mature high priest who remarked, "Bishop, I do not think I have really had many tribulations." Even though I was fairly well acquainted with him, I didn't know if his life trials had been sufficient to warrant his exaltation; we are never qualified to make that judgment. However, I have thought about his remark over the years and have been prompted with many questions related to my interview with him. Had he failed to see his trials for what they were? Had he endured his trials so well that he was merely basking in the joy of self-mastery? Had he not yet faced his greatest tests? Was he merely comparing temporal things without analyzing the battles within his soul? I don't know the answers to those questions.

This much I *do* know: Every son and daughter of God will have sufficient testing and trial to allow the necessary exercise of agency to gain exaltation. God, in His tender mercy, will tutor us with our own specific challenges in our own specific time and place. Our Father in Heaven's great plan of happiness provides ample opportunity for tribulation and growth sufficient for His purposes. Our task is not to unduly compare or complain but to come out of great tribulation.

Some tribulation will come to us in the form of physical suffering. In my office I have a small four-ounce bag of flour on which is printed the words *Faith in Every Footstep*. This small bag commemorates the faith and dedication of the handcart pioneers, who had their rations cut to a mere four ounces of flour per day per person. The bag seems so small that I wonder how they could have survived—and, of course, some did not. That is, they did not *temporally* or *temporarily* survive. However, as we know from the accounts of their faithful lives and their promised blessings, they are assured of a glorious resurrection in the kingdom of God because of their "faith in every footstep" of life. They came out of their tribulation. In the spiritual sense, even though their trials were sore, they hungered and thirsted after righteousness.

*How do we deal with those who mistreat us?* Often tribulation comes from others who mistreat or abuse us. I was recently inspired by my reading of *The Peacegiver,* a profound book by James L. Ferrell. It is a wonderful illustration of the need for forgiveness and healing in our lives. A sort of a multilayered parable, it is set in the context of a struggling marriage, but is designed to apply to all people in all circumstances of life. The thesis of the book is stated, "Being mistreated is the most important condition of mortality, for eternity itself depends on how we view those who mistreat us."[11]

Think of a time in your life when you have been mistreated. Perhaps you have been taken advantage of by a business partner, or maybe you have been publicly or privately gossiped about or maligned. Maybe your spouse or loved one betrayed your trust. Perhaps you have been the victim of a serious crime. If we are misdirected by the adversary in our response to mistreatment, we may find ourselves hungering for justice to come to our assailant. In a figurative and even perhaps a literal sense, we may find ourselves developing a lust for blood against those who do us wrong.

I recently read a sad yet fascinating history of the 1821 sinking of the whale ship *Essex.* The story of the destruction of the large ship by an attacking sperm whale gave inspiration to Herman Melville to write his classic *Moby Dick.* Those who survived the wreck of the *Essex* endured one of the most grueling sea disasters in history. In their extreme hunger and thirst they cut their daily rations of hardtack bread to one and a half ounces per person per day. Many of the survivors succumbed to feelings of anger and bitterness, and some even turned to cannibalism in an effort to survive. In the Melville classic, we see the folly of choosing a course of anger and revenge as Captain Ahab hungers for the life and thirsts for the blood of the avenging whale. Sadly, he did not come out of his tribulation in the Lord's way—he did not choose the path of forgiveness and humility.

In our constant struggle to *come out of tribulation* we must have the faith and courage to turn our hungering and thirsting away from evil and revenge and toward righteousness. Jesus taught, "And blessed are all they who do hunger and thirst after righteousness, for they shall be filled with the Holy Ghost" (3 Ne. 12:6). If we thirst after the Living Water, it will become to us "a well of water springing up into everlasting life" (John 4:14). If we hunger for the Bread of Life, we will not die but will have everlasting life (see John 6:47–50). John the Beloved—who later recorded these teachings for us as John the Revelator—saw further application of these saving principles as he learned that "he that sitteth on the throne shall dwell among them. They shall hunger no more, neither thirst any more" (Rev. 7:15–16).We must have the faith and courage to allow Him to wash our robes and have them made white in the blood of the Lamb. In response to John's question "who shall be able to stand?" (Rev. 6:17), we have received the answer that we must "[come] out of great tribulation" (Rev. 7:14).

## GOD WILL WIPE AWAY ALL TEARS

*How many tears have you shed in your life? Why? What is the source of your comfort?* Chapter 6 concludes with one of the most touching and poignant illustrations in the Revelation of the theme of hope, healing, peace, and triumph. As we struggle to endure our great tribulation we will undoubtedly experience many times of sorrow and tears. As an illustration, consider several questions. *Is there anything in your life that has caused you tears this very day? Have you shed tears of loneliness or despair? Is someone you love moving in a wrong and dangerous direction?* Now think of the tears you have shed during the past year of your life. Now think about your mortal lifetime—how many tears have you shed?

Now consider all those you love—how many tears have they shed today? This year? In their lifetimes? Have they shed tears for you? Because of you? Have your loved ones sorrowed and cried for reasons of poor health? Of sin? Of poverty? Of crime and oppression? With all those combined, how many tears have been shed?

Now extend your imagination to include all the tribulation and sorrow of all the people of the earth. How many tears do you think have been shed today? As you consider that question, remember all the war, evil, famine, and oppression in the world. What about the sorrow portrayed just in today's issue of your state or local newspaper? Now try to imagine all of the tears shed by all people of all time. It is an awesome and solemn thought to contemplate all the sorrow of all the people of all time. The thought in itself may bring tears.

It is my experience and my testimony that the healing power and capacity of our Father in Heaven and of our Lord and Savior

Jesus Christ are sufficient to heal every heart and right every wrong through all of the world's history. The late Carl Sagan said, "in some respects, science has far surpassed religion in delivering awe. How is it that hardly any major religion has looked at science and concluded, 'This is better than we thought! The Universe is much bigger than our prophets said—grander, more subtle, more elegant. God must be even greater than we dreamed'? Instead they say, 'No, no, no! My god is a little god, and I want him to stay that way.' A religion, old or new, that stressed the magnificence of the Universe as revealed by modern science might be able to draw forth reserves of reverence and awe hardly tapped by the conventional faiths. Sooner or later, such a religion will emerge."[12]

To heal the hearts and souls and dry the tears of all people of all ages is an awesome and daunting task requiring the power not of a "little god" but of exalted beings who are omniscient, omnipotent, and omnipresent. The only way to even imagine being saved from all of our sins and sorrows and being healed of our heartaches is by a Savior who has Himself "descended below" all things (D&C 122:8). Such a mission could only be accomplished by "Jesus the mediator of the new covenant, who wrought out this *perfect atonement* through the shedding of his own blood" (D&C 76:69; emphasis added).

I know that all the tears of all the world throughout all time can be dried by our God and our Christ. John clearly saw this perfect Atonement in action when he witnessed, "For the Lamb which is in the midst of the throne shall feed them, and shall lead them unto living fountains of waters: and God shall wipe away all tears from their eyes" (Rev. 7:17).

# Chapter Eight
# A Dreadful Time for the Wicked

THE LONG-ANTICIPATED TIME HAS arrived for the opening of the seventh seal. This great millennium, the capstone of the ages, will be a glorious season. We will eventually see the earth renewed in paradisiacal glory—but at the outset of this seal and before the coming of the Lord, there is much yet to be made of the ongoing battle between good and evil. In the heading of chapter 8 we read, "John sees fire and desolation poured out during the seventh seal and preceding the Second Coming."

The events of the seventh seal are to be so magnificent and yet so horrendous—so great and yet so dreadful—that heaven itself pauses in reverent silence: "And when he had opened the seventh seal, there was silence in heaven about the space of half an hour" (Rev. 8:1).

## A SILENT PAUSE

*When have you felt tremendous anticipation during the silent time before a great event?* Although it has not been revealed what is specifically meant by the *half hour of silence,* we are certainly aware of other quiet pauses in our individual lives, in our collective history, and in the prophecies of the Restoration that may lend us some insight and feeling about this solemn time. The words of the Lord to the Prophet Joseph Smith in 1831 make a connection between the angels who will reap the earth and a time of silence: "For all flesh is corrupted before me; and the powers of darkness prevail upon the earth, among the children of men, in the presence of all the hosts of heaven—Which causeth silence to reign, and all eternity is pained, and the angels are waiting the great command to reap down the earth, to gather the tares that they may be burned; and, behold, the enemy is combined" (D&C 38:11–12).

*What are the significant silent pauses of our lives and what do these times do for us? What are some of the great silent pauses of the history of the world and why were they significant?* I personally appreciate and enjoy the quiet time at the end of the day when our street is silent, the phone is no longer ringing, and conversations are subdued and peaceful. This is a time of rest and meditation—a time of pondering the events of the current day and of anticipating the events of the next day.

Some of the most memorable times of my life have been the reverent silence that has accompanied meetings in the presence of our living prophet. Particularly humbling and inspiring have been the two occasions I have been privileged to attend solemn assemblies in the Salt Lake Temple, during which we were instructed by prophets, seers, and revelators. The time of silence that existed from the time we arrived until the meeting began was a time of great anticipation; we knew we were about to hear profound messages from inspired leaders. The relatively *silent* hour of the actual meeting was a time of great reverence and quiet inspiration.

The crown jewel of my week is the time from the prelude before sacrament meeting until the closing prayer, a time during which I can contemplate with gratitude the atoning sacrifice of my Savior. I feel especially blessed on those occasions when there is relative silence during this time.

I recall a moment of peace and anticipation at a performance of Handel's *Messiah* in a large church in our community. At that performance, the conductor held a rather extended pause of silence following the tune-ups and preceding the opening notes of the performance.

Impressive and inspiring is the account of Jesus standing before Herod; for a long time Herod had desired to see this renowned prophet perform a miracle. As Herod "questioned with him in many words," the Savior simply and silently "answered him nothing" (Luke 23:9). Silence is often the most appropriate response to the proud and bawdy bearing of the wicked.

How wondrous must have been the time just after Christ proclaimed His divinity and mission in the Americas when "all the people of the land did hear these sayings, and did witness of it. And after these sayings there was silence in the land for the space of many hours; For so great was the astonishment of the people that they did cease lamenting and howling for the loss of their kindred which had been slain; therefore there was silence in all the land for the space of many hours" (3 Ne. 10:1–2).

Sweet is the counsel from the Psalmist, "Be still, and know that I am God" (Ps. 46:10).

What a witness of faith it must have been for the distressed camp of Israel as Moses, their prophet, admonished them to "fear ye not, stand still, and see the salvation of the Lord . . . The Lord shall fight for you, and ye shall hold your peace" (Ex. 14:13–14).

In our hectic lives, we can often draw guidance and strength from past moments of peace and silence. Think of the plea of Oliver Cowdery for a "further witness" of the truth of the cause he was beginning to align himself with. The Lord instructed him to "cast your mind upon the night, that you cried unto me in your heart, that you might know concerning the truth of these things. Did I not speak peace to your mind concerning the matter? What greater witness can you have than from God?" (D&C 6:22–23).We, like Oliver, can remember the times when we have felt peace and reassurance and gain from these times of inspiration the strength and courage to go forward.

We learn much from reflecting on the destruction of ancient Jericho. Before the actual destruction, "Joshua had commanded the people, saying, Ye shall not shout, nor make any noise with your voice, neither shall any word proceed out of your mouth, until the day I bid you shout; then shall ye shout" (Josh. 6:10). When the appointed time came for the actual destruction, Joshua commanded, "Shout: for the Lord hath given you the city" (Josh. 6:16).

Whatever the actual time and nature the half hour of silence may be at the opening of the seventh seal, we can confidently rest assured that it will be, as in ancient Jericho, a time of great pensiveness and anticipation—and if we are faithful and worthy, a time of peace, gratitude, and joyful longing for the advent of the Son of God into our troubled and noisy world.

## THE PRAYERS OF ALL SAINTS

John records, "And I saw the seven angels which stood before God; and to them were given seven trumpets" (Rev. 8:2). The Prophet Joseph Smith asked, "Q. What are we to understand by the sounding of the trumpets, mentioned in the 8$^{th}$ chapter of Revelation? A. We are to understand that as God made the world in six days, and on the seventh day he finished his work, and sanctified it, and also formed man out of the dust of the earth, even so, in the beginning of the seventh thousand years will the Lord God sanctify the earth, and complete the salvation of man, and judge all things, and shall redeem all things, except that which he hath not put into his power, when he shall have sealed all things, unto the end of all things; and the sounding of the trumpets of the seven angels are the preparing and finishing of his work, in the beginning of the seventh thousand years—the preparing of the way before the time of his coming" (D&C 77:12). What a time of joyful anticipation it will be to live in the time just before His coming.

*When have you felt answers to your prayers? How is it that God hears and answers the prayers of all His children?* Next came an angel with a golden censer who burned incense on the golden altar—incense that would ascend with the prayers of the righteous. "[A]nd there was given unto him much incense, that he should offer it with the prayers of *all* saints upon the golden altar which was before the throne. And the smoke of the incense, which came with the prayers of the saints, ascended up before God out of the angel's hand" (Rev. 8:3–4; emphasis added). The prayers of *all* Saints would certainly result in a sky full of prayers.

The word *all* is one of the biggest little words in the scriptures. For example, "*all* that my Father hath" will be given to those who keep the oath and covenant of the priesthood (D&C 84:38; emphasis added). In the Lord's law of forgiveness, we are commanded to "forgive *all*" (D&C 64:10; emphasis added).

Remember, we learned in the preceding chapter of the Revelation that "God shall wipe away *all* tears from their eyes" (Rev. 7:17; emphasis added). Awe-inspiring is the thought of the scope and magnitude implied by the word *all*. Because Christ "inviteth . . . *all* to come unto him and partake of his goodness" (2 Ne. 26:33; emphasis added), we could search through *all* the world for *all* time and not find a single soul excluded from His grace, mercy, and invitation. When our Savior says *all,* He really does mean *all.*

Let's blend this thought of *all* prayers with the thought of *all* tears. If we are to liken our prayers to the rising smoke of the burning incense, how much smoke would there be in a day? How about in a year? A decade? A lifetime? What about the prayers of all of our loved ones for a day, a year, a decade, and a lifetime? It would be a futile attempt to try to imagine the cumulative sum of "the prayers of all saints" throughout all the world and throughout all time.

*What is the sincere desire of your soul?* The thought of an omniscient and omnipotent God standing with His Only Begotten Son and proffering love, understanding, and answered prayers to all people of all time should fill our souls with gratitude. When I consider the tender mercies I have received as my personal prayers—offered over many years—have been heard and answered, I am left to stand with amazement at the love Jesus offers me. The thought that His love is sufficient to redeem my life and the lives of my loved ones is more than I can comprehend—but not more than I can believe. I am confident that *all* of the sincere prayers of imperfect but striving Saints really do ascend up before God and that He does hear and does answer. Is it any wonder that prayer really is the sincere desire of the souls of the Saints?

## A BITTERSWEET ANSWER

In response to the prayers and pleadings of all of the Saints of all time, the angel fills his censer with the fire of the altar and pours it out upon the wicked earth: "And the angel took the censer, and filled it with fire of the altar, and cast it into the earth: and there were voices, and thunderings, and lightnings, and an earthquake. And the seven angels which had the seven trumpets prepared themselves to sound" (Rev. 8:5–6). At first glance, fire cast down to earth seems a strange response to the prayers of the Saints. But God is true to His purposes and, although the response is bitter, it is also sweet.

*Why is this such a bitter time?* There is no delight in the sad condition necessitating such drastic destruction as now must come upon the wicked. We might think of the prophet Mormon as he was called to witness the final destruction of the Nephite nation. In the depth of his sorrow and his stance as an "idle witness" (Morm. 3:16), he wished, "And I would that I could persuade all ye ends of the earth to repent and prepare to stand before the judgment-seat of Christ" (Morm. 3:22). He found it "impossible for the tongue to describe, or for man to write a perfect description of the horrible scene of the blood and carnage which was among the people . . . and every heart was hardened, so that they delighted in the shedding of blood continually" (Morm. 4:11). Our mortal world sinks into bitter conditions wherein "conspiring men" with "evils and designs" in their hearts (D&C 89:4) perpetrate much evil upon mankind. It is no wonder that at one point, Mormon rejoiced when he saw the lamentation and mourning of his people—for he hoped, "knowing the mercies and the long-suffering of the Lord . . . that he would be merciful unto them that they would again become a righteous people. But behold this my joy was vain, for their sorrowing was not unto repentance, because of the goodness of God; but it was rather the sorrowing of the damned, because the Lord would not always suffer them to take happiness in sin" (Morm. 2:12–13). When the people of the earth become *fully* ripened in wickedness, then only the Lord's *full* measure of justice can correct the evil and stop the forward march of wickedness.

To witness the *spiritual death* of a loved one can be a more bitter trial than to experience the *physical death* of a truly righteous soul. As the angel pours out the plagues and destructions upon the wicked who have died spiritually, and as the seven angels signal the specific destructions with their trumpets, is it any wonder that John "heard an angel flying through the midst of heaven, saying with a loud voice, Woe, woe, woe, to the inhabiters of the earth" (Rev. 8:13)? Yes, "woe, woe, woe"—*sorrow, sorrow, sorrow*—will come to the wicked and, in some degree, to those who love and care for them. This is a bitter time and would seem hopeless without the sweet assurance we gain from our eternal perspective of the great plan of happiness.

*Why is this such a sweet time?* It is sweet because of our eternal perspective of God's mercy. How sweet it is to know the end from the beginning and to understand some basic principles that will guide us safely through. For example, Saints may draw comfort knowing that for the most part, the righteous will escape the terrible destructions to come upon the wicked. Since we have used Mormon as an example, let's gain peace and assurance from his teaching that in general the wicked will destroy each other: "But, behold, the judgments of God will overtake the wicked; and it is by the wicked that the wicked are punished; for it is the wicked that stir up the hearts of the children of men unto bloodshed" (Morm. 4:5).

We also find sweetness from our eternal perspective that God creates all life and takes all life. All of the wicked who are destroyed and all of the righteous who have fallen prey to the evil influences of the wicked will be left in His hand and will be subject to His judgment, justice, and tender mercy. Because of the atoning sacrifice of His Son, new life will come from the ashes of the destructive fires wherein "the third part of trees was burnt up, and all green grass was burnt up . . . and as it were a great mountain burning with fire was cast into the sea" (Rev. 8:7–8). As souls die, we find comfort in the knowledge that, in death, their lives continue in the hands of God. We know He will bless them to the fullest extent possible under His justice and mercy.

## WORMWOOD—CLEANSING FIRE
Although Wormwood is portrayed as a subordinate tempter in C.S. Lewis's classic *The Screwtape Letters,* John's Wormwood is a great star who wields enormous power and influence in the fallen world. John records, "and there fell a great star from heaven, burning as it were a lamp, and it fell upon the third part of the rivers, and upon the fountains of waters; And the name of the star is called Wormwood: and the third part of the waters became wormwood; and many men died of the waters, because they were made bitter" (Rev. 8:10–11). But no matter how powerful and influential Satan may seem, we must take hope from the promise to the righteous "that no combination of wickedness shall have power to rise up and prevail over thy people upon whom thy name shall be put in this house" (D&C 109:26).

Several years ago, a huge fire engulfed much of Yellowstone National Park. This destruction initially caused me to sorrow, as I have always loved the beauty and grandeur of the park. For many days as the fire raged, so did the debate as to the cost of the fire and the future of the park. I was encouraged by many experts who explained that fire is a very natural renewal process and that the park would ultimately be better off because of this so-called disaster. Several months after the fire, I took my family there to visit and, sure enough, we witnessed many signs of rebirth and renewal springing from the ashes of the devastating fire. We are now a few decades away from this great fire, and the park is as beautiful as ever—probably more so.

So will be the destruction of the wicked of the earth—of course, there will be bitter tears of sorrow for the wicked souls and the wicked influence they have had upon mankind. However, we must not lose sight of our eternal perspective and knowledge that all life is in God's hands and that he will make something far greater out of the lives of both the wicked and the righteous than we could ever imagine with our limited mortal perspective. Though we presently experience the world as *bittersweet* (and sometimes seemingly more bitter than sweet), we must remember that the lasting and healing effects of the Atonement of Christ are propelling us toward a totally *sweet* world in which the bitter will be long resolved and forgotten. Through faith and endurance, we will emerge from the ashes of life—and, like the rebirth of Yellowstone Park, we will become more beautiful and more glorious than ever before. What joyful anticipation we have for that day!

# Chapter Nine
# The Bottomless Pit

CHAPTER 9 PRESENTS US WITH at least two dilemmas. First is the struggle common to much of the Revelation: is John seeing real scenes from our modern world and attempting to describe them in his own language, or is he describing what he is actually seeing and leaving us with the task of deducing the real from the figurative? Second is our effort to seek out the message of hope, healing, peace, and triumph from such a destructive condition that seems so hopeless, chaotic, and beyond healing. We might wonder, "How could anyone triumph over such a terrible day?"

**OPEN MINDS**
We may approach the challenge of literal versus figurative by keeping our minds open to both viewpoints and then trying to transcend both to view the greater dimension and the general theme. We may not know if John's scorpions and chariots were really modern tanks, aircraft, and missiles or if he was literally seeing scorpions and chariots as figures of the wars and plagues being poured out upon the wicked in the last days. The more important task for us would be to focus on the big picture and remember that the wicked really will be destroyed and that the earth really will be cleansed in preparation for the millennial reign of the Savior.

The most effective way to fully understand not only this chapter but the entire Revelation will be to faithfully and patiently live through the times spoken of and then come back in the day when "the earth shall be full of the knowledge of the Lord as the waters cover the sea" (2 Ne. 30:15). We need to study it as history—perhaps even with John himself as our professor! In the meantime, I am personally content to keep some questions on the back burner and to keep my focus on my quest for peace, direction, and strength to endure the day.

As for the second task of seeking hope, healing, peace, and triumph—granted, these themes are not always so easily recognizable in the words of John alone. To discover them, we must blend our knowledge of the Revelation of John with all our other knowledge about the latter day of trial and triumph as found in the standard works and the words of the prophets. The beauty and blessing of our open-ended and ever-expanding canon of scripture is that it can lead to a greater understanding and perspective of the events of our times and of the glorious day of the coming of the Lord. Often the messages of hope and peace come from what a Book of Mormon prophet or a modern prophet has spoken concerning an event or a condition. The peace and hope are to be found if we will but seek them out.

## WHEN ARE THESE THINGS TO BE ACCOMPLISHED?

*What is the time frame of the events of chapter 9—When will they occur?* Joseph Smith asked the question, "Q. When are the things to be accomplished, which are written in the 9th chapter of Revelation? A. They are to be accomplished after the opening of the seventh seal, before the coming of Christ" (D&C 77:13). This answer may serve to help unburden any obligation we may feel to attempt to pinpoint the opening of the seventh seal or the coming of Christ. We recall, as Paul taught the Thessalonians, that those who lose their focus on what matters most will experience the coming of the Lord as a "thief in the night," while the faithful who properly set their course on a gospel-centered life "are not in darkness, that that day should overtake you as a thief" (1 Thess. 5:2, 4). We should keep our perspective focused on the grand view of life and not get so caught up in counting the trees that we fail to see the forest. We will be better served by being about the business of building the kingdom and properly enduring our trials than by attempting to pinpoint every speed bump in the road to the millennial day.

## SMOKE FROM THE BOTTOMLESS PIT

*How are we shielding ourselves against the polluting smokes of Satan's influence?* One of my boyhood chores was to carry coal in large steel buckets from our coal shed—located way out behind the barn—into the basement of our home, where I then poured it into the hopper of the old coal furnace that heated our home. (I was quite intrigued that as soon as I outgrew this chore, my father tore down the old coal shed and began storing the coal in a basement room adjacent to the furnace so all he had to do was shovel it from the room directly into the hopper. I have wondered why he didn't receive this flash of inspiration years earlier!) Occasionally I shirked my duty and the hopper was empty. When that happened, the furnace smoked, and the smoke drifted up through the entire house.

Each year at spring cleaning time my mother assigned me the job of washing and scrubbing the walls and ceilings. As I worked, I thought about my carelessness and vowed to be more diligent in keeping the coal hopper full. We still needed to do the spring cleaning, of course, but it would have been much less intense if we had confined most of the smoke and mess to the basement furnace room. When I married and moved away and my parents became more burdened by age, I remember how grateful and relieved I was that clean-burning natural gas was available in their community. They no longer had to shovel the coal or work as hard at spring cleaning.

Life would be so much more pleasant if we could confine Satan to his bottomless pit and keep the many "smokes" of his influence confined and restricted. We long for such a day, and surely such a day will come. But for now, we have his dirty and polluting influence to deal with: "And the fifth angel sounded, and I saw a star fall from heaven unto the earth: and to him was given the key of the bottomless pit. And he opened the bottomless pit; and there arose a smoke out of the pit, as the smoke of a great furnace; and the sun and the air were darkened by reason of the smoke of the pit" (Rev. 9:1–2). In our fallen world, it seems as though Lucifer has opened a great pit and—like smoke from a great furnace—it is spewing every imaginable evil throughout our society.

*What is our reaction to the rising smoke of Satan's evil influence? How are we doing as a nation? As a community? As individuals?* We seem to be working hard and making some real progress on matters of physical pollution. In many areas we seem to be taking action to regulate the toxins that cause harm to our water, our plants, our soil, and our air. Our laws restrict us from dumping waste oil into storm drains. We can't burn toxic waste that would contaminate the air. We aren't permitted to place items out as trash if they contain chemicals that need special recycling.

Even more critical is how we deal with society's mass of spiritual pollutants. For example, we may purchase pornography and bring it into our home without hardly any legal restriction. We are free to go into many public places and converse in profane and bawdy language. We may choose to be grossly immoral—and even parade our philosophy and our rights down Main Street—with scarcely a whimper or a comment from the law or from society. These types of smoke come from Lucifer. Such immoral activities do not "hurt the grass of the earth, neither any green thing, neither any tree" (Rev. 9:4) as do physical pollutants, but these kinds of evil activities are distant and contrary to those who have chosen Christ as their king and who have and keep His sealing—or His everlasting covenant—in their foreheads. Those to be hurt by the destroying locusts are "only those men which have not the seal of God in their foreheads" (Rev. 9:4).

Paul described well our latter-day condition of contending with the spiritual smokes of Satan: "For we wrestle not against flesh and blood, but against principalities, against powers, against rulers of the darkness of this world, against spiritual wickedness in high places" (Eph. 6:12). The prophets Lehi and Nephi taught us that the "mists of darkness are the temptations of the devil, which blindeth the eyes, and hardeneth the hearts of the children of men, and leadeth them away into broad roads, that they perish and are lost" (1 Ne. 12:17). The smoke and mists of Satan form a deadly poison.

*What is the antidote for this poisonous smoke? From whence cometh our hope, peace, and triumph?* We gain peace and hope in remembering that Christ Himself has the power and authority to keep Satan in check. He said, "I am he that liveth, and was dead; and, behold, I am alive for evermore, Amen; and have the keys of hell and death" (Rev. 1:18). Satan gets the keys to the bottomless pit only with the Savior's permission, and then he gets them only temporarily. His evil influence and destruction is set within bounds. This restriction is illustrated by the life of one of the servants of Satan—Adolf Hitler, who ranted and raved up and down the earth, bringing to bear all the smoke, weaponry, and power he could muster from his evil master. Yet in due time he was checked and defeated and cast back into his pit by the united force of some who were more righteous and more worthy of the gift of freedom. So it will be with Satan—even though he has opened the pit and his polluting smoke is spewing forth, it will have an end as we will be saved by the authority, power, and influence of the Savior. The fire of the Lord's wrath on the wicked will ultimately deliver us from their awful smoke. The scriptures remind us that "the righteous need not fear; for thus saith the prophet, they shall be saved, even if it so be as by fire" (1 Ne. 22:17).

## REFUGE IN ZION

*How can we find a safe dwelling place in a troubled world?* We find protection and peace by moving away from the great and spacious building and seeking refuge in Zion. How grateful we are for the concept of Zion and the efforts made by so many like-minded Saints who strive to build Zion in their hearts and homes. Those with the sealing of eternal life in their foreheads will seek and find protection and refuge in Zion.

Of this safe community of Zion, the Lord revealed, "And with one heart and with one mind, gather up your riches that ye may purchase an inheritance which shall hereafter be appointed unto you. And it shall be called the New Jerusalem, a land of peace, a city of refuge, a place of safety for the saints of the Most High God; And the glory of the Lord shall be there, and the terror of the Lord also shall be there, insomuch that the wicked will not come unto it, and it shall be called Zion. And it shall come to pass among the wicked, that every man that will not take his sword against his neighbor must needs flee unto Zion for safety. And there shall be gathered unto it out of every nation under heaven; and it shall be the only people that shall not be at war one with another. And it shall be said among the wicked: Let us not go up to battle against Zion, for the inhabitants of Zion are terrible; wherefore we cannot stand. And it shall come to pass that the righteous shall be gathered out from among all nations, and shall come to Zion, singing with songs of everlasting joy" (D&C 45:65–71).

Although we may not know the exact form, shape, and status of our protective Zion community in the future, we are wise to consider how it is now. We learn from scripture "that the gathering together upon the land of Zion, and upon her stakes, may be for a defense, and for a refuge from the storm, and from wrath when it shall be poured out without mixture upon the whole earth" (D&C 115:6). We are wise not to think that *someday when the smoke and evil are so bad, I will flee to Zion,* but to consider that *the smoke and evil are bad now and thus, this very day I am gathering to Zion.* In other words, *I am gathering to my stake with my stake president and my bishop as my leaders and guides.* Rather than imagining that a marvelous *Oz-* or *Brigadoon-*like city will suddenly appear and swing open its gates for the righteous to enter, it is better to consider that our Zion is already here.

The city of Zion will be built and Enoch's Zion will return, but we need not wait for a personal and family place of Zion—such a place can be here and now. The charge from the Savior that we are to "stand in holy places, and . . . not be moved" (D&C 45:32) has more present and practical application to *how* we are living rather than to *where* we are living. If we are living righteously, the Lord will tell us if He wants us to seek a new residence—but in the meantime, we are to continue to live righteously and build Zion where we are.

## CROWNS "LIKE GOLD"

*In our quest for eternal life, are we seeking the real deal or the counterfeit?* Some years ago, I wanted to grant my daughter's Christmas wish by getting her a special bracelet she wanted. I found the bracelet and, once I recovered from my sticker shock at the price tag, I ordered it for her. As I dealt with my mixed feelings about such an expensive purchase, I happened to come across an "exact replica" of the bracelet at a significantly reduced price. I also ordered the replica and then struggled with the decision of which to give my daughter and which to return. To me, the bracelets looked exactly the same; I doubted she would know the difference.

In my dilemma, I decided to put the problem to the test: I decided to show the two bracelets to my wife. As I presented her with both, she examined them for a brief instant and then, with an authoritative and unequivocal statement, declared the authenticity of the real one. She obviously saw what I did not see. I subsequently followed her counsel by returning the replica and presenting the real thing to my daughter. As I have seen how much this bracelet has come to mean to my daughter over the years and how well it has withstood the wear and tear of life, I have become even more grateful that I sought counsel from someone who knew the difference between real and replica and that I made the correct choice.

Earlier in the Revelation, we saw the "four and twenty elders" who were wearing "crowns of gold" that they "cast . . . before the throne" of God (Rev. 4:4, 10). We discussed how this action was symbolic of the righteous and sanctified Saints presenting their perfected lives to Father in Heaven—thus bringing Him continuing joy and fulfillment. They had been true and authentic in their progress and life decisions and had thus earned true crowns of true gold. These are the true believers who inherit the true glory and peace of the Lord.

In contrast to these real crowns of the truly righteous, Satan always offers a counterfeit. John now records, "And in those days shall men seek death, and shall not find it; and shall desire to die, and death shall flee from them. And the shapes of the locusts were like unto horses prepared unto battle; and on their heads were as it were *crowns like gold*, and their faces were as the faces of men" (Rev. 9:6–7; emphasis added). The phrase *crowns like gold* suggests to us that these pseudo-crowns of the wicked have some appearance of gold, but lack authenticity. William Shakespeare wrote in *The Merchant of Venice*, "All that glitters is not gold." Although something may be appealing or resplendent, it may lack true value.

Alma, in counsel to his wayward son Corianton, certainly caught the spiritual essence of "crowns like gold" with his enduring doctrinal declaration that "wickedness never was happiness" (Alma 41:10). Anyone who has struggled with a loved one in the depths of sorrow and loss from drug addiction, for example, can certainly see the contrast between real and authentic striving for life success and the succumbing to the lure of artificial coping. Strong is the allure of brightly packaged pornography, but dark and terrible are the rewards and sorrows of choosing this phony attempt at happiness. Enticing may be the thought of new romantic adventure, but heart-wrenching are the terrible consequences of adultery in the lives of betrayed innocents. Sad is the plight of a man who has squandered his precious resources on the toys and gadgets of our modern world while neglecting the faithful payment of tithes and offerings, thus forfeiting the opening of the windows of heaven.

I am reminded of two simple examples of people seeking crowns like gold. The first is of a young seminary student. At the conclusion of his senior year in high school, I asked him if he had plans to serve a mission. He casually responded, "No, I have just purchased a new sport utility vehicle and must work to make the payments." The second example was a man I visited as a home teacher. One day as we were roofing his house, I invited him to prepare to renew his long-expired temple recommend. He pointed to his flashy and extravagant motor home in the driveway and commented, "There is my tithing money." Had I been more familiar with the Revelation of John at the time, I might have been prompted to ask, *Can you not see that you are purchasing crowns like gold in lieu of the authentic crowns of eternal life?* Could the two individuals not see that they were choosing to follow a "king . . . which is the angel of the bottomless pit?" (Rev. 9:11). Just as I have wondered how I would have fared had I given my daughter the phony bracelet, I have wondered these many years what the motor home and the SUV look like now after a few decades of corruption by moth and rust. Sad is the reward of someone who chooses to lay aside the authentic crown for a replica that merely looks like gold.

## "GODS" THAT NEITHER SEE, HEAR, NOR WALK

*How does our commitment to living true gospel principles correlate to our understanding of the true nature of God?* Just as we sometimes struggle with blurred lines of recognition between replica and real, we also blur the lines of the nature of those we worship if we choose not to follow God with full purpose of heart. If people choose to pursue phony crowns that glitter but are not gold, then it naturally follows that they will pursue phony "gods" that appeal but do not save.

It is a very seductive deception. After all, some might say, "I am not really wicked, or I would have been destroyed with the really wicked." From the Revelation, we learn that the voice of God commanded the destroying angels to harvest the earth and cleanse it of the really wicked: "And the sixth angel sounded, and I heard a voice from the four horns of the golden altar which is before God, Saying to the sixth angel which had the trumpet, Loose the four angels which are bound . . . And the four angels were loosed" "and out of their mouths issued fire and smoke and brimstone. By these three was the third part of men killed, by the fire, and by the smoke, and by the brimstone which issued out of their mouths" (Rev. 9:13–14, 17–18).

At that time, the remaining inhabitants of the earth might say, "Well, good riddance to this bad rubbish—the terribly evil and profoundly wicked are gone!" But the paradisiacal glory of the Lord is not yet fully arrived—for many who remain are yet unrepentant: "And the rest of the men which were not killed by these plagues yet repented not of the works of their hands, that they should not worship devils, and idols of gold, and silver, and brass, and stone, and of wood: which neither can see, nor hear, nor walk: Neither repented they of their murders, nor of their sorceries, nor of their fornication, nor of their thefts" (Rev. 9:20–21).

I recall gaining a very simple yet profound insight years ago as I was pondering the motivation of men who would be so blind as to choose to worship an inanimate figure of wood, stone, or metal. I wondered, *Why would someone waste his time and energy praying to a God who cannot hear or speak?* Almost immediately came my answer: *The question itself contains the answer—the very reason people worship such gods is that the gods will not* hear *them or* speak *to them! If we choose a course of rebellion and sin, we do not want God to see our evil or to hear our profanity. We want a god who is blind, deaf, and dumb.*

All ancient and modern prophets have raised the warning voice against idolatry. Through Jeremiah, the Lord said, "Hath a nation changed their gods, which are yet no gods? but my people have changed their glory for that which doth not profit. Be astonished, O ye heavens, at this, and be horribly afraid, be ye very desolate, saith the Lord. For my people have committed two evils; they have forsaken me the fountain of living waters, and hewed them out cisterns, broken cisterns, that can hold no water" (Jer. 2:11–13).

Through Joseph Smith came the warning voice, "And the arm of the Lord shall be revealed; and the day cometh that they who will not hear the voice of the Lord, neither the voice of his servants, neither give heed to the words of the prophets and apostles, shall be cut off from among the people; For they have strayed from mine ordinances, and have broken mine everlasting covenant; They seek not the Lord to establish his righteousness, but every man walketh in his own way, and after the image of his own god, whose image is in the likeness of the world, and whose substance is that of an idol, which waxeth old and shall perish in Babylon, even Babylon the great, which shall fall. . . . The weak things of the world shall come forth and break down the mighty and strong ones, that man should not counsel his fellow man, neither trust in the arm of flesh" (D&C 1:14–16, 19).

Our prophets have repeatedly counseled us about our modern-day idols. Anything that takes us from the true gospel path can become an idol for us. We are sometimes seduced by the accolades of the world into a feeling that all is well with us—that we are invincible. As we amass money and possessions, we are lured in to a false sense of security—believing that our possessions will shield us from harm.

I recently read a biography of a lady who had become disaffected with the Church. It was quite revealing as, from the very outset, I saw red flags and warning signs of her reinventing a god to match her deteriorating morals and lifestyle. In the beginning, she seemed to have everything—education, intellect, strong family, meaningful work, opportunity for service, children, and so on. But strewn through her life path was this unmistakable quest for a crown *like* gold. In her progress toward this pseudo-crown, she continued to fall short of the true glory, peace, and fulfillment promised to the faithful by our true God. I wished she could step back and view her own life from the view I was experiencing. I wondered if she would ever get it. I wondered if her mind and spirit had become so clouded by the accolades of the world that she completely missed the true and steady assurance from our Father in Heaven that we can overcome all things of the world if we will but choose to not be *of* the world—even though we are constantly *in* the world.

A few years ago, I was attending a class taught by one of the volunteer institute teachers. He conducted a fascinating and thought-provoking chronological comparison of the great and renowned creeds and councils of the world in an effort to define the nature and character of God. His conclusion, which he so ably demonstrated, was that the longer they had to deliberate about the question of the true nature of God, the more confused they became. And so it is—if we, without faith and humility, seek to discover God on our own, we are at serious risk of being led astray down forbidden paths of misunderstanding and evil. However, if we set our sights on the true crown of eternal life and seek to obtain it by following our true and living God, we will not be deceived. We will indeed come to know and worship our true God and receive His reward of a true crown of glory and exaltation. And that is the greatest of all life quests—for we are promised, "And, if you keep my commandments and endure to the end you shall have eternal life, which gift is the greatest of all the gifts of God" (D&C 14:7).

# Chapter Ten

# John's Sweet and Bitter Mission

*OF WHAT VALUE TO US IS prophetic assurance of our success and triumph over our trials and challenges?* I recently enjoyed reading *1776*, the fascinating and insightful account of the American Revolution by the gifted author, David McCullough. This experience has prompted me to read other accounts of this decisive era in our early history. My readings have helped me gain new appreciation for the faith, courage, and ingenuity of our Founding Fathers. I realized that I had taken for granted the perilous and tentative task of creating our free nation.

Since we now have the advantage of what we might call twenty-twenty hindsight, as well as inspired prophecies such as those found in the Book of Mormon, it may be easy for us to see from the beginning the blessed destiny of our emerging nation. However, the participants of this noble quest of freedom had to rely on faith and didn't know with absolute certainty what the outcome would be.

It is natural for us to revere George Washington as the father of our country, but we must remember that in 1776, there was not yet a country—and no mortal knew with absolute certainty that there would be a new, independent nation. We look back with pride and confidence at the courage and bravery of those who pledged their all—even life—for the cause of freedom. We express our gratitude that the nation was born and that the patriots were spared the hangman's noose—but they did not know then that they would escape such fate.

It is inspiring to consider the hand of God in the work of leaders who wrested the slavery question through the decades and brought it to rightful conclusion with the preservation of the union. But the players on the Civil War field of battle struggled for years without the personal assurance that the union would be preserved.

It is one thing to read, understand, and believe that, as Daniel states, "a stone was cut out without hands . . . [and] became a great mountain and filled the whole earth" (Dan. 2:34–35), but we must realize that we have a significantly different perspective as thirteen million Church members who are blessed with relative acceptance and tolerance in the world. Ours is much different from the perspective of the small handful of faithful Church members who were being persecuted, mobbed, and driven from one place to another in the early days of the Church. What a blessing it is for us of the latter days to have within our view two hundred years of documented history of the kingdom of God and of our free nation.

It is a great blessing when someone who is enduring life trials gets a spiritual glimpse of a successful outcome that is still in the future. I recall such an occasion of sweet assurance offered to the Prophet Joseph Smith as he received a blessing at the hands of his father. In the midst of the blessing, as his father promised him that he would live to the completion of his sacred work, Joseph was so touched and overwhelmed with the joy of this promise that he cried out for a reconfirmation of the promise. At this, his father spoke again the promise to the great joy and delight of his son. How sweet it is to gain the Lord's assurance of our future potential and success.

## THE LITTLE BOOK

Chapter 10 provides for John a peaceful and reassuring glimpse of his life and mission as it relates to the vision of the time span of the earth. In the midst of the destructive smoke and fire and brimstone, he is given pause to reflect on his own calling and ministry. He is blessed with the reassuring grace of the Savior to help him stay focused on his mission and to complete his work as a Revelator and as a special witness to all the earth. He is given this personal offering in the form of a "little book."

John records, "And I saw another mighty angel come down from heaven, clothed with a cloud: and a rainbow was upon his head, and his face was as it were the sun, and his feet as pillars of fire: And he had in his hand a little book open: and he sat his right foot upon the sea, and his left foot on the earth . . . And I went unto the angel, and said unto him, Give me the little book. And he said unto me, Take it, and eat it up" (Rev. 10:1–2, 9).

In seeking understanding of this passage, Joseph Smith asked, "Q. What are we to understand by the little book which was eaten by John, as mentioned in the 10$^{th}$ chapter of Revelation?" He was told, "A. We are to understand that it was a mission, and an ordinance, for him to gather the tribes of Israel; behold, this is Elias, who, as it is written, must come and restore all things" (D&C 77:14). Thus, the little book John was given to eat was his personal mission, yet future to him at his time of exile on Patmos.

It is satisfying to have meaningful work to accomplish. I recently read an essay by a faithful Church member who was sharing his personal statement of why he belongs to the Church. He helped verbalize how I have always felt about our church and the way it is organized to provide its members with opportunities to serve. He contrasted our true and living church organization, comprised of a lay ministry, to the organization and opportunities to serve in a church where a clergyman is paid to tend the flock. How sweet is the work of having our lives intertwined with the lives of so many others as we serve in our callings and teach and nurture one another. How reassuring it is to know that Saints throughout the world have opportunity for continued Christian service in this Church.

It must have been encouraging to John to know that the Lord trusted him and that he would have many future opportunities to love and serve his fellow men. He was told by the angel, "Thou must prophesy again before many peoples, and nations, and tongues, and kings" (Rev. 10:11). We can only imagine how countless such opportunities would be for John, who had the promise that he would not die but would remain on the earth until the Second Coming of the Lord.

We are taught from Church history that on one occasion at the conference on June 3–6, 1830, "The Spirit of the Lord fell upon Joseph in an unusual manner, and he prophesied that John the Revelator was then among the Ten Tribes of Israel who had been led away by Shalmaneser, king of Assyria, to prepare them for their return from their long dispersion, to again possess the land of their fathers."[13] We consider with admiration and reverence the wanderings and sweet ministry of John in the hundreds of years before and after Joseph uttered that statement.

When I consider all of the blessings that have come personally to me from my work and service, I am profoundly grateful for Heavenly Father's plan that we must earn our bread by the sweat of our brow—and that when we are able to retire from our job, the great plan and organization of the kingdom affords us ample opportunity to continue to spend our days in active service to the Lord. I think often of the recounting of gospel covenants we make at baptism as taught by Alma the Elder at the Waters of Mormon wherein he said that we "[enter] into a covenant to serve him until you are dead as to the mortal body" (Mosiah 18:13). How sweet it is to be able to be anxiously engaged in the good gospel cause!

## SWEET AND BITTER

*When and how has your gospel service been sweet? When and how has it been bitter?* The joy and peace of gospel service in mortality is often tempered by the reality of the need for "opposition in all things" (2 Ne. 2:11). For all of the sweetness of our work and service, dark clouds of bitterness and disappointment often hover in our path. After John was told to eat the little book, he was told that "it shall make thy belly bitter, but it shall be in thy mouth sweet as honey. And I took the little book out of the angel's hand, and ate it up; and it was in my mouth sweet as honey: and as soon as I had eaten it, my belly was bitter" (Rev. 10:9–10).

Such is our mortal circumstance—we may feel sweet peace as we observe the innocent prayers of our young children. We may then feel bitter disappointment when they later abandon prayer for pride and cash in their obedience for the sins and pleasures of the world. It is joyous to teach and testify truth to a new convert—it is heart-wrenching to see a new convert drawn back into the lure of the great and spacious building of pride and sin. Few things can compare to the happiness and peace of a young couple kneeling at a holy altar in the Lord's temple as they make sacred covenants for time and all eternity. Few things could be more bitter than to see such commitment wither and die in a matter of just a few short years, falling far short of eternity. It is sweet to watch our healthy and strong children run and play the wholesome games of youth with joy, stamina, and vigor. Sorrow comes from seeing the same children with ravaged lives and souls from the deadly effects of drug addiction. The events of our mortal lives can certainly taste sweet as honey and yet can sometimes be bitter in our belly.

## TIME NO LONGER

*How willing are we to endure a life of bitterness in order to gain the lasting sweetness of eternal life?* The gospel good news is that no matter how much bitterness we encounter along the way, the end result can be sweet as honey. I once learned that a teaspoon of honey represents an entire lifetime of production for a honeybee. Just as the honeybee must struggle for a lifetime, so must we endure for a lifetime to overcome the bitter and gain the sweet.

A former teacher of mine taught me a profound but simple lesson some years ago. He heard of a time of bitterness in my life and graciously took the time to write me an encouraging note. It was brief and simple and the information it contained was really nothing new—but the fact that it came from him and that he cared enough to take the time to share it made it valuable beyond measure to me. He wrote, "I want to share with you something I heard a member of the Quorum of the Twelve share recently with someone going through a similar struggle—'Always keep your eternal perspective.'" That was it—*keep your eternal perspective!* If we are willing to live the gospel and keep an eternal perspective, all of our bitterness can be endured and our lives can be made eternally and everlastingly sweet.

To help John keep his eternal perspective about his bittersweet mission, the Lord said through the angel, "And sware by him that liveth for ever and ever, who created heaven, and the things that therein are, and the earth, and the things that therein are, and the sea, and the things which are therein, that there should be time no longer" (Rev. 10:6).

From latter-day revelation, we learn the significance of the phrase *time no longer:* "And so on, until the seventh angel shall sound his trump; and he shall stand forth upon the land and upon the sea, and swear in the name of him who sitteth upon the throne, that there shall be time no longer; and Satan shall be bound, that old serpent, who is called the devil, and shall not be loosed for the space of a thousand years" (D&C 88:110). There is much time yet for the sweet millennial reign of the Savior with the righteous, but there will be no more delay in the execution of the Lord's justice upon Satan and those who uphold his work.

Herein we find the theme of hope, healing, peace, and triumph. As bitter and difficult as life can be at times, the bitterness will not last. Satan will be bound and cast back into his pit—for him, there will be time no longer. The day of his power and influence will come to an end. We will overcome the bitter and rejoice in the sweet for a thousand-year period. If we are among the faithful, this millennial reign will simply serve to acclimate us to an eternity of sweetness and joy, during which all bitterness will be gone.

In this day, "the mystery of God should be finished, as he hath declared to his servants the prophets" (Rev. 10:7). What a great day this will be to have full understanding of the mystery of God. *Have you any mysteries you want to more fully understand?* I want to know many things about the events of the history of the world. But more than that, I want to know why my life has played out as it has. Why was I called to serve in certain places at certain times? Why was I disappointed by some who should have kept their covenants, but did not? I know generally—because they have their agency. But I really want to know someday all of the specifics and intricacies of how and why people have chosen to do as they have done. I want to more fully understand why I have done as I have done. I want to someday see my life as the Lord sees it. I long for the day prophesied by Isaiah when "They shall not hurt nor destroy in all my holy mountain, for the earth shall be full of the knowledge of the Lord, as the waters cover the sea" (2 Ne. 21:9).

This condition of full disclosure as spoken by Isaiah and as seen in vision by John offers great hope. We have likely heard the analogy of our lives being compared to a work of embroidery. God as the artist knows what He is about and sees the full and perfect view from the top side. We have a limited view as though we are simply looking at a portion of the underside of the work. All we see is a tangle of unattractive strings and knots, with no clue as to the beauty of the whole.

Years ago, this principle was well illustrated in one of our seminary manuals by this brief verse from an anonymous author:

My life is but a weaving
Between my God and me
I let Him choose the colors
He worketh steadily
And I, within my heart,
Forget He sees the pattern
While I see only part.
The dark threads were as needful
In the Weaver's skillful hand,
As the threads of gold and silver
In the pattern He had planned.
Not till the loom is silent
And the shuttles cease to fly
Shall God unroll the canvas
And explain the reason why.

This little verse gives me much cause for hope and peace in my life.

Many years ago, I decided to follow the counsel from President Spencer W. Kimball to record the events of my life in a personal history. It has been a challenging but very rewarding task. Now that I have three completed and bound volumes and am working on a fourth, I can see the wisdom of the prophet's counsel and I can more clearly see the application of the tapestry analogy. As I have worked on this project, I have come to more fully recognize and appreciate my enduring testimony. Yes, there have been many dark threads and times of bitterness, sorrow, and trial in my life. But there are also bright threads of great blessings and of joys beyond measure. Running through the whole is a golden thread of testimony that seems to bind it all together and give direction and hope for the future.

In summary, as John ate the little book he was "eating," or internalizing, his calling and mission. His mission would be bitter at times and sweet at other times. He would sorrow at the wickedness and rebellion of those he was called to serve. He would rejoice at the faith and conversion of those committed to the gospel. As long as he ate or feasted on the true word of the Lord, he would be protected and go forward in the accomplishment of his mission.

And such is life—we will each taste the bitter and the sweet. Through it all, we must hope on and work on and be true to our God and our covenants. May we ever feast on the Bread of Life. May we always let the sweet peace and joy of the gospel guide us and carry us through the bitterness of trial and disappointment. May we overcome and gain the day when the earth shall be full of the knowledge of the Lord.

# Chapter Eleven

# The Testimony of Prophets— The Reign of Christ

*WHAT ARE WE TO LEARN from the martyrdom of prophets?* My wife and I are blessed to live merely a half day's drive from Nauvoo—The City Beautiful. In context of my profession, my ward and stake service, and my family activity, I usually find myself making a pilgrimage to this sacred city at least two or three times a year. We always visit the Carthage Jail, and as I mentioned in chapter 6, I try to sit on the windowsill in the upper room where Joseph and Hyrum were murdered. This has become a very sacred experience for me as I reverently contemplate how the beloved Prophet of the Restoration here sealed his testimony of the gospel with his own blood. Recently my wife and I experienced an added testimony while in that upper room as the wife of one of our CES colleagues played a beautiful violin rendition of "A Poor Wayfaring Man of Grief," which helped us sense the mood and sounds of the day of martyrdom so long ago.

Even with all our knowledge and feeling about the martyrdom, it still seems so unfathomable and so distant. Such a great span of time since it occurred and the relative peace and security of our prophets since that day make it difficult to imagine the martyrdom of a modern prophet. All prophets have been maligned and some even threatened, but none have actually been martyred in our day.

As a result, we may sense that martyrdom of a prophet is a relic of the past. Then we come to the eleventh chapter of Revelation and learn that yet in our future, two of the Lord's Apostles will be slain in Jerusalem. What a solemn thought! It's a thought that causes us to wonder. Who will they be? How will their families cope with this terrible event? When will it occur? How will we respond? How will it impact the Church?

Although we can't fully answer all of these questions, we can gain understanding and guidance from the many doctrines and principles we *do* know about the ministering of modern prophets. And, as always, we can find hope and peace in the doctrines and principles of the Restoration. As we focus on the greater view of the ministry of our Apostles and couple that view with our knowledge of redemption through the Atonement, we will be better prepared to endure the pending day of martyrdom.

## Measuring Up

*Are we measuring up to the Lord's expectation of us? How may we find protection in being measured by the Lord's servants?* A common phrase in our society is that of *measuring up.* We speak of measuring up to our full potential. A new Marine experiencing the rigors of boot camp may be reminded by his cadre that he is not measuring up. A priesthood leader may learn from a progress report that his ward or stake unit may have some distance to go before measuring up to the desired degree of activity. We all take exams of one sort or another to see if we will measure up to the standard of the organization in which we are enrolled.

I have spent most of my adult life as a part-time tradesman; I am constantly measuring up the materials at hand in order to make proper installation and application to my project. In the trades, we have even formed a helpful little motto to guide and protect us in our work—"measure twice and cut once." (Some of us like to spoof this motto with the statement, "Oh, my, I've cut it off two times and it is still too short.")

John tells us that he "was given . . . a reed like unto a rod: and the angel stood, saying, Rise, and measure the temple of God, and the altar, and them that worship therein. But the court which is without the temple leave out, and measure it not; for it is given unto the Gentiles: and the holy city shall they tread under foot forty and two months" (Rev. 11:1–2). From John's task to "measure the temple of God," many things are suggested to us about the role and mission of prophets and Apostles.

As an Apostle, John the Revelator held the keys of the priesthood and the authority to exercise those keys in blessing and directing the people of the earth. He was to "measure" the conditions of the world and help give course correction as necessary. In our world of religious fervor and confusion, it's comforting to have true messengers at our head to give proper direction to our worship—to help us measure up.

I recall the experience of Karl G. Maeser leading a group of missionaries through a snowy mountain pass. The path had been marked by some wooden sticks or limbs placed at intervals in the snow. Once the group had passed this area and arrived at the top, Dr. Maeser had them look back at the sticks; then, using a simple metaphor, he said that the sticks were like the leaders of the priesthood. Priesthood leaders are just "sticks," or common men, but the priesthood they hold is of God and will give proper guidance to those who choose to follow them. So it is with our current Apostles—they stand to guide us and to give us direction. They measure and chart the path we are to follow to get us safely through life. The Apostles stand as our temporal and spiritual guardians. They set the safe passage for us if we will but demonstrate the humility, courage, and faith to follow them.

Under direction of the Apostles, our local authorized priesthood leaders apply the measuring rod of the temple recommend interview as a guide for our worthiness and progress toward eternal life. Although Gentiles may wander the outer courts of the temple, those who enter the inner court to receive the necessary qualifying ordinances of exaltation must meet the Lord's standard of worthiness. He will not allow His temple to be degraded and profaned by the evils of the world: "No unclean thing shall be permitted to come into thy house to pollute it" (D&C 109:20). Those who qualify themselves for entrance into the inner court of the temple are promised glorious blessings from the Lord. They will be "armed with thy power, and that thy name may be upon them, and thy glory be round about them, and thine angels have charge over them . . . no weapon formed against them shall prosper . . . no combination of wickedness shall have power to rise up and prevail over thy people" (D&C 109:22, 25–26).

This protective imagery upon those who enter the temple is also taught by the prophet Zechariah, who said, "I lifted up mine eyes again, and looked, and behold a man with a *measuring line* in his hand. Then said I, Whither goest thou? And he said unto me, To measure Jerusalem, to see what is the breadth thereof, and what is the length thereof. And, behold, the angel that talked with me went forth, and another angel went out to meet him, And said unto him, Run, speak to this young man, saying, Jerusalem shall be inhabited as *towns without walls* for the multitude of men and cattle therein: For I, saith the Lord, *will be unto her a wall of fire round about,* and will be the glory in the midst of her" (Zech. 2:1–5; emphasis added).

The measuring spoken of by Zechariah may well suggest the physical rebuilding of Jerusalem, but in this measuring the Lord also reminds us that His eyes are always on His people. To live in towns without walls suggests that we have a greater protection than bricks and mortar could offer. If we are willing to serve and obey Him, He will be to us as a wall of fire—a wall of protection around us. In our daily lives, we have access to the protective wall of fire round about through the guiding influence of the Holy Ghost in our lives.

As John measures—or, in a sense, circumscribes a protective measure around—the temple, he makes particular mention of "them who worship therein"—hopefully referring to us. If we are willing to worship in the temple and continually qualify for entrance therein, we are entitled to the protective care of the Lord. In His counsel to His Saints about enduring the trials of the latter days, He charges His disciples to "stand in holy places, and . . . not be moved" (D&C 45:32). Of course, we are to attend the temple often and renew our commitments with the protective spirit of this holy place, but it is not practical nor intended that we sequester ourselves in the temple, in a Church meetinghouse, or even in our own homes. The practical application of our standing in holy places is that we are to be out and about in the world in the business of life, but that we are to sequester ourselves from the evils of life.

Of His disciples, the Lord petitioned the Father "not that thou shouldest take them out of the world, but that thou shouldest keep them from the evil" (John 17:15). Alma taught this same principle to his flock at the Waters of Mormon when he said that they should "stand as witnesses of God at all times and in all things, and in all places that ye may be in, even until death" (Mosiah 18:9). We are blessed that our Savior, through His Apostles and prophets, has measured or drawn a wonderful protective shield around those willing to worthily worship in the temple.

## TWO OLIVE TREES AND TWO CANDLESTICKS

*Are we sufficiently grateful for the message, testimony, and guidance of our Apostles?* John now views the calling of the two Apostles to Jerusalem, their pending ministry, and subsequent martyrdom and resurrection: "And I will give power unto my two witnesses, and they shall prophesy a thousand two hundred and threescore days, clothed in sackcloth. . . . And if any man will hurt them, fire proceedeth out of their mouth, and devoureth their enemies . . . These have power to shut heaven . . . to smite the earth with all plagues. . . . And when they shall have finished their testimony, the beast that ascendeth out of the bottomless pit shall make war against them, and shall overcome them and kill them. . . . And after three days and an half the Spirit of life from God entered into them, and they stood upon their feet; and great fear fell upon them which saw them. And they heard a great voice from heaven saying unto them, Come up hither. And they ascended up to heaven in a cloud; and their enemies beheld them" (Rev. 11:3, 5–7, 11–12).

The Prophet Joseph Smith now gives us further light and knowledge concerning the ministry of these two prophets as he poses a question to the Lord: "Q. What is to be understood by the two witnesses, in the eleventh chapter of Revelation? A. They are two prophets that are to be raised up to the Jewish nation in the last days, at the time of the restoration, and to prophesy to the Jews after they are gathered and have built the city of Jerusalem in the land of their fathers" (D&C 77:15). It is instructive from this verse that the two witnesses are to be raised up "to" the Jewish nation, rather than "from" it. It is also instructive to remember that God's chosen prophet on the earth holds and exercises all priesthood keys and that the mission of these two witnesses to Jerusalem must happen under his direction: "Surely the Lord God will do nothing, but he revealeth his secret unto his servants the prophets" (Amos 3:7).

At the time of this writing, President Thomas S. Monson is the Lord's prophet on the earth and he is, in a very real sense, the *president of the world*—even though only just fewer than fourteen million of us currently recognize him as such. Whatever the identity and specific ministry of the two Apostles to Jerusalem will be, it will come under the direction of the president of the true and living Church. These two special witnesses, although they will die, will emulate the Savior and will stand "upon their feet" and "[ascend] up to heaven in a cloud" (Rev. 11:11–12).

We gain insight and inspiration from the fourth verse of this chapter as it describes these two Apostles: "These are the *two olive trees*, and the *two candlesticks* standing before the God of the earth" (Rev. 11:4; emphasis added). How fitting it is to refer to the two Apostles as olive trees and candlesticks. We recall from chapter 1 that Christ stood "in the midst of the seven candlesticks" and "had in his right hand seven stars" (Rev. 1:13, 16). We learned from the Joseph Smith Translation of the Bible that *stars* are "servants"—thus Christ holds His servants in His hand and gives them guidance and protection.

The candlesticks of John's day likely referred to a seven-branched menorah with a bowl at the top of each branch to hold olive oil and a wick. Olive trees and olive oil are associated with peace, healing, and light. The source of all peace, healing, and light is from the very Prince of Peace and the Light of the World—even our Savior. He administers and speaks this peace, healing, and light through His servants, the prophets and Apostles. Their very calling and ministry is to bear special witness of Him and of His Resurrection.

In the calling of a new Apostle after the death of Christ, we are told, "Beginning from the baptism of John, unto that same day that he was taken up from us, must one be ordained to be a witness with us of his resurrection" (Acts 1:22). From modern revelation, we are reminded that "the twelve traveling councilors are called to be the Twelve Apostles, or special witnesses of the name of Christ in all the world" (D&C 107:23).

And so the pattern of witnessing of Christ has continued through the ages and will continue in the witness and mission of these two special apostolic witnesses in Jerusalem, "which spiritually is called Sodom and Egypt, where also our Lord was crucified" (Rev. 11:8). They will be there in the very city of His life, His ministry, and His death to bear witness to the Jews and to all the world that He truly is the Divine Son of God. Although we do not now know of their specific identity or of the specific timing of this special mission, it is not difficult for us to know the specifics of the *message* they will deliver. It is the message they have always delivered as the olive trees and candlesticks of Christ. It will be the same message they are daily and constantly delivering to us today.

To give specific illustration of this message of the ages, I offer the following sampling of a few selected quotations from prophets and Apostles in the scriptures:

- From Moses: "Because I will publish the name of the Lord: ascribe ye greatness unto our God. He is the Rock, his work is perfect: for all his ways are judgment: a God of truth and without iniquity, just and right is he" (Deut. 32:3–4).
- From Joshua: "And now the Lord your God hath given rest unto your brethren as he promised them . . . take diligent heed to do the commandment and the law . . . to love the Lord your God, and to walk in all his ways, and to keep his commandments, and to cleave unto him, and to serve him with all your heart and with all your soul" (Josh. 22:4–5).
- From Job: "For I know that my redeemer liveth, and that he shall stand at the latter day upon the earth: And though after my skin worms destroy this body, yet in my flesh shall I see God" (Job 19:25–26).
- From Isaiah: "For unto us a child is born, unto us a son is given: and the government shall be upon his shoulder: and his name shall be called Wonderful, Counsellor, The mighty God, The everlasting Father, The Prince of Peace" (Isa. 9:6).
- From Jeremiah: "But the Lord is the true God, he is the living God, and an everlasting king" (Jer. 10:10).
- From John the Baptist: "I indeed baptize you with water: but one mightier than I cometh, the latchet of whose shoes I am not worthy to unloose: he shall baptize you with the Holy Ghost and with fire" (Luke 3:16).
- From Simon Peter: "Thou art the Christ, the Son of the living God" (Matt. 16:16). "Be it known unto you all, and to all the people of Israel, that by the name of Jesus Christ of Nazareth, whom you crucified, whom God raised from the dead, even

by him doth this man stand here before you whole. . . .
Neither is there salvation in any other: for there is none other
name under heaven given among men, whereby we must be
saved" (Acts 4:10, 12).

- From Paul: "That Christ should suffer, and that he should be
the first that should rise from the dead, and should shew light
unto the people, and to the Gentiles" (Acts 26:23). "For I
am not ashamed of the gospel of Christ: for it is the power of
God unto salvation to every one that believeth" (Rom. 1:16).

Our modern prophets and Apostles continue their charge from
the Lord to modern Israel as they constantly teach and testify of the
nature of the Godhead, the Restoration of the gospel, the divinity of
the Church, the Atonement and mission of Jesus Christ, the power
of the priesthood, the verity of the Book of Mormon, the need for
repentance, the power of forgiveness, and the pattern of true worship.

These beautiful and inspiring words give us faith, courage,
guidance, peace, and hope. They are not only the words of our
current living Apostles, but they are words of the Apostles of all past
and future dispensations who teach and testify of Christ and His
gospel—which testimony is to "worship God for the testimony of
Jesus is the spirit of prophecy" (Rev. 19:10). They were the words of
the Prophet Joseph Smith, who sealed his testimony with his blood in
Carthage; his final words of recognition and testimony were, "O Lord
my God!" (D&C 135:1). These words of testimony of Christ and of
invitation to accept His gospel will undoubtedly be the words of the
two special witnesses who will someday seal their testimonies with
their blood in the streets of Jerusalem.

## THE KINGDOMS OF OUR LORD

*What is your greatest wish for the world?* As I was recently visiting one
of the seminary classes under my supervision, I pondered what I
might say when the teacher offered me a few minutes to speak to the
students at the conclusion of class. I had the idea to ask the students
to pretend they had each just received a magic wand and that they
could use it to make any one significant change they wanted in the
world. I then asked each to respond.

One student said he would use his wand to end all war. Others said they would obliterate all harmful drugs, pornography, child abuse, racial prejudice—and so forth. I then asked them to imagine what the world would be like if the collective wishes of all could be granted. We all agreed that such a world would be a happy and glorious place. I then reminded them that such a world condition is possible through the cumulative effect and crowning achievement of the Atonement of our Lord and Savior.

After the two witness have born their testimony, sealed it with their blood, and been resurrected, then will come the day when "the kingdoms of this world are become the kingdoms of our Lord, and of his Christ; and he shall reign forever and ever" (Rev. 11:15). This millennial day will be a great time of rejoicing and will be a time of peace and joy throughout the earth.

Over the years of teaching seminary youth, I have often illustrated the advent of the great millennial day by asking students to go to the whiteboard with two colors of markers and there depict, graffiti-style, everything they despise and dislike about the world with one color. I ask that they use the other color to depict all of the beauty and goodness in the world. The finished product is a fairly good description of our present world condition—the beauty and goodness of life seems surrounded and overshadowed by the despicable and the evil. As I then erase selected portions of their work, we discuss the cleansing power of Christ in the renewal of the earth as it regains its paradisiacal glory. We bask in the joy of the day when drug abuse and alcoholism give way to health and freedom from addiction. We long for the time when the swords of war will be forged into plowshares of prosperity and the spears of destruction will give way to pruning hooks of productivity. We look forward to the day when all of mankind will live in love and harmony and when all are truly alike—not just in the eyes of God, but also in the vision and deportment of all humanity.

Such a millennial day will be a great day of rejoicing. The despots and tyrants of our fallen world will be gone. Their power and influence will yield to the righteous influence and reign of Christ. Of this time, John saw "the four and twenty elders, which sat before God on their seats, fell upon their faces, and worshipped God, Saying, We give thee thanks, O Lord God Almighty, which art, and wast, and art to come; because thou has taken to thee thy great power, and hast reigned" (Rev. 11:16–17).

## THE TIME OF THE DEAD—THE REWARD OF THE SAINTS

*"Do you look forward with an eye of faith, and view this mortal body raised in immortality . . . can you imagine to yourselves that ye hear the voice of the Lord, saying unto you, in that day: Come unto me ye blessed, for behold, your works have been the works of righteousness upon the face of the earth?" (Alma 5:15–16).* As I write this, I am in the time of the year that could perhaps best be typified by the word *commencement.* We have recently held our graduation at the institute. Next week will be our seminary graduation. The stake presidents and I have been signing diplomas and certificates to certify the accomplishment of our students. Many of our students are also graduating from their high-school or college programs. A few are even coming to the end of long, exhausting doctoral programs. They are tired and weary but joyful and well satisfied with their achievements. Despite their weariness, they are in happy anticipation of a rewarding future as a payoff for their long efforts.

Such comparisons can help us visualize the glorious time seen by John in vision: "the time of the dead, that they should be judged, and that thou shouldest give reward unto thy servants the prophets, and to the saints, and them that fear thy name, small and great; and shouldest destroy them which destroy the earth. And the temple of God was opened in heaven, and there was seen in his temple the ark of his testament; and there were lightenings, and voices, and thunderings, and an earthquake, and great hail" (Rev. 11:18–19).

As we muster the faith and courage to follow the lead and example of our Lord, we are enabled to endure the trials of life. As we measure up to the Lord's standard, we receive His protective barrier to shield and guide us through our trials. As we humble ourselves to obediently follow the counsel and direction of the chosen Apostles, we are led to a better world and are given the reward of the Saints and are crowned with immortality and a most glorious resurrection. The eternal commencement awaiting the martyred prophets and those who sustain and follow them will put in true and eternal perspective the momentary triumphs of death and hell. The martyred prophets and their humble followers will "[stand] upon their feet" and will hear the "great voice from heaven saying unto them, Come up thither" (Rev. 11:11–12).

# Chapter Twelve
# A Woman Preserved By God

*WHY WAS THE TWELFTH CHAPTER of the book of Revelation so greatly revised during the inspired translation by the Prophet Joseph Smith?* The twelfth chapter of the book of Revelation has the distinction of being the chapter in the Bible most revised by Joseph Smith. Nearly every verse received some change. The sequence of the verses was altered in the Joseph Smith Translation, and some verses were corrected so as to shed new light and vision on the entire chapter. Whenever I personally study chapter 12, I respectfully turn past this chapter in my King James Version and go directly to page 812 of the appendix of my LDS edition, which contains the complete Joseph Smith Translation revision of the chapter.

This chapter was revised so thoroughly primarily because of its great doctrinal significance and its importance to an understanding of the need for the Restoration of the gospel in the last dispensation. In this chapter we learn of the war in heaven and the continuation of this tremendous battle on the earth. We learn of the Lord's manifestation to us of His love by the formation of His true Church—and of His tender, loving care to preserve the elements of the Church through a dark period of apostasy and then restore it in these latter days. We learn how we are to personally overcome Lucifer, the great dragon.

This chapter is an inspiring view of God's love and plan for His children. It is no wonder that the Prophet Joseph spent so much time, effort, and energy on getting it right for us.

## THE JOSEPH SMITH TRANSLATION
*Are we a Bible-believing people?* A belief statement of our Church says, "We believe the Bible to be the word of God as far as it is translated

correctly; we also believe the Book of Mormon to be the word of God" (A of F 1:8). Many misalign and misinterpret this statement to mean that we do not believe the Bible. In truth, we do believe the Bible and we do accept it to be true—with a few exceptions of items that were inadvertently or deliberately changed by mortal hands. We certainly trust the honor and diligence of the early prophets and Apostles who wrote the Bible—but unfortunately, those of the great and abominable church through their wickedness and carelessness "[took] away from the gospel of the Lamb many parts which are plain and most precious; and also many covenants of the Lord have they taken away" (1 Ne. 13:26). The Revelation of John, like much of the Bible, fell prey to the destructive hand of this great and abominable church. Much of the confusion and struggle to understand the book of Revelation is a result of changes made by unauthorized hands.

After the Prophet Joseph Smith successfully completed his translation of the Book of Mormon, the Lord gave him the task of correcting the mistranslations of the Bible. His extensive work on this project has become known as the Joseph Smith Translation of the Bible. Known commonly as the JST, it offers us much insight and inspiration and is a valuable key in the restoration of the Bible to the condition it once held of being "plain and pure, and most precious and easy to the understanding of all men" (1 Ne. 14:23).

Joseph's task of correcting the Bible also became the Lord's laboratory for Joseph; He provided the context and the motivation for the Prophet to inquire after doctrine and to receive further revelation, light, and knowledge. Much of the revelation now comprising our Doctrine and Covenants came as a direct result of Joseph's inquiry for further light and knowledge while working on the Bible translation. A specific and relevant example of this inquiry is section 77 of the Doctrine and Covenants, the question-and-answer session with the Lord specifically about the book of Revelation. Of this section, the Prophet said, "In connection with the translation of the Scriptures, I received the following explanation of the Revelation of St. John" (D&C 77, section heading). The same is true of many sections—Joseph continued to receive revelation because he continued in the path of humility in seeking knowledge and of asking God, "that giveth to all men liberally, and upbraideth not" (James 1:5).

**A WOMAN CLOTHED WITH THE SUN AND A MAN CHILD**

From the Joseph Smith Translation, here is a helpful key to the understanding of chapter 12:

- *A woman* represents the *Church of God.*
- *A man child* represents *the kingdom of God and Christ.*

"And the dragon prevailed not against Michael, neither the child, nor the *woman* which was the *church of God*, who had been delivered of her pains, and brought forth the *kingdom of our God and his Christ*" (JST, Rev. 12:7; emphasis added).

*How do we distinguish between the "Church of God" and "the kingdom of God and Christ"?* The Church of God is a spiritual organization directed by God through His inspired and called leaders. Membership in the Church of God requires the obtaining of ordinances administered by those in proper authority and adherence to the commandments of God. The kingdom of God is an outgrowth of the Church of God and is a political organization that will govern the inhabitants of the earth during the millennial reign of the Savior. Thus all living on the earth during this time will be subject to governance of the *kingdom of God* even though not all will be members of the *Church of God.* Just as now, the invitation to come unto Christ and receive baptism into His Church will be unto all the world. Many will accept the invitation and come into the Church. Many will choose not to be baptized but will nonetheless receive the blessing and joy of basking in the light of the Lord's governance.

With this understanding of the power and influence of the Church on the earth and the power and influence yet to come from the kingdom of God during the millennial reign of Christ, it is inspiring to contemplate such a world and such a life. To get from where we are now to that blessed condition will be a long road and a daunting task—but not an impossible dream. The Revelation tells us that, in delivering the kingdom of God, "the woman being with child, cried, travailing in birth, and pained to be delivered" (JST, Rev. 12:2). But we must remember that "with men, it is impossible, but not with God: for with God all things are possible" (Mark 10:27).

One of the great quests of the Church of God on the earth has been to strive to bring about Zion, a condition in which people will be, like Enoch's community of old, "of one heart and one mind, and dwelt in righteousness; and there was no poor among them" (Moses 7:18). And even though this effort to establish Zion in our telestial, immoral environment has not been universally successful, we can achieve a great degree of a Zion condition in our own personal lives, families, and wards and stakes.

In the joyful contemplation of what our fallen world is yet to become, we certainly find the theme of hope, healing, peace, and triumph. Try to imagine our future world when Christ will "rule all nations with a rod of iron" (JST, Rev. 12:3). (Remember that the "rod of iron" in Lehi's vision represents the "word of God." We have already learned in John's vision that those who preside will "rule them with the word of God" [JST, Rev. 2:27].) Imagine how sweet it would be, for example, to live in unity with all of the nations of Islam and be able to peaceably enjoy the beauty and diversity of their culture without the threat of jihad and terror as perpetrated by a minority of misguided souls. Imagine the joyous condition of the continent of Africa becoming free from famine and drought and from the spiritual and political oppression of warlords and tyrants.

Have we even the capacity to contemplate life in our own nation when it will be free of every evil? Think of peoples and cultures freely exchanging thought, food, festival, art, and philosophy in a climate where no one need fear those who would consider one race to be supreme over another. It will be a great day when Christ arises to rule the nations with the rod of iron! It certainly gives us abundant cause for hope in the healing and peace that will come from the triumph of the Lamb of God over the forces of the great dragon that now so bind and bewilder our societies.

## WAR IN HEAVEN, WAR ON EARTH

*How are we doing in our role in the raging battle of good over evil?* The context and circumstance of the splendid vision we have come to refer to as the First Vision have given me much cause for thought and wonderment over the years. One of the most profound lessons learned by the events of the vision is the importance placed on it by Lucifer, the great dragon. Think about it: Satan has so much to manage in the world—wars, injustice, fraud, murder, despotism, tyranny, oppression, the perpetrating of false philosophy, the corruption of souls far and wide—and yet he seems to make a priority rush to the scene of a simple and heartfelt prayer uttered by an obscure boy in the back woods of a small village. Joseph tells in his own words, "I kneeled down and began to offer up the desires of my heart to God. I had scarcely done so, when immediately I was seized upon by some power which entirely overcame me, and had such an astonishing influence over me as to bind my tongue so that I could not speak. Thick darkness gathered around me, and it seemed to me for a time as if I were doomed to sudden destruction" (JS—H 1:15). Satan knew that something significant was about to begin in this Sacred Grove. He realized that the long-raging battle, by now spanning the realms of premortal and mortal millennia, was about to be renewed in a new and dramatic context. The woman, or "Church of God," was about to emerge from the wilderness. In his diabolical scheme, the great dragon acted quickly and desperately to stop this advent.

In his vision, John sees the appearance of "another sign in heaven; and behold, a great red dragon having seven heads and ten horns, and seven crowns upon his heads. And his tail drew the third part of the stars of heaven, and did cast them to the earth. And the dragon stood before the woman which was delivered, ready to devour her child after it was born" (JST, Rev. 12:4).

And so the battle rages. Awesome and frightening are the forces of the dragon with his "seven heads and ten horns, and seven crowns upon his heads." Seven, we recall, is a number representing fullness and completeness. By the time of the First Vision, Satan had already had several centuries to establish his many kingdoms throughout the earth. He was now ready to fully and completely unleash his forces against the woman who was now coming forth.

Our battle with the dragon can't be defined only in terms of tanks, planes, and guns. Paul said, "Put on the whole armour of God, that ye may be able to stand against the wiles of the devil. For we wrestle not against flesh and blood, but against principalities, against powers, against the rulers of the darkness of this world, against spiritual wickedness in high places" (Eph. 6:11–12). As such rulers of darkness strive to protect and retain their treasures, they spend vast sums to build machines of war and destruction. They worship the idols of their own hands and the gods of their own making. They lose sight of the very truths that could save and protect them. They continue in their downward spiral of destruction until it becomes too late—until their fate is sealed by their own rebellion.

## THE WOMAN FLEES TO "A PLACE PREPARED"

*Do we have hope and confidence in the Lord's ultimate victory and triumph over evil?* We sometimes hear of diehard sports fans, who, being unable to view the live contest they are interested in, arrange to watch a delayed broadcast or taping of the event. They demand that no one tell them the final outcome so they may enjoy the suspense of the progressive play-by-play clear up to the end result. That's fine for less significant things like football or basketball games, but as for the battle of good and evil, we need the hope and peace of knowing that good will ultimately triumph over evil.

One of the great blessings of hope from the Revelation—one of the many reasons I love it so—is that it reveals to us the final outcome of the war with the dragon. As the Revelation unfolds, the following words of John about the premortal portion of the war serve as a pattern for the mortal and postmortal outcome: "And the dragon prevailed not against Michael, neither the child, nor the woman which was the church of God, who had been delivered of her pains" (JST, Rev. 12:7). We are assured that Satan will not win the war.

We may, however, sometimes wonder why the dragon is allowed to win even some of the battles along the way. A guiding principle on this matter is to remember that, as the Prophet Joseph so poignantly learned through his experience with the lost manuscript, "it is not the work of God that is frustrated, but the work of men" (D&C 3:3).

One of the foundation stones of the great plan of happiness is the granting of individual and collective agency. If mankind, individually and generally, had been faithful, would the woman have needed to flee into the wilderness? Would she and her man child even have been in danger of being devoured by the dragon? It is instructive to read these words of the Prophet Joseph as he dismissed the men who marched in Zion's Camp: "Had the members of Zion's Camp been more faithful, less contentious, more united; had the Saints in the eastern branches had more faith—faith to send up to Zion more men and more money with which to strengthen the hands of the Saints on the land of Zion—the history of Zion's Camp might have been different. But thus it is: what men and great movements might attain to is often defeated, sometimes by the actions of enemies, sometimes by the lack of devotion and faith and energy on the part of those into whose hands great enterprises are committed. While God's general purposes will never ultimately be defeated by man, still upon each side of the general purposes of God a margin somewhat wide seems to have been left in which those both for and against those purposes may write what history they please—one that will meet with the approval of God, or one that will meet only with condemnation—herein is the agency of man. But in the exercise of that agency God's purposes will not be thwarted, for man's agency will not extend so far as that; if it did, it would interfere with God's agency and decrees."14

As the general agency of man played out, and the forces of evil smothered and persecuted the forces of good in the world, the dragon chased the woman into the wilderness—or, in other words, the Church was driven into apostasy ("And the woman fled into the wilderness" (JST, Rev. 12:5).) But God, in His tender mercy, made provision for the day when men's hearts would once again turn to faith and seek righteousness. In His infinite wisdom, he nourished and protected the gospel, even through the dark ages of apostasy. The woman did not flee blindly or alone into the wilderness, but rather "had a place prepared of God, that they should feed her there a thousand two hundred and threescore years" (JST, Rev. 12:5). We are told further, "Therefore, to the woman were given two wings of a great eagle, that she might flee into the wilderness, into her place, where she is nourished for a time, and times, and half a time, from the face of the serpent" (JST, Rev. 12:14).

We have many examples of this time of the nourishing of the woman in the wilderness and of the keeping alive of the gospel flame in preparation for the day of restoration. There are many heroic aspects of the lives of the great reformers. There are many inspiring stories of those who fed her there for the thousand two hundred and threescore years—some at the very peril of their lives. Many of their lives were given in the peril.

Many events transpired that plowed the ground and prepared the seedbed for the gospel light to grow and shine once again in preparation for the return of the woman from her sojourn in the wilderness. One such example is William Tyndale, who studied the Bible and—contrary to the efforts of many in the closed clergy of his day—desired to bring forth the word of God for all people. In the face of much persecution and opposition to his efforts, he pressed on in his work—expressing that a plough boy would soon know more of the true word of God than the critics who opposed him. He was eventually martyred for his cause of proclaiming truth.

## OVERCOME BY BLOOD AND TESTIMONY

*How can we, individually and collectively, overcome the dragon? How can we insure that we are properly using our divine gift of agency to assist in the work and glory of God? How can we demonstrate the same courage as William Tyndale and others in moving forward the great gospel cause? How can we stay the proper course leading to eternal life?* A simple and profound answer to these questions is found in the Revelation of John if we ponder the image of the Church as represented by the woman. The woman was "clothed with the sun, and the moon under her feet, and upon her head a *crown of twelve stars*" (JST, Rev. 12:1; emphasis added).

The Church, symbolized by the woman, has twelve stars at its crown or head. Today, as anciently, the Church has twelve stars at its head—the twelve special witnessing Apostles of Christ. We recall from the first chapter of the Revelation how Christ held His stars or servants in His right hand. Stars are often used to literally guide us on physical journeys (as mariners before the use of modern electronic guidance took their bearings from the North Star) and to spiritually guide us to Christ ("I Jesus . . . am the root and the offspring of David, and the bright and morning star"—Rev. 22:16). The star of the east served to both physically and spiritually guide wise men to Christ. As demonstrated by a sampling of their words in the previous chapter of this book, the Apostles or twelve stars have as their overarching mission the charge to teach and testify of Christ and to lead us to Him.

President Gordon B. Hinckley often liked to speak of the stars and tell of his experience in youth of sleeping out under the stars at night. He learned of the North Star and how mariners guided their ships by it. This star became to him a symbol of constancy amidst turmoil and change. This example of President Hinckley beautifully expresses how we may feel about the prophets and Apostles who stand at the crown of our Church and give us constant and enduring guidance.

I have three friends who served as infantrymen in Vietnam. Two of them were members of the Church at the time and attracted the confidence of others who gravitated to them for protection, guidance, and leadership. The third was not a Church member at the time, but was influenced by one of his leaders who was a Church member, and he joined the Church as a result of the guiding influence of this leader. Today, all three of my friends continue to be stalwart and true members of the Church. If I had to go into physical battle, I would want to follow them. As I have been going through my spiritual life battles, I have tried to follow their example. So it is with our prophets and Apostles—they are tried, tested, and true. They stand firm as special witnesses of Christ. They will not lead us astray. They teach us, "by the word of their testimony," to "overcome . . . by the blood of the Lamb" (JST, Rev. 12:11). We can follow them with absolute confidence. They are true stars and stand firmly and humbly—in contrast to so many pseudo stars of modern society whose names and images often adorn the glossy covers of the checkout stand magazines.

John describes, "And I heard a loud voice saying in heaven, Now is come salvation, and strength, and the kingdom of our God, and the power of his Christ: For the accuser of our brethren is cast down, which accused them before our God day and night. For they have overcome him by the blood of the Lamb, and by the word of their testimony; for they loved not their own lives, but kept the testimony even unto death. Therefore, rejoice O heavens, and ye that dwell in them" (JST, Rev. 12:9–11).

*How do we overcome by blood and by testimony?* Central to the image of blood is the heart. When we speak of *heart* in the scriptures and in the general gospel sense, we are referring to the inner feelings and commitments of the soul. In order for us to be cleansed by the redeeming "blood of the Lamb," our hearts must be pure and right before Him. Our mortal charge and challenge is to always keep our hearts right before God. Alma taught, "And now behold, I say unto you, my brethren, if ye have experienced a change of heart, and if ye have felt to sing the song of redeeming love, I would ask, can ye feel so now?" (Alma 5:26). To "feel the song of redeeming love" is to have a testimony in our hearts of the atoning sacrifice and redemption of our Savior. If we have such a testimony, we could say that our heart is right before God.

And thus we have a key to overcoming the influence of the dragon in our personal lives—we must get our heart right. If we were to try to battle him without our hearts being right, we would surely fail. If we were to focus our fight and our energy on only one of his seven heads, we would be at risk of being blindsided by one or more of his other heads or evil influences. Even the one head we may conquer could be healed and attack us again if we do not effect complete victory. John "saw one of his heads as it were wounded to death; and his deadly wound was healed: and all the world wondered after the beast" (Rev. 13:3).

If our own heart is right before God, we will be granted the strength, courage, and wisdom to strike at the very heart of the dragon. That is how we deliver him the lethal blow—*we strike him in his heart!* A lethal blow to his heart disables all of his heads! Our weapon for striking him in the heart *is our own pure heart.* Of course, we acknowledge and remember that the complete and ultimate destruction of the dragon and his influence in the world comes from the divine power and intervention of God—by the blood of the Lamb.

Consider these words of the Psalmist: "Who shall ascend into the hill of the Lord? or who shall stand in his holy place? He that hath clean hands, and a pure heart; who hath not lifted up his soul unto vanity, nor sworn deceitfully" (Ps. 24:3–4). Certainly Alma knew how we are to conquer the dragon: "And behold, he preached the word unto your fathers, and a mighty change was also wrought in their hearts, and they humbled themselves and put their trust in the true and living God. And behold, they were faithful until the end; therefore they were saved" (Alma 5:13).

## FLOODING THE EARTH
*How curious are we to see in true perspective and broad panorama all the intricate and specific details of our life quest and of our battle with Satan? How is our battle going? How much longer will it last? Do we*

*have Satan on the run? Does he know that we will prevail and overcome? Is he more angry now than in years past? Has he hit his stride, or does he yet have untapped spurts of energy to spend?* It's impossible to know all of these specific details, but with millions of righteous Saints on the earth, we certainly must have Satan's attention. And he doesn't like it, as evidenced by his continual outpouring of the flood of evil upon the earth: "And the serpent casteth out of his mouth water as a flood after the woman, that he might cause her to be carried away of the flood. And the earth helpeth the woman, and the earth openeth her mouth, and swalloweth up the flood which the dragon casteth out of his mouth. Therefore, the dragon was wroth with the woman, and went to make war with the remnant of her seed, which keep the commandments of God, and have the testimony of Jesus Christ" (JST, Rev. 12:15–17).

*What is our individual and collective response to Satan's flood of evil? Are we to cower in the corner and do nothing? Do we panic and run to and fro, not knowing where to go or what to do?* No, we counter with our own flood—a flood of testimony, righteousness, courage, and faith.

Years ago, President Ezra Taft Benson issued marching orders to flood the earth with the message and teachings of the Book of Mormon. Not as many years ago, President Gordon B. Hinckley renewed this battle cry, asking us as Church members to reread the Book of Mormon and make a renewed effort to take the message of it to the world. And such is the message of our dispensation and our answer to the evil flood of Satan. We will continue forward in striving to seek out the Lamb of God and share the message of His atoning sacrifice with the entire world. We will strive to overcome by the blood of the Lamb and by the word of testimony.

# Chapter Thirteen
# The Economy and Mark of Satan

*WHAT IS THE ECONOMY OF SATAN?* The *economy of Satan* is simply the counterfeit of the Lord's program of prudent and provident living. The Lord blesses us in abundance with the good things of the earth: "For the earth is full, and there is enough and to spare; yea, I prepared all things, and have given unto the children of men to be agents unto themselves" (D&C 104:17). As return on the investment of His abundance with us, the Lord expects us "to do good—to clothe the naked, and to feed the hungry, and to liberate the captive, and administer relief to the sick and the afflicted" (Jacob 2:19).

The driving motivation of Satan's economy is to distort the purpose of material and temporal provision. He persuades men to satisfy their pride and "set [their hearts] so much upon the things of the world" that they seek "to cover our sins, or to gratify our pride, our vain ambition, or to exercise control or dominion or compulsion upon the souls of the children of men" (D&C 121:35, 37). The economy of Satan serves to destroy the souls of all who buy into his false and damning philosophy. The economy of God, in contrast, serves to nurture and mentor the souls of men in preparation for eternal life.

My older sister jokes that I likely have the first dollar I ever earned. I jokingly reply, "No, I don't still have it, but I *do* have a ledger account of how it was spent." My Depression-era parents greatly influenced my economic philosophy. I recall watching my mother open a cube of butter and scrape the microscopic remnants off the inside of the wrapper before discarding it. She darned our stockings. We ate everything on our plates. We turned off lights not in use. My father timed all long-distance calls so they wouldn't exceed his two-minute limit. He once got an unsolicited credit card in the mail and with some ceremony demonstrated to me the proper way of dealing with such things as he cut it up into small pieces and discarded it.

As I have grown older, I have adapted more to our modern economy. However, the basics of my parents' philosophy have remained with me. For me, a bargain is not a bargain unless it is something I really need and something I can pay cash for. I rarely buy toys—and never huge ones. I reverently believe that a personal blessing I have received is that of not feeling compelled to keep up with the proverbial Joneses.

I find that these feelings of my heart and thoughts of my mind on matters of economy drastically clash with much of the modern world in which I now live. I shake my head in disbelief at young married couples who amass huge debt in an effort to get a thirty-year jump-start on accumulating what it has taken their parents a lifetime to acquire. My heart aches when I hear stories of ruined marriages stemming from debt—sometimes in the six figures—expended on pornography. I have anguished when I have seen grocery money being wasted on harmful and destructive drugs. And so goes the modern economy of Satan. He is subtle. He is ruthless. He is calculating. He is a terrible beast. He is incessant in his efforts to disrupt and destroy the physical and spiritual well-being of God's children through his false and damning economy.

Gratefully, we have been guided by the Lord's true messengers in how to experience peace and stability. One of the main ways is to align ourselves with the true economy of God by striving to receive His "mark in our foreheads" rather than the destructive and damning mark of the devil.

## A BEAST NOT FULLY UNDERSTOOD

*Are we willing to postpone our desire to know of things not yet revealed?* We do not fully understand all of the details of the Revelation, and we should not try to get too specific on some matters, such as attempting to identify the nature of every beast. In chapter 13, John sees "a beast rise up out of the sea, having seven heads . . . and upon his heads the name of blasphemy. And the beast which I saw was like unto a leopard, and his feet were as the feet of a bear, and his mouth as the mouth of a lion . . . And there was given unto him a mouth speaking great things and blasphemies" (Rev. 13:1–2, 5). The Prophet Joseph Smith once referenced these verses in counseling the missionaries to avoid things that they do not understand (see *Teachings of the Prophet Joseph Smith*, 292).

With that counsel, let's not worry too much about the specific identity of the beast. Instead, let's be content with the knowledge that "John sees fierce-looking beasts which represent degenerate earthly kingdoms controlled by Satan—The devil works miracles and deceives men" (Rev. 13, chapter heading). Let's remember that the war in heaven continues on earth and that we continue, for the present day, to do daily battle with Satan and his economy. Then we can seek out the principles and doctrines that guide our lives and give us hope, peace, and healing.

## WONDER THAT A DEADLY WOUND IS HEALED

Early in the morning of January 17, 1994, a 6.7-magnitude earthquake struck Southern California; its epicenter was in Northridge, a suburb of Los Angeles. Until that date, it was one of the most expensive natural disasters in the history of the United States, with total damage estimated at $15 billion. Although there is always sadness at the loss of life and property from destruction and disaster, there was something from the news of this particular quake that gave me some degree of satisfaction—although I knew that my pleasure was more symbolic than real, because I knew the news would not significantly alter the overall ebb and flow of evil in the world. My satisfaction came from learning that the studios of nearly every major American producer and distributor of pornographic videos were destroyed. These studios had been located almost directly atop the earthquake fault line.

Common sense told me then (as it would today) that the evil and wicked men who produce something as sinfully lucrative as pornography would not let a setback like this interfere for long with their economy. I'm sure they used their enormous profits to quickly rebuild and get back in business. But the news was encouraging, nonetheless, as it gives portent of what will someday befall the total economy of Satan. We learn from the Doctrine and Covenants, "And thus, with the sword and by bloodshed the inhabitants of the earth shall mourn: and with famine, and plague, and earthquake, and the thunder of heaven, and the fierce and vivid lightning also, shall the inhabitants of the earth be made to feel the wrath, and indignation and chastening hand of an Almighty God, until the consumption decreed hath made a full end of all nations" (D&C 87:6).

Of the seven-headed beast seen by John, we learn, "And I saw one of his heads as it were wounded to death; and his deadly wound was healed: and all the world wondered after the beast" (Rev. 13:3). Although natural disaster or righteous activism in society may wound and even destroy a particular head of Satan's kingdoms, unfortunately the time is not yet for him to be completely destroyed and cast down. He will still be allowed to heal his wounded kingdom and continue his evil march.

But we must not despair. As individuals, families, and congregations, we can do much to hold him at bay and keep him out of our realm if our hearts are pure. We find hope in remembering "that no combination of wickedness shall have power to rise up and prevail over thy people upon whom thy name shall be put in this house" (D&C 109:26). We recall from our discussion in chapter 12 that the only way to annihilate the seven-headed beast is to strike him in the heart. To do this, we must ourselves be pure in heart.

## THE BOOK OF LIFE

*Are we living our lives so as to have our names written in the Lamb's book of life?* A few years ago at Christmastime I presented each of my children and each of my siblings a boxed set of my three-volume personal history—my autobiography to date. Does this autobiography represent my true life and character? Can it be considered my book of life? I'd answer, "Well, sure—I wrote it, so it must be true." Yet in reality, we know that all history—even autobiography—is biased. I have tried to accurately reflect my life, but the challenge is that *I* do not know *me* as *God* knows *me*.

Our book of life is not a book at all, as we know books. As we previously discussed in chapter 3, it is rather the summation of who we are—of what we have become. To have our name written in the

Lamb's book of life, we must have become His true followers and disciples. We must have become like Him, as He has charged us to be: "Therefore, what manner of men ought ye to be? Verily, I say unto you, even as I am" (3 Ne. 27:27).

As John saw the vision of the terrible beast, he saw that "it was given unto him to make war with the saints, and to overcome them: and power was given him over all kindreds, and tongues, and nations. And all that dwell upon the earth shall worship him, whose names are not written in the book of life of the Lamb slain from the foundation of the world" (Rev. 13:7–8). Since Satan will have power to overcome all whose names are *not* written in the book of life, and since the book of life is a record of absolute truth, there can be no hypocrisy. There can be no double standard. Though a man may associate himself with the Saints and may perform many impressive acts of service, if his heart is not right, then his book of life is void and blank. Our public and our private lives must be congruent.

Satan would have us be phony and incongruent. He who is the great imitator will attempt to get us to imitate works of righteousness. He likes us to attend church as long we don't apply what we learn. He revels in our profound speech as long as the language of our actions remains inconsistent with our words. He delights in our words of praise to God as long as we privately profane His name.

John tells us of the devil's tactics: "And he doeth great wonders, so that he maketh fire come down from heaven on the earth in the sight of men, And deceiveth them that dwell on the earth by the means of those miracles which he had power to do in the sight of the beast; saying to them that dwell on the earth, that they should make an image to the beast, which had the wound by a sword, and did live" (Rev. 13:13–14).

Satan is the master imitator—he works in opposition to all of the good things that come to us by the hand of the Lord. He presents a counterfeit path in opposition to our Father in Heaven's plan of happiness. Through his false miracles, he works to deceive and distract true disciples. The great imitator takes everything good and true and pollutes it, while packaging it in the glitz and glitter of the world. He even creates a phony imitation of the sacred mark "sealed . . . in their foreheads" (Rev. 7:3) of those who belong to the true fold of God—even the Church of the Firstborn.

## W<small>HICH</small> M<small>ARK</small> A<small>DORNS</small> O<small>UR</small> F<small>OREHEAD</small>?

*Where is our economic loyalty? With which mark do we adorn our foreheads?* Several years ago, while serving as bishop of my ward, I officiated and spoke at the funeral service of a dear friend, Sister Hazel Hakes. She and her husband had been the next-door neighbors I mentioned earlier for nearly twenty years. He had been our stake president and was then the patriarch of the stake. I had been sent to the community to teach seminary in his place upon his retirement. They were, and still are, my heroes. President Hakes passed away just a few years ago, and I long to see these great souls again someday.

They became almost as parents to me—in fact, they, like my own parents, were children of the Great Depression. Their righteous and good lives were the epitome of provident living. During his tenure as stake president, he consistently and eloquently taught by precept and example the gospel principles of provident living. I had the great blessing of sharing irrigation turns with him for most of twenty years and, for a few hours each week, was tutored by him as we waited for the water to run its course.

When President James E. Faust came to the stake to release President Hakes as president, he called on Sister Hakes to share her testimony. In speaking of the service and sacrifice of her husband, she said, "I have learned that it is better to have 10 percent of a 100- percent man than to have 100 percent of a 10-percent man." President Hakes was a 100-percent man, and she was a 100-percent woman. It gives me much joy to think of them now together forever.

Their provident lifestyle was inspiring. I watched them live prudently as they grew their own food and became mostly self-reliant. Rarely did they go to the store, and when they did, I think they hardly ever purchased anything wasteful or unnecessary. They certainly never bought anything harmful or evil from Satan's store. One of their mottos was, "Use it up, wear it out, make it do, or do without."

In John's vision, he tells of the last days when Satan will control so much of the economy of the world. Of this evil influence, he says, "And that no man might buy or sell, save he that had the mark, or the name of the beast, or the number of his name" (Rev. 13:17). I can imagine what the response of Brother and Sister Hakes might be to this diabolical threat. I can imagine them saying, in their deliberate and steadfast way, "Well, so what? Who would want to buy what Satan has to sell anyway?" They were certainly never interested in supporting the economy of Satan.

As I was preparing to speak at Sister Hakes's funeral, inspiration took me to the final chapter of Proverbs, which was likely written by King Solomon. It seemed to fit so well the life and legacy of my friend. In tribute to her, I shared with the congregation these words: "Who can find a virtuous woman? for her price is far above rubies. The heart of her husband doth safely trust in her . . . She will do him good and not evil all the days of her life. . . . She girdeth her loins with strength . . . Strength and honour are her clothing; and she shall rejoice in time to come. . . . In her tongue is the law of kindness. She looketh well to the ways of her household, and eateth not the bread of idleness. Her children arise up, and call her blessed; her husband also, and he praiseth her" (Prov. 31:10–12, 17, 25–28).

In the years since the occasion of my friend's funeral, I have had many continuing thoughts about her and her husband and also about my words at her funeral—particularly the words quoted from King Solomon. One day the thought entered my mind that the words seemed so incongruent with the later life of King Solomon. I wondered why King Solomon did not live by his own counsel. I wondered why he did not "find a virtuous woman," rather than marrying so many strange and corrupt women. Today I would answer, *Because he got the wrong mark in his forehead!* Let me explain.

As we examine the later life of the once-wise King Solomon, we learn that he became obsessed with the wealth of the earth and the economy of Satan. He acquired "targets of beaten gold . . . three hundred shields of beaten gold . . . a great throne of ivory . . . overlaid . . . with the best gold . . . drinking vessels . . . of gold . . . a navy of Tharshish . . . bringing gold, and silver, ivory, and apes, and peacocks. . . . So king Solomon exceeded all the kings of the earth for riches" (1 Kgs. 10:16–18, 21–23).

We further learn that he married multiple times out of the covenant, contrary to the law and warning of ancient Israel that "neither shalt thou make marriages with them . . . For they will turn away thy son from following me, that they may serve other gods"

(Deut. 7:3–4). King Solomon "loved many strange women . . . and he had seven hundred wives, princesses, and three hundred concubines: and his wives turned away his heart. . . . And Solomon did evil in the sight of the Lord, and . . . did build an high place for Chemosh . . . And likewise did he for all his strange wives, which burnt incense and sacrificed unto their gods" (1 Kgs. 11:1, 3, 6–8).

And then we find this fascinating verse: "Now the weight of gold that came to Solomon in one year was six hundred threescore and six talents of gold" (1 Kgs. 10:14). *Six hundred threescore and six*—666—a very interesting number! It occurs only three times in the Bible—two of them are used to describe the annual gold revenue of Solomon as we have just described, and the other is in the Revelation of John: "And he causeth all, both small and great, rich and poor, free and bond, to receive a mark in their right hand, or in their foreheads . . . Here is wisdom. Let him that hath understanding count the number of the beast: for it is the number of a man; and his number is Six hundred threescore and six" (Rev. 13:16, 18).

This intriguing number—666—is one of the most speculated-about concepts in the Revelation of John. What does it mean, exactly? How will it be administered? Why is it "the number of a man?" We don't fully know the answers to these questions, but it seems to be a relevant number in explaining the course followed by King Solomon. And it seems relevant that he stands as an example to us of how we should *not* engage in the economy of Satan.

I also know that my dear, old friends from across the fence had absolutely no interest in pursuing and obtaining the mark of the beast or in buying or selling his product. Their only interest throughout their righteous lives was in having the seal of the true God sealed in their foreheads as described to us earlier: "Saying, Hurt not the earth, neither the sea, nor the trees, till we have sealed the servants of our God in their foreheads" (Rev. 7:3).

Of this sealing of the true God, the Prophet Joseph Smith taught that the angels holding power over the earth would place a seal of the everlasting covenant upon families—fathers and mothers—so that their posterity could not be lost (see *Teachings of the Prophet Joseph Smith*, 321).

That is the mark I desire in my forehead. That is the mark I hope those I love will desire in their foreheads. That is the mark that so many Saints of all ages have sought for their foreheads—to be sealed by the everlasting covenant. As we consider the blessing of seeking the economy of God and of abandoning the economy of Satan, let's remember that those who keep gospel covenants have the sure promise that "the kingdom is yours and the blessings thereof are yours, and the riches of eternity are yours" (D&C 78:18). Any other course—or any other sealing that we might be tempted to pursue—must certainly pale in comparison. The economy of Satan pales greatly in comparison to the economy of God.

# Chapter Fourteen

# Restoration and Harvest

*HAVE WE "SUFFICIENTLY RETAINED IN remembrance" the "mercy and long-suffering" of the Lord for us (Alma 5:6)?* In the tugs and pulls of our lives, when we are being buffeted by the temptations of Satan, we may get discouraged and temporarily lose sight of our eternal goals. It thus becomes critical to our spiritual survival that we learn to regularly pause for spiritual refreshment and renewal. We are often counseled about the importance of remembering our daily prayer and scripture study and of the importance of regular sacrament meeting and temple attendance. A computer search of the word *remember* shows that it appears 352 times in the scriptures. As I reviewed how the word was used, it so often was to remind us of the great blessings our Father in Heaven has reserved for those who keep His commandments. It is mostly used to encourage us.

Provision has been made by the Lord for us to regularly gather to be refreshed and to remember. Twice a year in general conference, we are able to personally hear the Lord's words of blessing and renewal from our leaders. We are given direction about the things we must do so that we will not lose our bearings and lose our hope. In the Book of Mormon, we are instructed to "feast upon the words of Christ; for behold, the words of Christ will tell you all things what ye should do" (2 Ne. 32:3).

I have often heard people say about a particular class, meeting, or temple session, "Oh, I wish I could just stay here all day!" But our mortal mission is not to always sequester ourselves in peaceful places, but to be out on the battlefields of life serving, sharing, and learning. Nevertheless, how glorious it is to have those intermissions of peace, renewal, refreshment, and remembrance in our lives.

In looking at the Revelation of John, we have studied much of the battle with the dragon and the destruction of those who choose to follow his course. We have much of destruction and battle yet to experience. But the next few chapters provide an intermission of peace, renewal, and joy.

## STANDING WITH THE LAMB ON MOUNT ZION
*Do we live in joyful anticipation for the day of our salvation and triumph over the world?* I believe one of the biggest misunderstandings of many Church members is the false notion that the celestial kingdom is reserved for prophets and for little children who die before the age of accountability. We must remember that there is no maximum seating capacity in the celestial kingdom. As I have taught this principle to my seminary and institute students, my motive has been to prompt discussion about the doctrine that our Father in Heaven has the capacity and the power to save and exalt all who will come unto Him.

As chapter 14 of the Revelation begins, we see Christ standing on Mount Sion with "an hundred forty and four thousand" who have all chosen to follow Him and receive "his father's name written in their foreheads." They are joyful and rejoicing in the happy contentment of knowing that they have charted their life course in following Christ and resisting the temptations of Satan: "And I looked, and, lo, a Lamb stood on the mount Sion, and with him an hundred forty and four thousand, having his Father's name written in their foreheads. And I heard a voice from heaven, as the voice of many waters, and as the voice of a great thunder: and I heard the voice of harpers harping with their harps: And they sung as it were a new song before the throne, and before the four beasts, and the elders: and no man could learn that song but the hundred and forty and four thousand, which were redeemed from the earth" (Rev. 14:1–3).

We recall that the 144,000 are not members of an exclusive gated country club of saved souls, but rather a vast army of humble servants who are "ordained unto the holy order of God, to *administer* the everlasting gospel; for they are they who are ordained out of every nation, kindred, tongue, and people, by the angels to whom is given power over the nations of the earth, to bring *as many as will come* to the church of the Firstborn" (D&C 77:11; emphasis added). This symbolic number is not to be taken literally as any kind of a cap or quota; it reflects those who are called to administer the saving ordinances to the vast multitudes that choose to come unto Christ.

Those who will have endured their trials and overcome the world will be so jubilant and joyful that they will offer their praise and gratitude to the Lord in music of harps and of a new song. I don't often hear the music of harps in my world, but I did on two recent occasions, and I have a new sense of reverence and awe for this beautiful instrument of worship of the Lord. On one occasion—that of a special Christmas service in our ward—a talented sister brought her harp and was there playing as we entered the chapel. The attitude of the congregants seemed more subdued and worshipful than usual. The mellow and beautiful tones of the music stirred our souls and lifted our spirits. The second occasion was at a recent seminary graduation where one of the graduates played on her harp a beautiful medley of hymns to remind us of the course of study for the year. Her sharing of her talent brought an uplift and feeling of joy. What a beautiful expression to speak gratitude to the Lamb, through music, for His redemption of our souls.

Not only do the saved worship with the music of the harp but also with the singing of a new song of praise and adoration. We are given more description of this blessed event in latter-day scripture, introduced by the heading to Doctrine and Covenants 84, which reads, "The New Song of the Redemption of Zion." The Lord gives this introduction to the new song in words consistent with the context of the verses of our focus in the Revelation:

> For I, the Almighty, have laid my hands upon the nations, to scourge them for their wickedness. And plagues shall go forth, and they shall not be taken from the earth until I have completed my work, which shall be cut short in righteousness—Until all shall know me, who remain, even from the least unto the greatest, and shall be filled with the knowledge of the Lord, and shall see eye to eye, and shall lift up their voice, and with the voice together sing this new song, saying:

The Lord hath brought again Zion;
The Lord hath redeemed his people Israel,
According to the election of grace,
Which was brought to pass by the faith
And covenant of their fathers.
The Lord hath redeemed his people;
And Satan is bound and time is no longer.
The Lord hath gathered all things in one.
The Lord hath brought down Zion from above.
The Lord hath brought up Zion from beneath.
The earth hath travailed and brought forth her
strength;
And truth is established in her bowels;
And the heavens have smiled upon her;
And she is clothed with the glory of her God;
For he stands in the midst of his people.
Glory, and honor, and power, and might,
Be ascribed to our God; for he is full of mercy,
Justice, grace and truth, and peace,
Forever and ever, Amen. (D&C 84:96–102)

## FOLLOWING THE LAMB WHITHERSOEVER HE GOETH

*How willing are we to follow the Lord "whithersoever he goeth"?* Years ago, the Church Educational System produced an exhilarating video presentation designed to help teach students the principle of following the prophet. The context of the video was an adventure of helicopter skiing; the participants were flown by helicopter to a jagged mountain top, and then they daringly skied down the snowy slopes. A mature and very experienced elderly man was serving as the guide. He led the way as his followers excitedly skied through new adventures and thrills like never before experienced.

Partway down the mountainside, one young man decided he wanted even more adventure, so he left the group to pursue his own path. He was excited about his new-found freedom—the high adventure of charting his own course. He paused to enjoy the moment of his independence. After some contemplation, he wisely chose to rejoin his party and follow his guide.

As the group further descended the mountain, the guide soon stopped and had them look up. The young man was astonished as he realized that had he continued his own course, he would have plunged to certain death over a rocky ledge. In the closing narration, the young man humbly expressed his gratitude at the wise decision he made to be "willing to follow an old man down the hill." The video powerfully taught the need to follow the prophet.

If we are to overcome the world and join the redeemed from the earth in gaining exaltation and in singing the song of redeeming love, we must learn to follow the prophet. Our earnest question is, *Where will the prophet lead us?* Most Church members, if asked to state the mission of the Church, could readily respond, "To invite all to come unto Christ and be perfected in Him and receive the saving ordinances of the gospel."

We may rightly conclude that the role of the prophet is to lead us to Christ, that we may follow Him. As Jesus Himself said to the well-to-do ruler, "Yet lackest thou one thing: sell all that thou hast, and distribute unto the poor, and thou shalt have treasure in heaven: and come, follow me" (Luke 18:22). Now our earnest question becomes, *If we choose to follow Christ, where will He lead us?* John gives us the answer: "These are they which were not defiled with women; for they are virgins. These are they which follow the Lamb *whithersoever he goeth*. These were redeemed from among men, being the firstfruits unto God and to the Lamb" (Rev. 14:4; emphasis added).

"To follow the Lamb whithersoever he goeth"—that is what is required of us! Now we might ask, *Where does He go?* We gain answer to this question from the dark and smelly depths of the Liberty Jail. The Prophet Joseph and his companions had spent months of unjust confinement in this terrible dungeon while their families and beloved Saints were being persecuted and driven from their homes. Joseph, in his anguish, had cried out to the Lord, "O God, where art thou? And where is the pavilion that covereth thy hiding place?" The Lord had responded, "My son, peace be unto thy soul; thine adversity and thine afflictions shall be but a small moment; And then, if thou endure it well, God shall exalt thee on high; thou shalt triumph over all thy foes" (D&C 121:1, 7–8).

The Lord goes on to counsel Joseph with great empathy that He understands and feels the pain and anguish of His beloved Prophet—the derision, the rage of hell, the blasphemy, the lies, the betrayal, the robbery, the rape, the plunder, the murder, the false accusation, the unjust imprisonment—and much more. Then the Lord teaches Joseph this great lesson: "If the very jaws of hell shall gape open the mouth wide after thee, know thou, my son, that all these things shall give thee experience, and shall be for thy good. *The Son of Man hath descended below them all.* Art thou greater than he? . . . fear not what man can do, for God shall be with you forever and ever" (D&C 122:7–9; emphasis added).

We must be willing to follow Christ wherever He takes us. We must remember that He has suffered all of the pains and afflictions of all mankind. In our suffering, He will understand us and He will not forsake us. If we are willing to make and keep this commitment to follow our Savior, then our blessing will be to gain the status spoken of by John: "And in their mouth was found no guile: for they are without fault before the throne of God" (Rev. 14:5).

## A<small>N</small> A<small>NGEL</small> F<small>LYING IN THE</small> M<small>IDST OF</small> H<small>EAVEN</small>

*Do we fully appreciate the significance of the mighty angel bringing the everlasting gospel to be preached to all the world?* There are many examples of people who have been lost and even presumed dead who have miraculously and triumphantly returned. I heard such a story a few years ago about a young man in the Navy who walked out on deck in the middle of the night; and at a sudden pitch of the ship, he was hit by a swinging door and knocked overboard. No one saw or heard his mishap and no one discovered him missing for many hours—not even at morning muster. By the time they did discover his absence, the ship had traveled so far beyond the point of his falling overboard that the crew had little chance of finding and rescuing him. His family was finally notified that he was missing, and as the hours passed, almost all hope of finding him vanished. He was presumed dead. But because of the young man's survival training, he did many things to keep himself alive—such as repeatedly inflating his pants and using them as a life preserver. After several days of grief and sorrow, the phone rang in the home of his parents and the young man announced to them his safety. He had been discovered and rescued by the crew of a small fishing boat and taken to their village. The grateful parents were soon rejoicing in a glorious reunion with their son.

We now come to a glorious reunion in the Revelation of John. We recall from chapter 12 how the "woman clothed with the sun" (Rev. 12:1), symbolizing the Church of God, had been chased into the wilderness by the great dragon. Even though there were many dark days and many of early and later Christians lost hope of ever reuniting with the true Church, we recall that she was in a place "prepared of God" and, "given two wings of a great eagle," was there "nourished" (JST, Rev. 12:14). In the Lord's due time came the glorious day of rejoicing and jubilation as the woman returned through the ministering of the Lord's appointed angels, commencing on that beautiful spring morning of 1820 with the appearance of the Father and the Son to the new Prophet of the Restoration.

John records, "And I saw another angel fly in the midst of heaven, having the everlasting gospel to preach unto them that dwell on the earth, and to every nation, and kindred, and tongue, and people, Saying with a loud voice, Fear God, and give glory to him; for the hour of his judgment is come: and worship him that made heaven and earth, and the sea, and the fountains of waters. And there followed another angel, saying, Babylon is fallen, is fallen, that great city, because she made all nations drink the wine of the wrath of her fornication" (Rev. 14:6–8).

In modern revelation, the Lord speaks more of the great work of the Restoration of the gospel by His angel: "And now, verily saith the Lord, that these things might be known among you, O inhabitants of the earth, I have sent forth mine angel flying through the midst of heaven, having the everlasting gospel, who hath appeared unto some and hath committed it unto man, who shall appear unto many that dwell on the earth. And this gospel shall be preached unto every nation, and kindred, and tongue, and people. And the servants of God shall go forth, saying with a loud voice: Fear God, and give glory to him, for the hour of his judgment is come; And worship him that made heaven, and earth, and the sea, and the fountains of waters" (D&C 133:36–39).

Following the appearance of the Father and the Son and the introduction of the Book of Mormon record by the angel Moroni, many more angels of the Restoration appeared, including John the Baptist, Peter, James, Moses, Elijah, Elias, and even John the Revelator himself. (I have wondered how much he knew of the full and specific significance of his future ministration when he saw in vision the angel fly in the midst of heaven.)

We are truly as one great family as we declare the message of the Restoration throughout the world. We of the latter days joyfully welcome the woman back with us after her long time of preparation in anticipation of this beautiful day of restoration. What a triumphant and wonderful day! What a glorious reunion!

## THE PATIENCE OF THE SAINTS—THE REST OF THE LORD

*How do we envision the time of rest promised to the faithful Saints? How do we envision the unrest of those who follow Satan?* Even though we now bask in the glorious day of restoration, we are not yet free of Babylon and cannot yet fully rest from our labors. The wrath of God is yet to be poured out on those who will not hear and accept the message of the restoring angels. Those who "worship the beast and his image, and receive his mark in his forehead . . . shall drink of the wine of the wrath of God, which is poured out without mixture into the cup of his indignation; and he shall be tormented with fire and brimstone in the presence of the holy angels, and in the presence of the Lamb: And the smoke of their torment ascendeth up for ever and ever; and they have no rest day nor night, who worship the beast" (Rev. 14:9–11).

How frustrating and disappointing that many in the world—even some among our own families—will not recognize the message of the flying angels and the gift and blessing of the woman returned. But God will never usurp the gift of agency. We must each worship "according to the dictates of our own conscience, and allow all men the same privilege, let them worship how, where, or what they may" (A of F 1:11). God honors our agency with patience and longsuffering, but the day of His judgment will surely come. C. S. Lewis said, "I believe that if a million chances were likely to do good, they would be given. But a master often knows, when boys and parents do not, that it is really useless to send a boy in for a certain examination again. Finality must come sometime, and it does not require a very robust faith to believe that omniscience knows when."[15]

We must trust our omniscient God to know when justice and mercy will have full sway. One of the greater trials of our mortality is knowing when and how to help those we love. We always love, of course, but we cannot determine what course another will take. The very best thing we can do to help the ones we love is to *show* them the way—to constantly hold up to them the love and light of our Savior. "Therefore, hold up your light that it may shine unto the world. Behold I am the light which ye shall hold up" (3 Ne. 18:24).

*What will be the reward and the outcome of our striving?* John sees the outcome and tells us, "Here is the patience of the saints: here are they that keep the commandments of God, and the faith of Jesus. And I heard a voice from heaven saying unto me, Write, Blessed are the dead which die in the Lord from henceforth: Yea saith the Spirit, that they may rest from their labours; and their works do follow them" (Rev. 14:12–13). The reward for righteous endurance will be a blessed death and a time of rest.

*What is the meaning of "blessed are the dead which die in the Lord"?* From modern revelation, we learn, "And it shall come to pass that those that die in me shall not taste of death, for it shall be sweet unto them" (D&C 42:46).

*What is a "sweet death"?* Sometimes good and righteous people suffer long and painful deaths. Sometimes not-so-good and not-so-righteous people seem to pass through death's door so peacefully and simply that it seems no trial at all. So the promise of *sweet death* must refer to the spiritual rather than the physical aspect of death. In the previous chapter, I referred to my dear friends, President and Sister Hakes. She died after many long months of suffering. I'm not sure about the specifics of President Hakes's suffering, as I lived in another part of the country at the time—but he had his own serious ailments. I am sure they hoped for a much easier time when it came to physical death. But I am confident that once their physical death was accomplished, they had a very sweet experience in graduating from this troubled world and being united in glory forever after. Sweet it is for a righteous couple to go forward in Heavenly Father's plan with the assurance that they have kept their gospel covenants and endured the trials of life and are now free from the pain, suffering, trials, and temptations of mortality.

*What is "the rest of the Lord"?* My father sometimes jokingly spoke of the eternal day of rest as the time when he could sleep his days away and, during his waking hours, float lazily and peacefully on a cloud, sipping lemonade. I doubt that there will be much sitting around doing nothing. I believe that there will be much good work to do. We know from modern scripture "that the faithful elders of this dispensation, when they depart from mortal life, continue their labors in the preaching of the gospel of repentance and redemption" (D&C 138:57). The rest involved will be rest from the trial, sin, evil, sorrow, and depression of our fallen world. Gathered Israel has the promise of the day when "the Lord shall give thee rest, from thy sorrow, and from thy fear, and from the hard bondage wherein thou wast made to serve" (2 Ne. 24:3).

A respected teacher of mine once taught that *rest* could equate with *remainder*. For a simple example, if I contracted to pay you $1,000 and have already paid you $600, then I owe you a remainder of $400—or the *rest* of what I contracted to pay. Think of all that Heavenly Father has *already* given us. If we get on the gospel path and stay there until we die, He will give us the rest, or remainder, of what He has prepared for us. This remainder will be added to what we already have, for "their works do follow them" (Rev. 14:13). From what we call the "Oath and Covenant of the Priesthood," we learn, "And he that receiveth my Father receiveth my Father's kingdom; therefore all that my Father hath shall be given unto him" (D&C 84:38). We have only part right now; we may then have it all. What a glorious rest to have all that our Father in Heaven has to offer us.

## THE SHARP SICKLE OF THE SON OF MAN

*Are we preparing ourselves for the Lord's harvest?* Some of the more pleasant memories from my boyhood are the times of fall harvest on our little farm. Occasionally I got to miss school and go with my dad to watch the combine harvesting the wheat that was ripe, nearly white and ready to harvest. Often I helped my dad dig the potatoes from our garden. When we raised sheep, we had a spring harvest during which we sheared and sacked their wool. A few days before my son departed for his mission, I sent him down to help Grandpa harvest the potatoes and told him, "Mark, enjoy this day, for it may be the last you will have on earth with your grandpa." I was right—Dad died while Mark was on his mission.

These times of harvest were times of high adventure for me. I felt peace and gratitude to see the harvest safely gathered—to have the barn, the root cellar, and the fruit cellar all full. John, in describing the harvest of the earth, said, "And I looked, and behold a white cloud, and upon the cloud one sat like unto the Son of man, having on his head a golden crown, and in his hand a sharp sickle. And another angel came out of the temple, crying with a loud voice to him that sat on the cloud, Thrust in thy sickle, and reap: for the time is come for thee to reap; for the harvest of the earth is ripe. And he that sat on the cloud thrust in his sickle on the earth; and the earth was reaped" (Rev. 14:14–16).

The long-anticipated day is here—the time of the harvest of souls is at hand. The righteous have had ample time to ripen and mature in their righteousness. The wicked have had ample time and warning about the consequence of continuing to ripen in their iniquity. The Lord now sets His sickle to the task.

How grateful we will be that our perfect Savior is Lord of the Harvest. Occasionally when helping my father at harvest time, in my youthful exuberance I inadvertently ruined a good potato, spilled a shovel full of wheat, or wasted a bucket full of milk. But we can trust that our Savior will conduct a perfect harvest. We are promised that we need "fear not, little children, for you are mine, and I have overcome the world, and you are of them that my Father hath given me; And none of them that my Father hath given me shall be lost" (D&C 50:41–42).

We can also rest assured that the timing of the Lord's harvest will be perfect. John says of this timing, "Thrust in thy sharp sickle, and gather the clusters of the vine of the earth; for her grapes are fully ripe" (Rev. 14:18). *Fully ripe* does not mean "fully perfected." Once grapes are picked, there is still much to be done in the refinement of the final product. Once we are harvested, we still have far to go—but we will go with the blessed assurance that our mortal growth, trial, and progress is fulfilled and complete.

We also have assurance that the harvest will be full and complete. John saw that "the winepress was trodden without the city, and blood came out of the winepress, even unto the horse bridles, by the space of a thousand and six hundred furlongs" (Rev. 14:20). We may calculate "a thousand and six hundred furlongs" to be about the length of Palestine. The city of Dan lies at the northern end and the city of Beersheba at the southern end of the land. A common phrase, ancient and modern, to describe the *whole* land of Israel was and is to say, "from Dan to Beersheba." We are reminded of the notion discussed in chapter 1 that Christ's title, *Alpha and Omega,* means "the first and the last and everything in between." The Lord of the Harvest will certainly gather all—even "from Dan to Beersheba" and from Florida to Alaska and from Canada to Antarctica. He will measure with perfect measure, and His justice and mercy will be perfectly blended to offer just reward to each individual soul.

In summation of the great Restoration and harvest, our Lord and Savior loves us with perfect love. For us, He "wrought out this perfect atonement through the shedding of his own blood" (D&C 76:69). He has restored His gospel once again to the earth. He invites us to patiently endure our trials and tribulations. If we are true and faithful, He promises us a sweet death and receipt of the rest of all that He has prepared for us. At the time of harvest, He will completely, fairly, justly, and mercifully effect the law of the harvest, awarding to each and every individual soul the greatest reward possible according to our individual works, as enabled by His abounding grace.

# Chapter Fifteen

# The Song of the Lamb

*HOW INTENSE IS OUR DESIRE for victory over evil? Can we imagine our future victory celebrations?* Four decades ago, my rural high school basketball team won the state championship—a David and Goliath match as our squad went up against larger and more favored schools. The players on the team were my friends, and I rejoiced in their success. They all fought hard and, against great odds, battled on to victory. The resulting celebration was enormous, and the entire community gathered to welcome home the victors. Even though it was four decades ago, we haven't forgotten that victory, and we still talk about it with awe and respect. The coach's son told me of a recent gathering of the players to honor his father, who has been a good man and a great role model for these many years. This championship was a sweet victory, worthy of celebration and remembrance.

Although I have always doubted whether I could have qualified for the winning basketball team had I made a serious effort to do so, I have learned to not doubt my potential—nor the potential of every son and daughter of God—to be part of the Lord's victory over evil. Unlike basketball, success in gaining exaltation requires no specific physical shape, condition, or coordination—admittance to exaltation is open to one and all who are willing to make and keep sacred covenants. The promise of victory to the faithful is assured. There will be no limits of race, physical prowess, gender, or economic status. The Lord has told us that He "inviteth them all to come unto him and partake of his goodness; and he denieth none that come unto him, black and white, bond and free, male and female; and he remembereth the heathen; and all are alike unto God, both Jew and Gentile" (2 Ne. 26:33).

Chapter 15 of the Revelation of John portrays a time of rejoicing in the day of the Lord's victory over evil. It is a victory that will never be forgotten. It will be a perpetual celebration of joyous proportion wherein all of the celebrants will be active participants of the team—a team who, seemingly against all mortal odds, has won a fantastic victory over Satan and his forces. These "exalted saints praise God in celestial glory forever" (Rev. 15, chapter heading).

## THE LAST PLAGUES

*How do we find hope, healing, peace, and triumph amidst the pouring out of God's wrath upon the wicked?* The stage is now being set for the final assault on and destruction of the rebellious. John records, "And I saw another sign in heaven, great and marvelous, seven angels having the seven last plagues; for in them is filled up the wrath of God" (Rev. 15:1). This pouring out of the wrath of God will take center stage during the coming few chapters, culminating in the final battle of Armageddon.

We may find hope in striving to understand the nature of God's perfect justice. The word *wrath,* deriving from the Greek *thumos,* indicates anger, rage, fury, intense feeling, intense displeasure, or indignation. Further contemplation of God's wrath could suggest *vindication* or *retribution* or *fair payment to meet the demands of justice.*

In chapter 15, John seems to be describing more of the justice of God upon the wicked than His tender mercy for the righteous. It is a time, as taught by the prophet Alma, when "justice exerciseth all his demands" (Alma 42:24). When we someday have full understanding of all things, we will more fully realize that the justice and mercy of God are perfectly and constantly blended in all of His dealings with His children.

Many years ago, when our children were small and still nearly perfect, our stake presidency asked my wife and me to serve as instructors for a "Becoming a Better Parent" class, under the supervision of LDS Family Services. As we fulfilled this calling, we had opportunity to learn and practice many great principles of child-rearing and of general human relationships. One of the basic lessons of the class that I have found particularly useful through the years was the discussion of natural and logical consequences. It not only helped in rearing children, but these principles have helped me better understand such things as the wrath, justice, and mercy of God. I certainly have a more positive feeling about the destructive plagues being cast down upon the wicked when I realize that they are just and fair and even merciful.

To illustrate natural and logical consequences, I recall when my children were small. In my love for my toddler son and my desire that he be protected from evil and danger, I didn't want him to play in the street. The natural consequence of him doing so could be serious injury or death. Since he was too young and inexperienced to be trusted to keep himself safe from serious injury or death, I chose to substitute a *logical* consequence in place of the destructive *natural* consequence. My logical consequence was that I wouldn't allow him to play alone outside until he had grown up some and I was confident that he was mature and responsible enough to choose to stay out of the street. I knew the day would come when he would be independent and would need to experience the natural consequences of all of his actions. At that time, I would no longer be able to protect him from natural consequences with my logical consequences.

Our Heavenly Father deals with us in much the same way. His love for us is always unconditional. His desire for us is that we will always be protected from physical and spiritual harm. He provides for us many safeguards to help us escape physical and spiritual injury or death. But because of His great love for us and His desire for us to attain His status of exaltation, He honors our agency and leaves us to our own management. He allows us to learn, through proper exercise of our agency, the things we will need to know to become as He is. If we are wise and learn and keep the lessons of life, then we will join the exalted Saints who will praise Him forever. If we are unwise, then we will suffer and lose our opportunities for eternal progression—in other words, we will suffer the wrath or natural consequence of our behavior.

When we see that "one of the four beasts gave unto the seven angels seven golden vials full of the wrath of God, who liveth for ever and ever" (Rev. 15:7) and we realize that this wrath is about to be poured out upon the wicked, we will know that God is not being impulsive. His anger is not out of control—He is simply giving a just, fair, and measured response commensurate to the agency and work of each individual. He is letting natural consequences play out in the lives of His children. Those who are destroyed have always been in His hands, are still in His hands, and will yet receive the full measure of His love and mercy.

The scriptures often speak of God's recompense: "Yea, verily, to seal them up unto the day when the wrath of God shall be poured out upon the wicked without measure—Unto the day when the Lord shall come to recompense unto every man according to his work, and measure to every man according to the measure which he has measured to his fellow man" (D&C 1:9–10).

In another time and place, the Lord said, "Vengeance is mine, and I will repay; and because this people repented not after I had delivered them, behold, they shall be cut off from the face of the earth" (Morm. 3:15).

I find peace and hope in my knowledge that God loves us with perfect love and wants the very best for us that He can possibly give. The obedient will be spared destruction: "Nevertheless, Zion shall escape if she observes to do all things whatsoever I have commanded her" (D&C 97:25). Even after the fullness of God's wrath is poured out upon the wicked in measured response to their life choices, He will continue loving them unconditionally and will give them the very greatest reward that He can give, according to what they have merited through their agency. I am grateful that an omniscient and perfect God will be my final judge and the final judge of all of mankind. All will know that His recompense has been just, fair, and merciful.

## THE VICTORIOUS PLAY THE HARPS OF GOD AND SING THE SONG OF MOSES

*How deep is our trust in the capacity of our Father in Heaven and His Son to put right all that goes wrong and to heal all that is damaged? Do we look to the Lord for our strength and salvation?* A few years ago, a beautiful and talented young lady who is a member of the Church was kidnapped by a perverse religious fanatic and his accomplice. Her tragic story quickly gained the focus and the prayers of the entire nation. Search efforts seemed to be in vain, but the family, the police, and a multitude of supporters did not lose hope and kept looking, praying, and trying to find her. After many months, and thanks to the effort and enduring faith of many people, the young lady was identified walking along a city street with her captors. She was quickly taken to safety and the kidnappers were arrested. What a glorious day and sweet reunion!

Shortly after the return of the young lady to her family, I heard one professional offer the opinion that she would never be able to fully heal from her trauma. I appreciated the professional's opinion and wondered if she might be right—but was then reminded of my enduring testimony that Christ, who descended below all things, can heal all things. Then I witnessed this young lady in what I think was her first public national interview. She was calm, bright, and self-assured. Few could have guessed from observing her strong demeanor and sweet countenance that she had endured such an awful trauma. She radiated confidence and a spirit of healing and moving forward. She exuded a feeling of forgiveness and mercy for those who had done her harm. She seemed very content to leave them to God's justice and mercy. By choosing to follow this course of forgiveness and healing through the Atonement, she has certainly won great victory over her captors and over Satan, their master. It seemed as if God had purged hatred and evil from her soul. She later accepted a mission call.

Another pleasing detail of this rescue story—a detail that tied this example to the Revelation of John for me—was the added information that this young lady loves playing the harp. After her rescue, she was joyfully reunited with this worthy pursuit. What comfort this must have been for her to be able to express and exercise her talents once again. In fact, she told the talk-show host that she desires to play the harp professionally. My opinion is that if she continues on the healing path she has begun, she will not only become a professional harpist but will qualify to be with those who play the harps of God and sing the song of Moses.

John records, "And I saw as it were a sea of glass mingled with fire: and them that had gotten victory over the beast, and over his image, and over his mark, and over the number of his name, stand on the sea of glass, having the harps of God. And they sing the song of Moses the servant of God, and the song of the Lamb, saying, Great and marvelous are thy works, Lord God Almighty; just and true are thy ways, thou King of saints" (Rev. 15:2–3). The young lady in our example has by her character, life, and actions certainly "gotten victory over the beast." It is comforting and inspiring to think of the personal application that may be drawn from the "song of Moses" in the life of this young lady and into the lives of all of us who struggle to overcome the trials of mortality.

Let's ponder and consider a sampling of the joyful doctrines recorded in the song of Moses as rendered in the book of Exodus: "Then sang Moses and the children of Israel this song unto the Lord, and spake saying, I will sing unto the Lord, for he hath triumphed gloriously: the horse and his rider hath he thrown into the sea. The Lord is my strength and song, and he is become my salvation: he is my God, and I will prepare him an habitation; my father's God, and I will exalt him. . . . Thy right hand, O Lord, is become glorious in power: thy right hand, O Lord, hath dashed in pieces the enemy. And in the greatness of thine excellency thou has overthrown them that rose up against thee: thou sentest forth thy wrath, which consumed them as stubble. . . . Who is like unto thee, O Lord, among the gods? who is like thee, glorious in holiness, fearful in praises, doing wonders? . . . Thou in thy mercy hast led forth the people which thou hast redeemed: thou hast guided them in thy strength unto thy holy habitation. . . . The Lord shall reign forever and ever" (Ex. 15:1–18).

## THE SEA OF GLASS MINGLED WITH FIRE

*What is the significance of the "sea of glass, mingled with fire"?* We learned previously that the "sea of glass spoken of by John . . . is the earth, in its sanctified, immortal, and eternal state" (D&C 77:1). It represents the celestial earth. It, and similar orbs, will become the residence of exalted beings.

*What is meant by "mingled with fire"?* We learn from the Old Testament that "the Lord thy God is a consuming fire" (Deut. 4:24). *What does His fire consume or burn away?* Sin and evil. We learn from the scriptures that "none were received unto baptism save they took upon them the name of Christ, having a determination to serve him to the end. And after they had been received unto baptism, and were wrought upon and cleansed by the power of the Holy Ghost, they were numbered among the people of the church of Christ" (Moroni 6:3–4).

*How does the Holy Ghost burn or cleanse sin from our souls?* He reveals truth to us and comforts and guides us in the path of true repentance. Until a few years ago, I assumed that I had never really experienced the "burning in the bosom" spoken of in the ninth section of the Doctrine and Covenants. Then through the inspired words of one of our prophets, I learned that *comfort* and *serenity* are prime words in describing the "burning in the bosom." I now realize that I have many times experienced this manifestation of the Spirit.

The Lord, through the Holy Ghost—that wonderful cleansing agent of our souls—gives us needed revelation to help us repent and know the path we must follow. If we demonstrate humility and commitment to follow that path, we will one day find our residence with God in His eternal glory, which is as "a sea of glass mingled with fire." With our harps of God we will joyfully sing the song of Moses in praise and gratitude to our Father and our Savior for the wonderful and saving plan They have provided for us. We will have triumphed over sin and death. Our broken hearts will be healed of all that needs healing. We will feel the eternal, joyful peace of exaltation. Our hope of a glorious resurrection will have come to enduring fulfillment.

## THE TEMPLE IS CLOSED FOR CLEANING

*From whence is the justice of God executed? Why is this significant?* We recall that Christ has stewardship of "the keys of hell and of death" (Rev. 1:18). He also holds the keys of salvation: "Yea, verily I say unto you, if ye will come unto me ye shall have eternal life" (3 Ne. 9:14). The mission of the Church is to help Heavenly Father in His work of offering "immortality and eternal life" (Moses 1:39) to all of mankind by inviting all to come unto Christ. Our quest to come unto Christ leads us to the temple.

Our leaders have often taught us that in all we do, we lead people to the temple. Just as the righteous plot a life course *toward* the temple to gain eternal life, the wicked plot a life course *away* from the temple in their hollow quest for the pleasures of the world. The temple, in essence, is the Lord's central command post. Just as Christ seeks out and invites the righteous to *come to the temple* to receive their salvation, He, *from the temple,* seeks out the wicked to allot them their justice.

John said, "And after that I looked, and, behold, the temple of the tabernacle of the testimony in heaven was opened: And the seven angels came out of the temple, having the seven plagues, clothed in pure and white linen, and having their breasts girded with golden girdles. And one of the four beasts gave unto the seven angels seven golden vials full of the wrath of God, who liveth for ever and ever. And the temple was filled with smoke from the glory of God, and from his power; and no man was able to enter into the temple, till the seven plagues of the seven angels were fulfilled" (Rev. 15:5–8).

We are reminded that this is *God's* plan and that it is *His* justice, mercy, and vengeance that is being fulfilled upon the nations of the earth. The angels with the last plagues come out of His temple, dressed in His holy robes of recompense. We may trust that all will be accomplished in perfect order and that no unfairness or injustice will befall any person from the hand of God. We may also trust that all unfairness and injustice received by mortals at the hand of other mortals will receive recompense and healing from the hand of God. Undoubtedly, this will be a time of awe and wonder—but those grounded in the gospel foundation will endure with faith and understanding and will know that this too will pass in preparation of the millennial day.

This notion of the justice of God going forth from His temple is reaffirmed in modern revelation: "Behold, vengeance cometh speedily upon the inhabitants of the earth, a day of wrath, a day of burning, a day of desolation, of weeping, of mourning, and of lamentation; and as a whirlwind it shall come upon all the face of the earth, saith the Lord. And upon my house shall it begin, and from my house shall it go forth, saith the Lord; First among those among you, saith the Lord, who have professed to know my name and have not known me, and have blasphemed against me in the midst of my house, saith the Lord" (D&C 112:24–26).

A few years ago, I had some brief business in Chicago and reasoned that I could get an early start, transact my business, and then spend a peaceful day in the temple. All went as planned until I arrived at the temple and discovered that it was *closed for cleaning*. How disappointing! Yet my disappointment was short-lived and I was soon able to return to the temple. Since it is only a few hours away, we are blessed to be able to go most anytime we choose.

Near the time of my *minor* disappointment at the brief closing of the Chicago Illinois Temple, I was reminded of the *major* disappointment of the early Saints at the closing of the Nauvoo Temple. What a sad day this was for the Saints who so wanted to continue their worship therein. But they had to leave for a time. My wife and I were recently in Nauvoo at a conference where we sat around a campfire at the river's edge with our colleagues. Among the fifty of us who were there, we discovered that most had ancestors who had lived in old Nauvoo. We shared stories of how they were willing to follow the Lord at all costs. They demonstrated every ounce of patience and courage they could muster as they crossed the river and followed the Lord to a new land. Their faith and courage were rewarded when in the new land they built a new temple.

As we visited at the river's edge, not too far from the newly constructed Nauvoo Temple, our group had the solemn and humbling realization that *we are back!* We, the descendants of those pioneers, are back—scattered throughout the Midwest and working with hundreds of wonderful and dedicated volunteer teachers and priesthood leaders in the work of teaching the gospel to thousands of bright, worthy students. Tens of thousands of Latter-day Saints are back, having *crossed the river in reverse,* and are here building the kingdom of God. President Hinckley once eloquently spoke of the two grand temples—the Salt Lake Temple, or "Brigham's temple," facing east to "Joseph's temple" in Nauvoo, which faces west. He reminded us of the suffering and the sacrifice of our pioneer Saints who have bequeathed us such a powerful spiritual heritage.

Yes, the plague, trials, and sufferings will come. Recompense will reign from the Lord's temple. I often wonder how the vile and wicked men who drove our ancestors out of Nauvoo will fare. Thankfully, they will be measured in the Lord's balance. The Lord will not forget His Saints. The day of peace will come once again. The plan of our great God is marching forward.

What a glorious time when we will worship forever in His house without distraction or interruption. Yes, the temple of our God will, in perhaps a figurative sense, be *closed for cleaning*—that is, the cleaning of the entire earth, starting from the temple. "And no man was able to enter into the temple, till the seven plagues of the seven angels were fulfilled" (Rev. 15:8). This may be a time requiring great patience as we await the fulfillment of God's justice, but the temple will be opened once again, and the righteous Saints will *be back* and will enter and enjoy the great reward that there awaits them. With the temple as the great symbol of our faith and devotion, we will forever sing "the song of the Lamb, saying, Great and marvellous are thy works, Lord God Almighty; just and true are thy ways, thou King of saints" (Rev. 15:3).

# Chapter Sixteen
# Armageddon—It Is Done

HOW DO WE PREPARE FOR *the battle against the armies of Satan?* On June 6, 1944, most often remembered as D-Day, one of the largest combined military forces in history crossed the English Channel to attack the coast of Normandy in northern France. Theirs was an effort to dislodge Hitler's army and secure a battlefront from which to continue the effort to strangle the German war machine. It truly was a *great* day, because it was a major step in ridding the world of one of the most evil tyrants we have ever known. It truly was also a *dreadful* day because of the massive loss of life and the tremendous sacrifice made by so many. More than 150,000 men in command of a fleet of approximately 5,000 ships, 11,000 aircraft, and 50,000 vehicles attacked the beaches with all the force they could muster. A masterful deception plan confused Hitler and his generals into thinking that the attack was to be centered elsewhere. Nevertheless, the Germans were still able to respond with ample fury to cause nearly 9,000 D-Day casualties among the Allied forces.

The most inspiring aspect of D-Day for me personally has been to learn of the dauntless courage, tenacity, and genius of the individual Allied soldiers. No matter how great the battle plans of the combined force may have been, the actual battles were won by the commitment and courage of individuals. On D-Day, nearly everything that could go wrong *did* go wrong to one degree or another—yet the individual soldiers reassessed, regrouped, and pressed forward in their quest for freedom from tyranny. The men and women of World War II were certainly a great generation.

In a sense, we now come to D-Day in our study of the Revelation of John. The long-promised judgment of the wicked is now commencing with the seven angels pouring out their vials of destruction upon the earth. The final battle has begun. It is not a pleasant day to learn of. However, if we are alert, we still find our theme of hope, healing, peace, and triumph.

Over the years, I have pondered an impossible question: *Had we not joined forces with our allies to stop the destructive march of Hitler, how would our world be different today?* Another question we might ask is, *If the current downward spiral of evil and wickedness in our world is not stopped, will our world even survive?* Although we don't know how bad conditions will yet become before the final cleansing of the earth, we do know that it will be cleansed in the Lord's own due time and in His own way. That is where I find the theme of hope, healing, peace, and triumph from these chapters of destruction—from remembering that all life is in the hands of Him who created life, and that He will take back life as needed to prepare the earth for the great millennial day. That millennial day of peace and rest is something to hope for!

## POUR OUT THE VIALS OF WRATH

*Are we able to keep an eternal perspective of the purpose and mission of the destruction of the wicked?* We are reminded that the destruction of the wicked is at the hand and order of the Lord as the commander and originates from His command post—the temple—and goes from there throughout the earth. "And I heard a great voice out of the temple saying to the seven angels, Go your ways, and pour out the vials of the wrath of God upon the earth" (Rev. 16:1).

This pattern of cleansing from the inside out is consistent with the work of the Lord. Moroni wrote to Pahoran during a time of needed cleansing of the interior government, "Do ye suppose that God will look upon you as guiltless while ye sit still and behold these things? Behold I say unto you, Nay. Now I would that ye should remember that God has said that the inward vessel shall be cleansed first, and then shall the outer vessel be cleansed also" (Alma 60:23). From the great allegory of the olive tree, we learn of the necessity that the "bad be hewn down and cast into the fire, that they cumber not the ground of my vineyard; and thus will I sweep away the bad out of my vineyard" (Jacob 5:66).

So the great and final cleansing of the earth begins. John sees each of the seven angels pouring out his vial in turn: "And the first went, and poured out his vial upon the earth; and there fell a noisome and grievous sore upon the men which had the mark of the beast, and upon them which worshipped his image. And the second angel poured out his vial upon the sea; and it became as the blood of a dead man: and every living soul died in the sea. And the third angel poured out his vial upon the rivers and fountains of waters; and they became blood. . . . And the fourth angel poured out his vial upon the sun; and power was given unto him to scorch men with fire. . . . And the fifth angel poured out his vial upon the seat of the beast; and his kingdom was full of darkness; and they gnawed their tongues for pain. . . . And the sixth angel poured out his vial upon the great river Euphrates; and the water thereof was dried up, that the way of the kings of the east might be prepared. . . . And the seventh angel poured out his vial into the air" (Rev. 16:2–17).

This will be a time of great horror and bloodshed. And yet, it is a necessary time and must occur in order for the eternal purposes of the Lord to take place. In all of this destruction upon the wicked, we must remember that all life is in God's merciful hands as great hosts are cleansed from the earth in preparation for the joyful Millennium.

The world cannot continue to grope in spiritual darkness. How many times have we heard, "The world is so much worse now that it was back in my generation?" or "Conditions are far worse today than they were even five years ago?" We know that the downward spiral of wickedness cannot continue to exponentially grow without severe repercussions upon the Saints. There must be a time of winding up, even a time of full and complete judgment.

We have hoped and worked and prayed that the wicked would repent so that they might be spared the awful personal destruction from their acts and that we might be spared the awful consequences of their wickedness. Some, gratefully, will repent. However, as John saw, many "blasphemed the name of God, which hath power over these plagues: and they repented not to give him glory. . . . And blasphemed the God of heaven because of their pains and their sores, and repented not of their deeds" (Rev. 16:9, 11).

Although it seems harsh and unpleasant, it is true that those who will perish are deserving of their punishment. John recounts, "For they have shed the blood of saints and prophets, and thou hast given them blood to drink; for they are worthy" (Rev. 16:6). Joseph Smith, one of the prophets whose blood was shed, specifically gave warning that the wicked would have their fill of death. Shortly before he was martyred, several of the officers of the Carthage militia visited him in his jail room. Joseph asked them to tell him if they thought he was the despicable character his enemies had described to them. "The reply was, 'No, sir, your appearance would indicate the very contrary, General Smith but we cannot see what is in your heart, neither can we tell what are your intentions.' To which Joseph replied, 'Very true, gentlemen, you cannot see what is in my heart, and you are therefore unable to judge me or my intentions; but I can see what is in your hearts, and will tell you what I see. I can see that you *thirst for blood,* and nothing but my blood will satisfy you. It is not for crime of any description that I and my brethren are thus continually persecuted and harassed by our enemies, but there are other motives, and some of them I have expressed, so far as relates to myself; and inasmuch *as you and the people thirst for blood, I prophesy, in the name of the Lord, that you shall witness scenes of blood and sorrow to your entire satisfaction. Your souls shall be perfectly satiated with blood,* and many of you who are now present shall have an opportunity to face the cannon's mouth from sources you think not of; and those people that desire this great evil upon me and my brethren, shall be filled with regret and sorrow because of the scenes of desolation and distress that await them. They shall seek for peace, and shall not be able to find it'" (emphasis added).[16] We know that this prophecy of Joseph was in part fulfilled by the Civil War, where many of the wicked murderers in Carthage faced the canon's mouth. Complete fulfillment will yet come in the day of the pouring out of the final plagues of destruction.

*Do we feel compassion for the wicked?* A significant sign of our own spiritual maturity is the degree to which we are willing to forgive those who trespass against us, leaving their justice in God's hands. Our yearning for His perfectly blended formula of justice and mercy is enhanced as people we personally love choose to follow forbidden paths. We must remember that all of our friends and loved ones are children of God and were so long before they belonged to us. He loves them and cares about them with perfect love and will give them the greatest reward and the least punishment that He can possibly give. From modern revelation, we learn the Lord suits "his mercies according to the conditions of the children of men" (D&C 46:15).

As previously discussed, we can gain peace and hope from remembering that all life is in the hands of God and that He will be just and merciful to all. John reminds us, "And I heard another out of the altar say, Even so, Lord God Almighty, *true* and *righteous* are thy judgments" (Rev. 16:7; emphasis added).

## BLESSED IS HE THAT WATCHETH

*How may we prepare for the day of the coming of the Lord?* To instruct in the important doctrine of being prepared for the Second Coming of Christ and the attendant destructions upon the wicked, the Church Educational System once produced a short video segment about a gardener of a large estate. One day as he was going about his pruning and digging, he noticed a man outside the fence taking photos of some of the plants. The gardener, sensing that the man had a special interest in his master's estate, invited him to come in for a tour of the grounds.

After the tour of the impressive estate, the two men stood on a balcony overlooking the property. The visitor complimented the gardener on how well he kept things up. The gardener acknowledged the compliment and said he was motivated by the pleased look on his master's face on the occasions he visited the estate. The visitor, astonished that the master did not actually live at the estate, asked if the gardener knew when the master was returning. "No," the gardener commented. The visitor then said, "Well, the way you keep this place up, you would think he were returning tomorrow." To this, the wise old gardener responded, "No; today, Sir, today."[17] The lesson is obvious—we are to live our lives each day as though that is the day of the Lord's coming.

After John has witnessed the pouring out of six of the seven plagues, the Lord says, "Behold, I come as a thief. Blessed is he that watcheth, and keepeth his garments, lest he walk naked, and they see his shame" (Rev. 16:15). Remember that those who are watching and who are prepared and worthy "are not in darkness, that that day should overtake you as a thief" (1 Thess. 5:4). For the Saints who study, know the word of the Lord, and are watching for the signs of the times, the winding-up scenes will not come as a great surprise. For the wicked who have blinded eyes and hardened hearts, the pending destruction of the wicked and the advent of the Savior of the world will indeed come by surprise, much as would a thief in the night.

Just as only a privileged few across the earth knew of the exact plan and course of the D-Day invasion of Normandy before June 6, 1944, many will remain in blindness as to the D-Day showdown of Armageddon. Nearly everyone will be able to see that conditions are worsening—but for the wicked, the day sneaks a bit closer as they ignore or rationalize away the warning signs. Nonetheless, ready or not, Armageddon will come. John saw "the spirits of devils, working miracles, which go forth unto the kings of the earth and of the whole world, to gather them to the battle of that great day of God Almighty. . . . And he gathered them together into a place called in the Hebrew tongue Armageddon" (Rev. 16:14, 16).

*Armageddon* refers to the Mountain of Megiddo, about fifty miles north of Jerusalem, which is to be the scene of a great battle at the Second Coming. As in so much of the Revelation, there are both figurative and literal aspects of Armageddon. Paul taught that "we wrestle not against flesh and blood, but against . . . spiritual wickedness" (Eph. 6:12). The day may yet be future when the armies of the earth will gather to the valley of Megiddo, and elsewhere across the world—but certainly we need not wait for the spiritual forces of good and evil to engage the final battle. We are now waging that war, as we have always done. To survive, we must take up "the whole armour of God . . . having your loins girt about with truth, and having on the breastplate of righteousness . . . your feet shod with the preparation of the gospel of peace . . . the shield of faith . . . the helmet of salvation . . . the sword of the Spirit . . . praying always . . . with all perseverance and supplication for all saints" (Eph. 6:13–18).

For us spiritually, Armageddon is the present. Like the greatest generation who disembarked on the beaches of Normandy, we must be brave. We must give our total commitment. We must pray always and place our trust in the Lord, our God—the only sure commander. If we are to survive the day, we must keep the commandments of our sure commander.

## It Is Done

*Do we joyfully anticipate the glorious and triumphant end of the wickedness of the earth?* In his gospel account, John the Revelator recorded for us the triumphal day when Jesus entered Jerusalem at the beginning of the last week of His mortal ministry: "On the next day much people that were come to the feast, when they heard that Jesus was coming to Jerusalem, Took branches of palm trees, and went forth to meet him, and cried, Hosanna: Blessed is the King of Israel that cometh in the name of the Lord" (John 12:12–13). This was most certainly a triumphal entry of our Savior. He had triumphed over His enemies, who at that very hour were sneaking around in darkness concocting plans of how to seek out this Jesus, their enemy. He confounded them by His public, daytime entry—servants of darkness are bewildered and blindsided by the glorious light of day. On this occasion, they were indeed baffled by the Light of the World. Before this week would end, He would triumph over not only these wicked locals, but over the great enemies of all mankind—even death and hell!

John the Revelator also records that once the Savior, in supreme loving sacrifice, had effected the Atonement for you and for me and for all mankind—including those who crucified Him—"he said, *It is finished*: and he bowed his head, and gave up the ghost" (John 19:30; emphasis added).

John the Revelator also recorded that "the seventh angel poured out his vial into the air; and there came a great voice out of the temple of heaven, from the throne, saying *It is done*" (Rev. 16:17; emphasis added). As previously discussed, the number *seven* represents completeness. Once the seventh angel has delivered the seventh plague—or the completeness of the destruction—then the final pronouncement of triumph comes from the very throne of God. What a triumph! What a glorious day of peace and rest! It is the day the righteous have lived for and prayed for and hoped for throughout mortal time. And now, "It is done!"

Remember that the Revelation of John is not always chronological. Even though *It is done* has been pronounced, we still have some destruction and plague yet to discuss—but the glorious end is in sight. A sneak preview of the rest of the Revelation would reveal to us that it soon gets much better. In fact, it becomes so great that we may rejoice to think about it.

### THE GREAT EARTHQUAKE—ISLANDS FLEE AND MOUNTAINS NOT FOUND

*Are we quake-proofing our lives by building on the sure foundation of Jesus Christ?* I have a personal sacred shrine that I have frequently visited throughout my life. My father first took me there when I was a young child; it is not a well-known place and likely would not have much meaning to most people. It is located about a dozen miles east of my birthplace of Fairview, Utah, where the old Mammoth Dam and reservoir used to be. In 1918, at the outbreak of World War I, the dam washed out, killing one woman and causing a great flood of the railway access to several coal mines. About one-fourth of the old dam still stands.

The dam has become sacred to me for several reasons. My grandfather gave his heart and soul to the project for eleven years as the construction foreman. The construction and subsequent disaster did much to define his life and the life of my father—the dam binds me to them. But the greatest reason why the dam is sacred to me is the massive object lesson it has taught me, including the personal thoughts and commitments I have made while visiting the site.

The disruption of the downstream coal mines gave the engineers a convenient alibi—war-time sabotage. However, any observant individual can stand downstream and look up to the dam—with its eroded streambed—and quickly ascertain that the foundation was faulty. It was not built solidly on bedrock.

I have often climbed out onto the ruins of this dam to ponder the lesson it teaches. I have also taken my children there on occasion to teach them the lesson of the Mammoth Dam. When I served as bishop, our ward youth were camped in the area, and I assigned them to go examine the ruins of the dam and report their theories of the disaster back to the group at the evening campfire. I then shared my lesson.

The events and disasters of the latter days will shake the physical and spiritual foundations of our society. Physical structures that are not founded on bedrock will be at great risk of collapse and destruction. Spiritual philosophies symbolized by Babylon and not founded on the bedrock of Christ and His gospel will be exposed and supplanted by truth.

After the seventh angel pours out the seventh vial, John records, "And there were voices, and thunders, and lightnings; and there was a great earthquake, such as was not since men were upon the earth, so mighty an earthquake, and so great. And the great city was divided into three parts, and the cities of the nations fell: and great Babylon came in remembrance before God, to give unto her the cup of the wine of the fierceness of his wrath. And every island fled away, and the mountains were not found. And there fell upon men a great hail out of heaven, every stone about the weight of a talent: and men blasphemed God because of the plague of the hail; for the plague thereof was exceeding great" (Rev. 16:18–21).

As we speak of the last days and the signs of the times, we often quote statistics to show that the occurrence of major earthquakes has dramatically increased over recent decades. We speak of tsunamis and hurricanes with the attendant flooding as valid evidence of prophecies fulfilled. I recently toured the Gulf Coast of the southern United States and examined the aftermath of the destruction of hurricane Katrina—a terrible tragedy and a vivid reminder of the times in which we live.

We may accept these many physical disasters as fulfillment of latter-day prophecy. The Lord said, "For after your testimony cometh the testimony of earthquakes, that shall cause groanings in the midst of her, and men shall fall upon the ground and shall not be able to stand. And also cometh the testimony of the voice of thunderings, and the voice of lightnings, and the voice of tempests, and the voice of the waves of the sea heaving themselves beyond their bounds" (D&C 88:89–90).

I have great empathy and respect for the victims of physical disaster. My sincere hope and prayer for them is that they will continue to be nurtured by the tender mercies of the Lord through the charitable goodness of so many people who help them. And although the physical destructions of the latter days are valid and real, my study of the Revelation of John and other scriptures focuses my attention on the spiritual or metaphorical aspects of the prophecies. I do this in part, I suppose, because the spiritual trials seem so much more universal than the physical disasters, which are generally somewhat isolated to a specific location. There's another likely reason: spiritual trials often seem to have more profound and lasting effects on our hearts and souls—the destruction of a flood is usually corrected within a period of months or years, but the residual effects of spiritual disaster can persist for decades, if not a lifetime.

Speaking metaphorically, the prophet Helaman taught his sons the importance of establishing a sure foundation in our lives: "And now, my sons, remember, remember that it is upon the rock of our Redeemer, who is Christ, the Son of God, that ye must build your foundation; that when the devil shall send forth his mighty winds, yea, his shafts in the whirlwind, yea, when all his hail and his mighty storm shall beat upon you, it shall have no power over you to drag you down to the gulf of misery and endless wo, because of the rock upon which ye are built, which is a sure foundation, a foundation whereon if men build they cannot fall" (Hel. 5:12).

Many times, especially during dark days of my life, I have sat on the ruins of the old Mammoth Dam and pondered what I must do to keep my life founded on the bedrock of Christ.

As we contemplate the earthquakes described by John, we might consider the earthquake of apostasy, a situation in which the faith of the Saints is violently shaken. This earthquake seems to have an epicenter in every stake throughout the world. We might consider the heavy and destructive stones of the hailstorm of pornography that seem to be universally falling on every neighborhood in every community. The fierce winds of drug addiction have had horrible effects on so many people. We are being buffeted on every side by the evil and destructive forces of the dragon.

We as a nation have recently been following the sad story of the rise and fall of a large corporation. In the glory days of this company, it seemed to be the ideal of American free enterprise, standing as a mountain of strength and stability. Thousands of people were happily employed; many had even invested all of their retirement eggs in the one basket of this company. Their future and the future of the corporation seemed bright.

But all was not well. The destructive rot of greed and avarice was at play among the principals—even the chief officers. They now stand convicted of multiple counts of fraud and deception. The fall of this giant corporation took many down with it; many honest and loyal employees were unwittingly defrauded of their life savings. And so goes the sad story—this island has fled away and this mountain is no longer found.

As we consider the instability of the creations of man and compare them with the strength and fortitude of the creations and plans of God, we must keep our faith and our daily walk and talk centered in Jesus Christ and His gospel. If we are to withstand the mighty earthquakes and great hailstorms of the end of time—physical and spiritual—we must have our lives grounded in the teachings of Jesus Christ and founded on the bedrock of His gospel.

# Chapter Seventeen
# Babylon the Great

DO WE APPRECIATE THE DEPTH *of the Lord's sacred marriage metaphor?* Temple Square in Salt Lake City is an Eden-like place with magnificent displays of countless variety of trees, shrubs, and flowers. Everything is carefully and tastefully planted, groomed, and nurtured. The pure reflecting pools mirror the magnificent temple and other sacred and historic buildings. The entire ambience bespeaks reverence for the Creation and for the Creator.

It is of little wonder that many young couples choose to be married in the Salt Lake Temple. The magnificent flora provides a peaceful array of natural bridal décor, a ready photo studio where couples may capture the sweet memories of their marriage day amidst the symbols of the restored gospel, enhanced by the beauty of the earth.

The greatest symbol of all, however, is when the bride and groom present themselves worthy in the holy temple. Their white dress symbolizes purity, virtue, and their worthiness to partake of the ordinance of eternal union under the hand of God and Christ. Everything about the temple ceremony further symbolizes trust, love, devotion, light, protection, eternal union, exaltation, covenant keeping, unity of faith, common purpose, obedience to commandments, charity, and every good and holy aspect of a true marriage.

The Savior Himself chose marriage as a metaphor to teach of His enduring covenant relationship with those of His Church: "Then shall the kingdom of heaven be likened unto ten virgins, which took their lamps, and went forth to meet the bridegroom" (Matt. 25:1).

## THE WOMAN SITTING UPON THE BEAST

It is also of little wonder that a polluted marriage metaphor is used to describe Satan, the crown prince of counterfeit, in his vile attempt to destroy all that is good. *How alert are we to Satan's counterfeit marriage metaphor and its wide-reaching influence throughout the world?* In contrast to the beautiful and worthy bride adorned for her husband, John sees "the great whore that sitteth upon many waters; With whom the kings of the earth have committed fornication, and the inhabitants of the earth have been made drunk with the wine of her fornication. . . . [A]nd I saw a woman sit upon a scarlet coloured beast, full of names of blasphemy, having seven heads and ten horns. And the woman was arrayed in purple and scarlet colour and decked with gold and precious stones and pearls, having a golden cup in her hand full of abominations and filthiness of her fornication: And upon her forehead was a name written, MYSTERY, BABYLON THE GREAT, THE MOTHER OF HARLOTS AND ABOMINATIONS OF THE EARTH. And I saw the woman drunken with the blood of the saints, and with the blood of the martyrs of Jesus" (Rev. 17:1–6).

The metaphor of a harlot for Satan and his realm is most appropriate to describe his kingdom. After all, he prostitutes everything that the faithful and righteous hold to be "virtuous, lovely, or of good report or praiseworthy" (A of F 1:13). The great whore who commits fornication throughout the world brings a vivid message of mistrust, lack of devotion, darkness, vulnerability, eternal disunion, damnation, covenant breaking, disunity of faith, divergent goals, disobedience to commandments, hatred, and every evil and unholy aspect of an adulterous relationship. Anyone who has had his or her sacred marriage covenants betrayed by a once-beloved partner could speak volumes of the attendant heartache and agony that come from this fornication and betrayal. The terrible harlot described in chapter 17 is the very opposite of the woman of chapter 12, who represented the Church of God. The age-old battle of good and evil is depicted in the contrast between the woman clothed with the sun and the whore that sits upon the many waters.

We gain much insight as we view the scarlet-colored beast as representative of Satan's political influence and the woman who is the great whore as representative of his religious influence and power.

Remember that John saw "a woman sit upon a scarlet coloured beast"—or, in other words, false religion driving political movements. In these winding-up times of our fallen world, Satan directs and controls the government as much as he can.

How often do we see wicked kings and rulers who are spurred by the riders of false religion? A perfect illustration of this concept involves Iraq and the evil tyrant, Saddam Hussein. Some years ago at the height of his *political* reign, he constructed a *religious* shrine that he named the "Mother of All Battles" mosque. (How intriguing to note the similarity of his language to the "MOTHER OF HARLOTS" language in the Revelation of John.) Hussein's mosque was designed around the instruments of his political war, with the minarets formed in the shape of ballistic missiles and machine-gun barrels. Inside the mosque was a Koran supposedly written with a mixture of his own blood. Of this strange "holy place," Philip Smucker reported from Bagdad, "One diplomat said, 'Saddam is just supporting his ideology with religion. He plays the religious card just to stay in power.'"[18]

Examples like this help us easily see the influence of false religious belief on the political powers and kingdoms of the world. Like Saddam, many political tyrants often attempt to masquerade their evil terror as religion. Their atrocious acts against humanity are often proclaimed as the "will of God." *So where may we find peace and hope from this chapter, which describes the turmoil and darkness of the whore and the beast?* The hope and peace, of course, come from the Prince of Peace—the Lamb of God: "These shall make war with the Lamb, and the Lamb shall overcome them; for he is Lord of lords, and King of kings: and they that are with him are called and chosen, and faithful" (Rev. 17:14).

The Lamb of God places His steadying hand on the kingdoms of the earth. From modern revelation we are told, "And for this purpose have I established the Constitution of this land, by the hands of wise men whom I raised up unto this very purpose, and redeemed the land by the shedding of blood" (D&C 101:80). We are also told, "And that law of the land which is constitutional, supporting the principle of freedom in maintaining rights and privileges, belongs to all mankind, and is justifiable before me. Therefore, I, the Lord, justify you, and your brethren of my church, in befriending that law which is the constitutional law of the land" (D&C 98:5–6).

We gain confidence, peace, and hope from knowing that the hand of the Lord has guided our free land to endure as a beacon of freedom to the entire world. Despite our troubles, which are many, we have long endured and will continue to endure under God's protective hand. He gave us the inspiration and the leadership necessary to establish a free land. We are asked to befriend the Constitution so that we might keep the whore separate from the beast. The provision of separation of church and state by our Founding Fathers was never intended by them to remove God from government. The intent was to keep a *false* God from becoming the government. We must not have a state religion that would drown out all other religions until such state religion is the true religion of the Lamb of God.

Even a cursory look at the history of the world reveals a multitude of horrors and evils perpetuated on mankind in the name of false religion. As the terrible and wicked whore continues to ride through the nations on the opulent and fearsome beast, we must seek out the protection and safety offered by our true God through His true religion. We gain this protection and safety by our worthiness and obedience. We must remember that "no combination of wickedness shall have power to rise up and prevail over thy people upon whom thy name shall be put in this house" (D&C 109:26). We must learn the lesson that the beast cannot conquer us unless we give our lives over to sin. By repenting and coming unto Christ, we will experience peace, hope, healing, and ultimate triumph.

## THE BEAST THAT WAS, AND IS NOT, AND YET IS

*Do we properly recognize and appreciate the enduring kingdom of God in contrast to the fleeting kingdom of Satan?* During part of my boyhood, we raised purebred sheep on our little farm. We fought many hazards to our flock, including that of dogs. My father taught me that once a dog kills sheep, it develops a lust for blood and will continue to kill, even when it is not hungry. Once this happens, dogs kill just for the sake of killing. We experienced the truth of my father's teaching one night as a pack of local dogs got into our herd and killed or hamstrung half of the thirty lambs we were getting ready for market. They killed far more than they could eat—they were simply on a killing spree.

Those who sell themselves over to evil are at risk of developing this lust for blood. John describes the killing spree of the terrible whore: "And I saw the woman drunken with the blood of the saints, and with the blood of the martyrs of Jesus: and when I saw her, I wondered with great admiration. And the angel said unto me, Wherefore didst thou marvel? I will tell thee the mystery of the woman, and of the beast that carrieth her, which hath the seven heads and ten horns. The beast that thou sawest was, and is not; and shall ascend out of the bottomless pit, and go into perdition: and they that dwell on the earth shall wonder, whose names were not written in the book of life from the foundation of the world; when they behold the beast that was, and is not, and yet is" (Rev. 17:6–8).

In a letter to his son Moroni, the prophet Mormon offers us an example of such a killing spree in the final battle of the Lamanites and Nephites: "For so exceedingly do they anger that it seemeth me that they have no fear of death; and they have lost their love, one towards another and they thirst after blood and revenge continually" (Moro. 9:5).

As John witnesses the killing spree of the servants of Satan, note that he reacts with "admiration." The Greek word for *admiration* is *thauma,* meaning "astonishment" or "incredulous surprise." I was recently traveling with a colleague who shared an account of a terrible atrocity he had learned of from a news account. My reaction to his account was one of astonishment, or incredulous surprise. Granted, such things occur each day, but they are still so repulsive to our inner core of divine nature that we are left to wonder, *How bad must it get before the end?* Just when we think we have seen it all, the cycle of evil seems to spiral further downward.

It may seem a great mystery that the conditions of our mortal world could become so evil. Satan would have it be a mystery to us—he would have us believe that the downward spiral will continue and that he will be the ultimate conqueror. He shrouds his false religion in mystery in his vile attempt to deceive mankind. Even the name of the woman is written upon her forehead: *MYSTERY.* The false religious philosophies of the world have always been shrouded in mystery. The wicked leaders of such religions go to great lengths to keep their subjects confused and ignorant as to the true character and nature of God and of His plan of salvation for His children.

Although we have had revealed to us the truth of the mystery—for example, of the nature of God—we may continue to wonder at the mystery of how long Satan will be allowed to rule his realm. In some ways and to some people, his entrenchment will appear so deep-rooted that it would seem that he could never be dragged out to justice. Yet the righteous need not fear—the end will come. The mystery is solved. Wickedness will not be allowed to continue. The beast who ruled the nations will be destroyed and cast off forever: "The beast that thou sawest was, and is not; and shall ascend out of the bottomless pit, and go into perdition: and they that dwell on the earth shall wonder, whose names were not written in the book of life from the foundation of the world, when they behold the beast that was, and is not, and yet is" (Rev. 17:8). Someday we will say of him, he "was, and is not." Our consoling thought will be, *He is gone—and good riddance!*

We know that Satan will return again for a season after the Millennium—"and yet is." At that time, those on earth who have still not gotten the right mark in their foreheads—"whose names were not written in the book of life from the foundation of the world"— will wonder after him still. But wonder as they will, his final and permanent end will come. Once again, and this time in finality, we will be able to say of him that he "is not"—forever and ever!

Our solace, peace, and protection will come from the true King of Glory who, in contrast to Satan, has declared, "I am Alpha and Omega, the beginning and the ending, saith the Lord, *which is, and which was, and which is to come, the Almighty*" (Rev. 1:8; emphasis added). As the wicked political leaders and false religious zealots come and go and as their kingdoms change and crumble—seemingly with every wind of doctrine that blows their way—those who follow Christ and center their faith in Him will know and experience with more and more surety that He has *always been* and that He *is now* and that He *will always be* our Lord and Savior.

Mormon's fatherly counsel to Moroni is wise counsel for all of us as we seek the Lord's peace and protection in the midst of evil. Mormon said, "My son, be faithful in Christ; and may not the things which I have written grieve thee, to weigh thee down unto death; but may Christ left thee up, and may his sufferings and death, and the showing his body unto our fathers, and his mercy and long-suffering, and the hope of his glory and of eternal life, rest in your mind forever. And may the grace of God the Father, whose throne is high in the heavens, and our Lord Jesus Christ, who sitteth on the right hand of his power, until all things shall become subject unto him, be, and abide with you forever. Amen" (Moro. 9:25–26).

## THE LAMB WILL OVERCOME

*Who are the agents of the destruction of the wicked?* Those who are righteous may gain a certain sense of peace and comfort from knowing that, as a general rule, the Lord allows the wicked to destroy the wicked. Agents of destruction are often destroyed by other agents of destruction. This action is consistent with revealed scripture: "And the blood of that great and abominable church, which is the whore of all the earth, shall turn upon their own heads; for they shall war among themselves, and the sword of their own hands shall fall upon their own heads, and they shall be drunken with their own blood" (1 Ne. 22:13).

We are also told that "it is by the wicked that the wicked are punished; for it is the wicked that stir up the hearts of the children of men unto bloodshed" (Morm. 4:5). In his Revelation, John sees these same principles applied in the culminating destruction of the wicked as the evil beast battles the hateful whore: "And the ten horns which thou sawest upon the beast, these shall hate the whore, and shall make her desolate and naked, and shall eat her flesh, and burn her with fire. For God hath put in their hearts to fulfill his will, and to agree, and give their kingdom unto the beast, until the words of God shall be fulfilled" (Rev. 17:16–17).

*What is the role of the Lord of Hosts in the final destruction of the wicked? How does the commanding general of the armies of Israel accomplish His work of cleansing the earth? How may we qualify for enlistment in His victorious army?* Generally the miracles of God are not rational to mortal man. It made no sense to the wedding guests at Cana that Jesus turned water to wine. Neither did it make sense that the wine He so quickly made was of such quality that the ruler of the feast supposed that they had "kept the good wine" (John 2:10) until the end. Strange also are the notions that a man could be healed of leprosy by bathing in a muddy river (see 2 Kgs. 5:8–14) or that a poultice of spittle and dirt could be used to heal blindness (see John 9:6).

As the people of the world see the stranglehold of the whore of all the earth on the wicked and perverse leaders of nations, it would seem far-fetched and irrational to them that a humble lamb could battle to victory over a fierce and terrible dragon. A lamb versus a dragon—this would seem as strange as a lamb and a lion communing one with another without ire. Yet, so it is—and so it will be. John records, "These shall make war with the Lamb, and the Lamb shall overcome them: for he is Lord of lords, and King of kings: and they that are with him are *called*, and *chosen*, and *faithful*" (Rev. 17:14; emphasis added).

The depiction that the soldiers of the Lamb are *called*, *chosen*, and *faithful* seems to resonate with and connect us naturally to our modern-day scriptural language spoken from that temple/prison ironically named the "Liberty" Jail. From that dark dungeon, the Lord speaks to Joseph: "Behold, there are many *called*, but few are *chosen*" (D&C 121:34; emphasis added). After outlining how Joseph and those he leads were to become "called and chosen," the Lord counsels us to show forth "an increase of love . . . That he may know that thy *faithfulness* is stronger than the cords of death" (D&C 121:43–44; emphasis added).

At the time of my writing, I am just a few days back from a humbling and awe-inspiring visit to the Liberty Jail, where the Prophet Joseph and his companions were unjustly imprisoned for several months—and where they suffered, both physically and emotionally, the terrible oppression of the rulers of darkness of this world. During this same time of imprisonment, the Prophet received some of the grandest and most glorious revelations of all time. A summary and contrast of these Liberty Jail revelations helps us gain an understanding of the battle between the Lamb of God and the mother of harlots.

As we scan the revelations of the Liberty Jail seeking for descriptors of the battle waged by Satan—and the pain and sorrow he inflicts on the world—we find such phrases as *unlawful oppressions; the dark and benighted dominion of Sheol; suffering; hope shall be blasted; hearts are corrupted; love to have others suffer; swear falsely against my servants; they have offended my little ones; those that discomfort my people; hearts set upon the things of this world; aspire to the honors of men; cover our sins; gratify our pride; exercise control or dominion or compulsion; persecute the Saints; unrighteous dominion; fools shall have thee in derision; hell shall rage against thee; cast thee into trouble; tribulation; perils among false brethren; robbers; perils by land or by sea; accused with all manner of false accusation; enemies tear thee from thy wife; dragged to prison; cast into the pit; sentence of death passed upon thee; the very jaws of hell shall gape open the mouth after thee; weight of iniquity; iron yoke; fetters of hell;* and *lie in wait to deceive* (see D&C 121–123). Vicious, unrelenting, and terrible is the assault of Satan on the souls of mankind!

As we read these same revelations received at Liberty Jail looking for descriptors of hope, peace, and triumph for our *faithfulness* in the gospel of the Lamb, we find many qualifying and comforting words such as *peace be unto thy soul; thine adversity and thine afflictions shall be but a small moment; God shall exalt thee on high; thou shalt triumph over all thy foes; cursed are all those that shall lift up the heel against mine anointed; God shall give you knowledge by His Holy Spirit; nothing shall be withheld; all thrones and dominions, principalities and powers shall be revealed and set forth upon all who have endured valiantly for the gospel of Jesus Christ; shall enter into His eternal presence and into his immortal rest; pouring down knowledge from heaven; power; faithfulness is stronger than the cords of death; then shall thy confidence wax strong in the presence of God; the doctrine of the priesthood shall distill upon thy soul as the dews from heaven; the Holy Ghost shall be thy constant companion; thy dominion shall be an everlasting dominion; thy people shall never be turned against thee by the testimony of traitors; all these things shall give thee experience, and shall be for thy good; the priesthood shall remain with thee; fear not what man can do, for God shall be with you forever and ever;* and *then may we stand still, with the utmost assurance, to see the salvation of God, and for his arm to be revealed* (see D&C 121–123).

Yes, Satan is powerful and persuasive—but the Lord continues as the caretaker of "the keys of hell and of death" (Rev. 1:18). How blessed we are with the assurance that—even though the dragon will be strong and terrible—the Lamb of God will prevail, "for he is Lord of lords, and King of kings" (Rev. 17:14).

# Chapter Eighteen
# Come Out of Babylon!

HOW ARE WE RESPONDING TO *the Babylonian community so common to our world?* It is intriguing and instructive to observe how differently people respond to similar circumstances. For example, we learn in the Book of Mormon that "because of the exceedingly great length of the war between the Nephites and the Lamanites many had become *hardened,* because of the exceedingly great length of the war; and many were *softened* because of their afflictions, insomuch that they did humble themselves before God, even in the depth of humility" (Alma 62:41; emphasis added).

A few years ago, I heard the story of a senior couple who had dedicated their lives to missionary service. As they had served one full-time mission and were processing their application for the next, they were struggling with the challenge of what to do with the burden of their home and possessions. During these weeks of struggle, and in their absence, the home caught fire and burned to the ground, destroying everything. As family, friends, and neighbors gathered to offer condolence and assistance, they observed that these faithful folks were not particularly saddened by the event—they were actually somewhat relieved that this roadblock to their continued service had been removed. Of course, they must have experienced some pain and sorrow at the loss of some precious things—but overall, they saw the disaster as a blessing in their desire to return promptly to full-time missionary service.

The final verse of chapter 17 transitions our focus from the wicked woman as representing the marriage of false religion with political empires to the woman now taking the form of a great city called *Babylon:* "And the woman which thou sawest is that great city, which reigneth over the kings of the earth" (Rev. 17:18). Babylon represents the opulence and greed of Satan's earthly realm. In chapter 18, we experience the vivid fall of ostentatious Babylon: "And he cried mightily with a strong voice, saying, Babylon the great is fallen, is fallen, and is become the habitation of devils, and the hold of every foul spirit, and a cage of every unclean and hateful bird" (Rev. 18:2). Undoubtedly this fall will cause varied reactions among people of the nations. Many will mourn. Many will rejoice. Many who have attempted dual residency in Zion and Babylon will struggle as to whether to mourn or rejoice. As in all of life, we will do well to follow the example of our true messengers—even the prophets and Apostles—in how to deal with the destruction of Babylon.

## Come Out of Babylon

*Are we willing, unlike Lot's wife, to leave Babylon?* Babylon, the ancient capital of Babylonia, has stood throughout the ages as a symbol of the wickedness and corruption of world society. Oppressive and evil empires have often been nicknamed *Babylon.* Peter undoubtedly applied the fitting title of *Babylon* to the strangling rule of ancient Rome over the emerging Christian society: "The church that is at Babylon, elected together with you, saluteth you" (1 Pet. 5:13).

In the Lord's own preface to the Doctrine and Covenants, He offers us a description of modern Babylon and the pending destruction that will overcome this evil empire: "They seek not the Lord to establish his righteousness, but every man walketh in his own way, and after the image of his own god, whose image is in the likeness of the world, and whose substance is that of an idol, which waxeth old and shall perish in Babylon, even Babylon the great, which shall fall" (D&C 1:16). If we are not "seeking the Lord to establish his righteousness," are we not then building the kingdom of Babylon?

In continuation of Satan's corrupt counterfeit-marriage metaphor, John offers us this vivid description of the power and influence of Babylon throughout our modern world: "For all nations have drunk of the wine of the wrath of her fornication, and the kings of the earth have committed fornication with her, and the merchants of the earth are waxed rich through the abundance of her delicacies" (Rev. 18:3).

*How may we avoid committing spiritual fornication with Babylon?* The Lord's answer is simple and direct—we must have the courage and determination to leave and go someplace else. We must be willing to leave behind the stuff of Babylon. Lot's wife apparently did not have such determination. The Savior taught, in speaking of the destruction of the latter days, "In that day, he which shall be upon the housetop, and his stuff in the house, let him not come down to take it away: and he that is in the field, let him likewise not return back. Remember Lot's wife. Whosoever shall seek to save his life shall lose it; and whosoever shall lose his life shall preserve it" (Luke 17:31–33). John records a profound warning—so succinctly spoken in such a few words—of how we are to deal with Babylon: "Come out of her, my people, that ye be not partakers of her sins, and that ye receive not of her plagues" (Rev. 18:4).

*As we leave Babylon, or the "world," where are we to go?* We are to go to the great sacrament meeting at Adam-ondi-Ahman, along with all who flee the *world*. My son, in reference to his wanderings in the badlands of southern Utah, used to say, "You can never be lost if you don't care where you're going." In fleeing Babylon, it is essential that we *do* care where we are going and that we not get lost. It is not enough to just *exit* Babylon—we must *enter* the kingdom of God. It is not enough to just rid ourselves of the stuff of the world—we must replace evil with good. In the parable of the empty house, the Savior taught, "When the unclean spirit is gone out of a man, he walketh through dry places, seeking rest, and findeth none. Then he saith, I will return into my house from whence I came out; and when he is come, he findeth it empty, swept, and garnished. Then goeth he, and taketh with himself seven other spirits more wicked than himself, and they enter in and dwell there: and the last state of that man is worse than the first. Even so shall it be also unto this wicked generation" (Matt. 12:43–45).

As we leave Babylon, we should *figuratively* go to Adam-ondi-Ahman—"the land where Adam dwelt" (D&C 117:8). I have been privileged to visit this beautiful valley several times in recent years. I believe that someone who is seeking to follow the gospel path could not go there without feeling something of the powerful spirit associated with this historic and hallowed place. We learn from the

Doctrine and Covenants that "Spring Hill is named by the Lord Adam-ondi-Ahman, because, said he, it is the place where Adam shall come to visit his people, or the Ancient of Days shall sit, as spoken of by Daniel the prophet" (D&C 116:1). To figuratively go to Adam-ondi-Ahman is to prepare our lives to be worthy of invitation to the great spiritual gathering associated with the Second Coming of Christ. This will be a great sacrament meeting wherein the Lord will minister to His Saints.

*Who is invited to Adam-ondi-Ahman?* The Doctrine and Covenants holds the answer to this question. The Lord says, "Behold, this is wisdom in me; wherefore, marvel not, for the hour cometh that I will drink of the fruit of the vine with you on the earth" (D&C 27:5). He then goes on to give a partial listing of some who will be at this great sacrament meeting—people such as Moroni, Elias, John the Baptist, Elijah, Joseph, Jacob, Isaac, Abraham, Adam, Peter, James, and John. In the weakness of our mortality, we may be tempted to wonder if we could ever personally qualify to attend such an exclusive meeting with such an exclusive group. Our Savior goes on to explain, "And also with *all* those whom my Father hath given me out of the world" (D&C 27:14; emphasis added). In His plan and in His mercy, our Father in Heaven has provided opportunity for *all* of His children to escape Babylon and come unto Him in His kingdom!

*Specifically, how do we qualify ourselves for inclusion with the righteous Saints at Adam-ondi-Ahman and ultimately for exaltation in the celestial kingdom of God?* The Lord instructs us to "lift up your hearts and rejoice, and gird up your loins, and take upon you my whole armor, that ye may be able to withstand the evil day, having done all, that ye may be able to stand. Stand, therefore, having your loins girt about with truth, having on the breastplate of righteousness and your feet shod with the preparation of the gospel of peace, which I have sent mine angels to commit unto you; taking the shield of faith wherewith ye shall be able to quench all the fiery darts of the wicked; And take the helmet of salvation, and the sword of my Spirit; which I will pour out upon you, and my word which I reveal unto you, and be agreed as touching all things whatsoever ye ask of me, and be faithful until I come, and ye shall be caught up, that where I am ye shall be also. Amen" (D&C 27:15–18).

As we specifically and diligently apply this counsel of putting on the whole armor of God, we will be motivated and enabled to raise our shield of faith in protection from such fiery darts as gossip, profanity, pornography, and the ill effects of addiction. By having our loins girt with truth, we will be able to discern the lying and conniving treacheries of the prince of darkness, who would lure us to fame and fortune as the reward for abandoning our faith and commitment.

Wearing our breastplate of righteousness, we will protect our hearts from permanent disability as a result of betrayal from loved ones or depression from the daily struggles of our fallen state. Wielding the sword of the Spirit, we will be led through the darkness to those people and circumstances that can bless us and guide us peacefully along. If we choose to come out of Babylon and pursue the path to Adam-ondi-Ahman, great will be our reward, our peace, and our triumph over the great dragon. Sweet will be our joy and our rest in entering the true fold of God!

## WEEPING MERCHANTS AND FALLING STARS

*What are the guiding stars of our lives?* We now learn more of the reactions of both the good and evil ones to the fall of mighty Babylon. To illustrate these reactions, let's return to the imagery of stars. Remember that the Lord referred to those who serve him as stars: "And he had in his right hand seven stars" (Rev. 1:16). We recall that the woman representing the Church of God had "upon her head a crown of twelve stars" (Rev. 12:1). These twelve stars at the head of the Church have obvious reference to the Twelve Apostles. True to his course of counterfeit, Lucifer appoints his own stars—in fact, he himself is referred to as a falling star: "And the third angel sounded and there fell a great star from heaven, burning as it were a lamp, and it fell upon the third part of rivers, and upon the fountains of waters. . . . And the name of the star is called Wormwood" (Rev. 8:10–11).

How fitting and illustrative that we in our modern society, surrounded by the great city of Babylon, have affixed the title of *star* to many who are so popular and seemingly so powerful. (I speak in awareness of and deference to the many righteous stars who—even with fame and fortune—remain good and true to correct principles.)

Particularly illustrative of the fall of Babylon is the fall of some of the unrighteous stars. Consider some star athletes who have risen to positions of fame and fortune and have then fallen to the depths of drug abuse, deceit, and murder. Consider some of the stars of the corporate world who have tasted great success and even done many good things, only to fall from grace in a blaze of fraud, conspiracy, greed, and lust. One year they bask in opulent luxury at the side of their extravagant pools and in the shadows of their great and spacious mansions built from the sweat and toil of the hundreds of whom they have taken advantage. The next year, they weep bitter tears of grief and sorrow at the pronouncement of the judge and are led away in shackles to the confines of physical and mental prisons.

John describes the bitter fate of those who have taken up their residence in the great city of Babylon: "And the kings of the earth, who have committed fornication and lived deliciously with her, shall bewail her, and lament for her, when they shall see the smoke of her burning, Standing afar off for the fear of her torment, saying, Alas, alas, that great city Babylon, that mighty city! for in one hour is thy judgment come. And the merchants of the earth shall weep and mourn over her; for no man buyeth their merchandise any more. . . . The merchants of these things which were made rich by her, shall stand afar off for the fear of her torment, weeping and wailing. . . . For in one hour so great riches is come to naught . . . And cried when they saw the smoke of her burning, saying, What city is like unto this great city! And they cast dust on their heads, and cried, weeping and wailing, saying, Alas, alas, that great city, wherein were made rich all that had ships in the sea by reason of her costliness! for in one hour is she made desolate" (Rev. 18:9–11, 15, 17–19).

*Why do some not learn the lesson that safety and security will never come from the offerings and merchandise of Babylon?* The commerce and economy of Satan and the lure and splendor of Babylon are very seductive to the hearts and souls of mankind. John gives a sampling of what is for sale in Babylon: "And cinnamon, and odours, and ointments, and frankincense, and wine, and oil, and fine flour, and wheat, and beasts, and sheep, and horses, and chariots, and slaves." And then we read of the most costly of all the merchandise that is for sale: "and souls of men" (Rev. 18:13).

We may wonder with sadness at how many souls of men were prostituted by the evil and warped philosophy of Hitler's Reich. We may wonder with sadness, multiplied many times, at how many souls of the masses of humanity throughout the temporal span of the earth have been prostituted by Satan's hand on their shoulders. John saw that "a mighty angel took up a stone like a great millstone, and cast it into the sea, saying, Thus with violence shall that great city Babylon be thrown down, and shall be found no more at all" (Rev. 18:21).

### DISCIPLES REJOICE AT THE TRUE STARS WHO NEVER FALL

*How will the righteous respond to the fall of Babylon?* John, as he so masterfully does, weaves into his narrative that golden thread of peace, hope, and guidance. In reference to the fall of Babylon, he records, "Rejoice over her, thou heaven, and ye holy apostles and prophets; for God hath avenged you on her" (Rev. 18:20). We are to rejoice over the fall of Babylon! Of course we are saddened by those souls who will have fallen prey to the great city—but they will be in God's tender mercy. We are to rejoice! What a beacon of hope. What a day of triumph! In our rejoicing, we may well sing out with great joy our well-loved hymn, "Rejoice, the Lord Is King!" (see *Hymns*, 66).

The light of Christ will vanish from the great city of Babylon. Its inhabitants will be left to grope in the darkness of their greed: "And the light of a candle shall shine no more at all in thee; and the voice of the bridegroom and of the bride shall be heard no more at all in thee: for thy merchants were the great men of the earth; for by thy sorceries were all nations deceived. And in her was found the blood of prophets, and of saints, and of all that were slain upon the earth" (Rev. 18:23–24).

Babylon will be gone—this great city whose magistrates tried so hard to silence the voice and extinguish the light of the Bridegroom as manifest through the righteous and enduring lives and ministries of the holy Apostles and prophets. These are the true stars standing as the crown of the true and living Church. These stars, in contrast to the falling stars of Babylon, will never fall. Like the North Star, they stand true, steady, and firm. In their humble ministries, they lead and guide us through the darkness of Babylon and into the everlasting light and love of God. If we will but have the courage, faith, and fortitude to follow them, we will give thanks and triumph evermore.

Some years ago, I was spending some time with a struggling loved one at Temple Square. We went to the upper floor of the North Visitors' Center to sit quietly at the feet of the Christus statue. At the time, I was also in the midst of preparing to teach chapter 18 of the Revelation and had been pondering the fall of Babylon and the need for us to listen to the voice of the Bridegroom. This sacred place in the visitors' center is a visual portrayal of our Lord and Savior as He stands with His stars in the midst of the universe, giving order and offering salvation to all who will heed the invitation from His outstretched arms. We then went to a performance of *Music and the Spoken Word* with the Mormon Tabernacle Choir and Lloyd Newell.

Brother Newell's message that morning was a perfect message for my loved one to hear at that time and was most relevant to my lesson preparation. His message focused on the fact that we often hear only what we want to hear. A great example comes from sheep, who know the voice of their shepherd and respond only to his voice; if someone else calls, they simply go on grazing, oblivious to the unfamiliar voice. In a similar way, we pay attention to those things that are priorities for us. We need to determine our "shepherd"—do we pay attention to things like popularity, creature comforts, or the seeking of wealth or pleasure? Or are we oblivious to those things as we focus on and listen for the still, small voice of God? If we have established the Lord as our shepherd, we will hear the one true Shepherd. It is His voice that we will seek and follow—a voice that will never lead us astray.

As the great Babylon falls, let's stand firmly listening to the voice of the Bridegroom through His tried and true messengers—the prophets and Apostles. As we do so, we will have much cause to rejoice and adore our Lord and King.

# Chapter Nineteen
# The Fine Linen
# of Righteousness

*ARE WE JOYFULLY ANTICIPATING THE day of the Lord's salvation?* A few decades ago, I was trying to complete a graduate degree that I had struggled with for five years. Along with working on the degree, I was working to provide for my family and was serving in my Church callings. During many long and sometimes discouraging hours of work on my degree, I often wondered if it was really worth the effort, but time and reason motivated me to continue.

The years soon passed, and I arrived at a particular day when I had successfully completed my comprehensive exams and my writing projects. I still had some work to do, but I now knew I was going to make it. As a family, we celebrated this happy time. I joyfully anticipated the commencement and the peace and rest it would bring. I donned the cap and gown and took my place in the processional in an effort to model the value of education to my children. It was a time of happy celebration and of adjustment to a new life phase.

Similarly, we now come to a point in the Revelation of John where most of the blood and tears are to be left behind. We still have the battle of Gog and Magog to deal with, and we still have to get death and hell forever cast into the lake of fire and brimstone—but mostly, in these concluding chapters, the righteous are in the glorious position where they know they are going to make it. They can bask in their joyous knowledge of the salvation of the Lord. The end is in sight—and what a glorious end it will be! In the concluding chapters of the Revelation, John the Revelator provides us with a brilliant array of the glory and the beauty of the zenith of the great plan of happiness. Although we still have some tears of sorrow to shed, we approach the time when our tears will be forever wiped away by the perfect Atonement of our Lord and Savior.

This view of a glorious future was so well expressed by another revelator of more than a century ago—even President Lorenzo Snow, who said, "My hopes in reference to the future life are supremely grand and glorious, and I try to keep these prospects bright continually; and that is the privilege and the duty of every Latter-day Saint. I suppose I am talking now to some Latter-day Saints that have been sorely tried and they have thought sometimes, perhaps like the Savior felt, that he had no friends, that his friends had all gone; and everything was going wrong, and everything was disagreeable, and his circumstances were continuing to get worse and worse. . . . We know that in the future after we have passed through this life, we will then have our wives and our children with us. We will have our bodies fortified, made free from every sickness and distress, and rendered most beautiful. There is nothing more beautiful to look upon than a resurrected man or woman. . . . There is no Latter-day Saint within the sound of my voice but that certainly has this prospect of coming forth in the morning of the first resurrection and being glorified, exalted in the presence of God, having the privilege of talking with our Father as we talk with our earthly father."[19]

We thus enter the concluding chapters of the Revelation with joy and exaltation at the knowledge of pending triumph and the inevitable healing and peace to come through our Savior.

### ALLELUIA—PRAISE JEHOVAH!

John begins this portion of his vision by saying, "And after these things [referring to such things as the pouring out of the plagues upon the wicked and the fall of Babylon] I heard a great voice of much people in heaven, saying, Alleluia; Salvation, and glory, and honour, and power, unto the Lord our God: For true and righteous are his judgments: for he hath judged the great whore, which did corrupt the earth with her fornication, and hath avenged the blood of his servants at her hand" (Rev. 19:1–2).

*Alleluia* means "praise ye the Lord." What a fitting expression of our joy at the triumph of our Savior over death and hell. In looking forward to the mortal reign of Christ, King Benjamin declared what may well serve as a similar expression of praise at His Second Coming: "For behold, the time cometh, and is not far distant, that with power, the Lord Omnipotent who reigneth, who was, and is from all eternity to all eternity, shall come down from heaven among the children of men" (Mosiah 3:5).

Yes, the rightful King of Glory of heaven and of all the earth is returning! The hopeful promise of our theology is now being fulfilled, "that Christ will reign personally upon the earth; and, that the earth will be renewed and receive its paradisiacal glory" (A of F 1:10). After so many long and trying centuries of evil and corruption on the earth, the time of rest and renewal is at hand. Words can hardly express the relief and joy we will feel with the knowledge that the day of trial is now past and that the day of triumph is now at hand.

*How may we, as children, best honor our parents? How may we, as God's children, best honor Him?* Mere words pale in comparison to the righteous actions of the obedient. After a long time of heart-wrenching struggle with a disobedient child, there came a day of rebirth for her. She promised her father that she was now going to change. He was joyful—yet cautious. The reality of the past years tempered his joy, and his expression to her became simply, "Your words are as music to my ears—but I can now only trust actions. Please don't just tell me—show me." The greatest joy a parent can have is to witness the righteous actions, perhaps coupled with the sweet words, of obedient children. John records, "And the four and twenty elders and the four beasts fell down and worshipped God that sat on the throne, saying, Amen; Alleluia" (Rev. 19:4).

We recall earlier in the Revelation that the four beasts representing the whole of righteous creation gave "honour and thanks to him that sat on the throne, who liveth for ever and ever" and that the four and twenty elders, "cast their crowns before the throne, saying, Thou art worthy, O Lord, to receive glory and honour and power: for thou hast created all things, and for thy pleasure they are and were created" (Rev. 4:9–11). Receiving a "crown" refers to the crown of eternal life. What greater praise could a child sing to parents than to earn a "crown of glory," or eternal life, and present this crown to the joyful and grateful parents? There really is no honor greater that a child could show for a parent than this, for we know that "eternal life . . . is the greatest of all the gifts of God" (D&C 14:7). The four and twenty elders thus not only spoke their allegiance to the gospel cause, but they *lived* the gospel cause and presented themselves as righteous heirs of eternal life before the throne of the Father.

John then records, "And I heard as it were the voice of a great multitude, and as the voice of many waters, and as the voice of mighty thunderings, saying, Alleluia: for the Lord God omnipotent reigneth" (Rev. 19:6). Yes, Alleluia—praise Jehovah for His perfect Atonement. What a glorious day! What a joyous time!

## Fine Linen and the Marriage of the Lamb

*Of all of the spiritual protective clothing we could wear, what is the most essential?* Several years ago, our family went on a four-day river trip down the Colorado River, embarking at Moab, Utah, and continuing through Cataract Canyon into Lake Powell. From this experience, I could offer much counsel to anyone planning a similar adventure— wear good shoes, drink lots of water, use sunscreen, and so on. But if I could only give *one* piece of advice, I would simply say, "Wear your lifejacket in the whitewater!" I would offer that advice with absolute confidence and unequivocal firmness. Why? Because our lifejackets literally saved our lives.

Most of the river is calm and easy, and lifejackets are not even worn except in the whitewater. The most treacherous of the whitewater consists of three sets of rapids, appropriately named Big Drop I, II, and III. At this point, the river constricts into the narrow Cataract Canyon as it dramatically drops in elevation. The water rushing down this channel provides one of the most exhilarating whitewater adventures on planet earth.

We did fine on Big Drop I. However, on the very first significant wave of Big Drop II, our boat stood straight up in the air and then fell back—upside down. We were thrown in all directions. I am a fair swimmer, but I'm not certain if that really mattered. The force of the waves and the draw of the currents were so powerful that the only way to even hope to keep our heads above water was with the help of the lifejackets. I'm not sure how others felt or would have fared—but I know that I could not have survived without my lifejacket. We have talked of someday running the river once again. If we do, I will get all things in order—but above all, I will make sure that I have a good and proper lifejacket and that I wear it in the whitewater!

In the Revelation of John, we now come to one of the most blessed and most hoped-for high adventures of all time—even the marriage supper of the Lamb. Let's now return to this profound metaphor wherein Christ as the Bridegroom has prepared the way for His bride—the righteous Saints—to be united with Him in eternal glory forever in the kingdom of the Father. If I could offer only one charge to those I love to enable them in their preparations for this glorious marriage, my charge would simply be, "Wear your fine linen—it's your spiritual lifejacket!"

What is that "fine linen"? John states, "Let us be glad and rejoice, and give honour to him for the marriage of the Lamb is come, and his wife hath made herself ready. And to her was granted that she should be arrayed in fine linen, clean and white: *for the fine linen is the righteousness of saints*. And he saith unto me, Write, Blessed are they which are called unto the marriage supper of the Lamb. And he saith unto me, These are the true sayings of God" (Rev. 19:7–9; emphasis added).

Throughout the dispensations, the righteous Saints, symbolized by the bride, have been joyfully anticipating this wonderful marriage. Those who have been converted to the gospel have been diligently storing away precious oil in their lamps with a drop of tithing here and an ounce of service there. Their lifetimes of dedication to the principles of the gospel have resulted in prepared lamps, full and trimmed and ready to present at the great marriage supper. Their lives are in harmony with gospel principles, and they are ready for a sacred union with their Lord and Savior in eternal glory. They are now dressed in their fine linen—their individual and collective righteousness.

A brief comparison of the characteristics of fine linen to the preparation of righteous lives should help us better understand this aspect of the marriage metaphor. Linen is a luxury fabric—beautiful, durable, and elegant. The ancient Egyptians used linen as a wrapping for their dead—not only to portray a display of wealth, but to symbolize light and purity. Since it is a natural fiber made from flax, its beauty and luster are natural and enduring. Such is the beauty and luster of righteous Saints—natural and enduring.

President James E. Faust illustrated this righteous luster when he told of a historic meeting in Jerusalem many years ago when Church leaders were trying to procure a lease agreement for the construction of the BYU Jerusalem Center for Near Eastern Studies. In order to obtain the lease, we as a Church had to promise that we would not proselyte. After the lease had been signed, one of the officials commented, "Oh, we know that you are not going to proselyte, but what are you going to do about the light that is in their eyes?"[20] He was speaking of the students who studied at the center. These students had adorned themselves with the fine linen of righteousness that naturally radiated through their countenances.

Linen is the strongest of the vegetable fibers, enabling it to be preserved and handed down through generations in the form of valuable keepsakes. The righteousness of the Saints is an enduring legacy, reverently endowed from one generation to another.

Linen is naturally smooth and soft, making the finished product essentially free of lint. Righteous disciples are smoothed and softened by life's trials; they learn to live in the world and to not be of the world. They naturally shed the lint and debris of our fallen environment—they put off the attributes and habits of fallen man.

Linen can be boiled without damaging the fiber—in fact, the more it is washed, the softer and finer it becomes. Righteous Saints can endure the boiling of adversity and actually become better and more refined as a natural result. As they choose a righteous course, their hearts are continually softened. As we learned earlier in the Revelation of John, the righteous "are they which came out of great tribulation, and have washed their robes, and made them white in the blood of the Lamb" (Rev. 7:14). Our lives are whitened and purified with repeated washings in the blood of the Lamb.

As mentioned before, the spiritual death of a loved one can be an even greater trial and heartache than physical death. As sad as physical death may be and as much as our hearts may ache at the loss of someone dear to us, we have the assurance that the Atonement will fix physical death—"yea, even a hair of the head shall not be lost; but all things shall be restored to their proper and perfect frame" (Alma 40:23). Of course, the Atonement can also fix the spiritual death of a loved one if they will come back to the fold and wash their garments in the blood of the Lamb. But will such a one come back? That is the perplexing question of concerned parents. If I *had* to choose between offering my loved ones the counsel of wearing a lifejacket in whitewater or of arraying ourselves in fine linen—the righteousness of Saints—I would choose the latter. May we all strive each day to put on our fine linen—the linen of righteousness—and thus prepare ourselves for entrance to the marriage supper of the Lamb.

## THE MARRIAGE SUPPER

*Where would you like to dine? Are we living so as to be called to the marriage supper of the Lamb?* Imagine yourself going out to dinner at a fine restaurant. The ambiance is bright, clean, and fresh. The air is clear and sweet. Fine linen adorns the table; the finest china and silver are tastefully placed. The servers and chefs are competent and courteous. The food is natural, delicious, and healthy—perfectly prepared and gracefully served. The water is pure. The conversation is appropriate and edifying. The entire setting bespeaks the Lord's desire for our happiness and well being. We gratefully acknowledge the promise of the Lord to us that "the fullness of the earth is yours . . . the herb, and the good things which come of the earth, whether for food or for raiment . . . in the season thereof, are made for the benefit and the use of man, both to please the eye and to gladden the heart; Yea, for food and for raiment, for taste and for smell, to strengthen the body and to enliven the soul. And it pleaseth God that he hath given all these things unto man" (D&C 59:16–20).

Now consider a setting chosen more from dire necessity or by accident than by design. This restaurant is dirty and filled with smoke. The talk is loud and bawdy. The fragrance here is the stench of tobacco and drunkenness. The food is stale and is sloppily prepared and served. The staff exudes disrespect and profanity. The whole of this greasy-spoon setting bespeaks gloom and depression. I suppose we have all likely dined here at least once.

In continuing the marriage metaphor, John now speaks of the wedding feast: "Blessed are they which are called unto the marriage supper of the Lamb" (Rev. 19:9). This feast will far surpass anything mortal man could imagine. It will be an occasion of utmost enjoyment and sociality. Those who come to the feast will have come to worship the Lord. As our beloved Bridegroom presides, He will provide all things. The guests at this table will recognize and reverence His power and glory. We will recognize that His miracle at the marriage feast in Cana so long ago was but a foreshadowing of the grand and multiple miracles of this marriage supper. We will stand in joyful awe as we see the panorama of our Savior's miracles of the changing of human souls. The guests at this table will be those who have been changed—who have put off the natural man and who have truly become Saints through the Atonement and Redemption of the Bridegroom.

At this feast, we will know and feel with surety the eternal joy of partaking of the fountain of living water, and it will be in us as "a well of water springing up into everlasting life" (John 4:14). At this feast, we will eat of the bread of life and learn firsthand the magnificence of the doctrine the Bridegroom taught long ago when he said, "He that believeth on me hath everlasting life. I am that bread of life. Your fathers did eat manna in the wilderness, and are dead. This is the bread which cometh down from heaven, that a man may eat thereof, and not die. I am the living bread which came down from heaven: if any man eat of this bread, he shall live forever: and the bread that I will give is my flesh, which I will give for the life of the world" (John 6:47–51).

In contrast to the peace, joy, and celebration of the marriage supper of the Lamb will be the agony, wailing, and sorrow of the feast of the damned. Those who have chosen and followed a life course that has brought them to this feast are there in loyalty to and adoration of the beast. In vivid contrast, the wicked souls who have rejected the marriage proposal of the Bridegroom will now be devoured at this frightful feast. John records, "And I saw an angel standing in the sun; and he cried with a loud voice, saying to all the fowls that fly in the midst of heaven, Come and gather yourselves together unto the supper of the great God; That ye may eat the flesh of kings, and the flesh of captains, and the flesh of mighty men, and the flesh of horses, and of them that sit on them, and the flesh of all men, both free and bond, both small and great. . . . And the beast was taken, and with him the false prophet . . . These both were cast alive into a lake of fire burning with brimstone. And the remnant were slain with the sword of him that sat upon the horse, which sword proceeded out of his mouth: and all the fowls were filled with their flesh" (Rev. 19:17–18, 20–21).

We who have the blessing of a knowledge of not only the Revelation of John but of countless testimonies from many prophets through the ages should wonder why anyone would choose to ultimately dine at the feast of the damned when we are universally invited to prepare ourselves for entrance into the marriage supper of the Lamb.

## KING OF KINGS AND LORD OF LORDS

*What chance do we, as struggling mortals, have of being included in the marriage supper of the Lamb? Do we recognize and accept the redemptive power of the Lamb of God?* We must not be deceived into the false and damning philosophy perpetuated by Satan and his angels that the invitation to the marriage supper of the Lamb is beyond our means. If we are not careful, we might despairingly exclaim, "I would really like to sup in the fine dining hall but, alas, I am poor and must confine myself to the greasy-spoon café." In other words, "I would really like to go to the celestial kingdom of God someday, but I fear that it is beyond my means and that it is a realm reserved only for others far more righteous than me." If this is our notion, we have somehow missed the grandeur and beauty of the doctrine of the Atonement. We have missed the true power and identity of our Lord of Lords and King of Kings.

Perhaps our challenge might be that we become so tainted by our lustful society, where everything seems to have its price tag, that we are naturally tempted to hang that price tag on the free gifts of redemption and salvation. If this is our error, these teachings of Jacob to his brothers should be particularly instructive: "Come, my brethren, every one that thirsteth, come ye to the waters; and he that hath no money, come buy and eat; yea come buy wine and milk without money and without price. Wherefore, do not spend money for that which is of no worth, nor your labor for that which cannot satisfy. Hearken diligently unto me, and remember the words which I have spoken; and come unto the Holy One of Israel, and feast upon that which perisheth not, neither can be corrupted, and let your soul delight in fatness" (2 Ne. 9:50–51).

Perhaps the challenge for some is to have been influenced by the damning social prejudice of our fallen world and to have transferred these evil practices into a warped perception that the marriage supper of the Lamb is to be held in some sort of an exclusive gated country club where only those of a particular race or economic status may dine. Listen instead to what Nephi had to say: "For none of these iniquities come of the Lord; for he doeth that which is good among the children of men; and he doeth nothing save it be plain unto the children of men; and he inviteth them all to come unto him and partake of his goodness; and he denieth none that come unto him, black and white, bond and free, male and female; and he remembereth the heathen; and all are alike unto God, both Jew and Gentile" (2 Ne. 26:33).

Christ, in His meekness and lowliness of heart, came riding into Jerusalem on a humble donkey in the triumphal entry at the conclusion of His mortal ministry. He was soon, through His suffering and sacrifice, to gain ultimate and eternal triumph over death and hell. Now, in the Revelation of John, we see our Savior riding in triumph once again as He begins His millennial ministry. John records, "And I saw heaven opened, and behold a white horse; and he that sat upon him was called Faithful and True, and in righteousness he doth judge and make war. His eyes were as a flame of fire, and on his head were many crowns; and he had a name written, that no man knew, but he himself. And he was clothed with a vesture dipped in blood: and his name is called The Word of God" (Rev. 19:11–13).

*Faithful* and *True* are certainly fitting and worthy titles for Christ. He has been *faithful* and *true* to all that the Father entrusted to Him, and He has now triumphed over the enemies of darkness. His "vesture dipped in blood" symbolizes His triumph through the blood of His Atonement. His "many crowns" symbolize the many kingdoms of this world, and of worlds without number, that He has overcome and the many glorious kingdoms awaiting those who have accepted of His offering and thus earned their own bright crowns of eternal life. At this end day, He rides not the humble donkey of Jerusalem but rather the white horse of purity and of victory over death and hell.

John then sees "the armies which were in heaven followed him upon white horses, clothed in fine linen, white and clean. And out of his mouth goeth a sharp sword, that with it he should smite the nations: and he shall rule them with a rod of iron: and he treadeth the winepress of the fierceness and wrath of Almighty God" (Rev. 19:14–15). The prerequisites of riding in triumph with the Savior are not gold nor silver nor social status but rather to be clothed in fine linen, white and clean. The fine linen of righteousness is our official invitation and entrance pass to the marriage supper of the Lamb. As we join the wedding party, we need no longer fear the swords of despots and tyrants of this fallen world. Christ will lead us with His "sharp sword"—"the word of his mouth" (JST, Rev. 19:15). We will rejoice in this glorious supper wherein we will "feast upon the words of Christ; for behold, the words of Christ will tell you all things what ye should do" (2 Ne. 32:3).

John records, "And he hath on his vesture and on his thigh a name written, KING OF KINGS, AND LORD OF LORDS" (Rev. 19:16). The station and victory of Christ are boldly proclaimed. He has overcome. He, through his true justice and tender mercy, has brought order, salvation, peace, and victory to the world. He has invited all who will to don their robes of righteousness and ride with Him to eternal glory. Let us put on our fine linen—the linen of righteousness. By so doing, we prepare to ride in triumph with the KING OF KINGS, AND LORD OF LORDS!

# Chapter Twenty
# Satan is Bound—
# The Righteous Live with Christ

FROM THE DEMISE OF THE IMAGINARY Wicked Witch of the North in the Wizard of Oz to the overthrow and death of the very real Führer of the Third Reich, a recurring theme of our mortal world seems to be that the reign of a terrible person is followed by a mighty sigh of relief and a sense of jubilation once the wicked reign is over and the perpetrator is dead or captured. In our post-911 era, and in the midst of our current accelerated war on terror, we anxiously anticipate the killing or capture of the most visible leaders of these terrorist regimes. A top general of terror was recently killed in a well-executed bombing raid on the "safe house" where he was staying. His death was hailed as a great victory in our enduring struggle. He will never kill again, and his own personal judgment is now squarely in the hands of God. And yet, the depressing reality seems to be that no matter how many of the ringleaders we eliminate, there seem to be countless successors ready to step up to fill the leadership voids. The terror continues—sometimes with renewed energy. There seems to be no end and no solution. *Where is the peace, the joy, and the hope in this prospect of never-ending terror?*

Of course, the enduring peace, joy, and hope are vested in our Lord and Savior, who holds the keys of death and hell. The only safe house is righteousness and faith in Him and in His gospel. Ultimately, all of the wicked tyrants will be ferreted out and brought to justice. Most exciting of all is that Satan himself, the commanding general of all that is wicked, will soon come to the end of his power. When he is cast out, then comes the great day of jubilation. Then we will have lasting and eternal peace and joy. What a glorious day of celebration throughout the earth!

## THE DRAGON IS BOUND, LOOSED FOR A SEASON, THEN BOUND FOREVER
*How do we imagine the joyous day when the enmity of men and beasts will be gone? Are we spiritually preparing to endure the great and last battles of good over evil?* John records, "And I saw an angel come down from heaven, having the key of the bottomless pit and a great chain in his hand. And he laid hold on the dragon, that old serpent, which is the Devil, and Satan, and bound him a thousand years" (Rev. 20:1–2).

Alleluia! The founder of every evil thing is now in the Lord's custody, and there is neither escape nor provision for perpetuating his evil from behind his bars. We are told that the angel "cast him into the bottomless pit, and shut him up, and set a seal upon him, that he should deceive the nations no more, till the thousand years should be fulfilled" (Rev. 20:3). This will be the happy time when "The wolf also shall dwell with the lamb, and the leopard shall lie down with the kid, and the calf and the young lion and fatling together; and a little child shall lead them. And the cow and the bear shall feed; their young ones shall lie down together; and the lion shall eat straw like the ox. And the sucking child shall play on the hole of the asp, and the weaned child shall put his hand on the cockatrice's den. They shall not hurt nor destroy in all my holy mountain, for the earth shall be full of the knowledge of the Lord, as the waters cover the sea. And in that day there shall be a root of Jesse, which shall stand for an ensign of the people; to it shall the Gentiles seek; and his rest shall be glorious" (2 Ne. 21:6–10).

Try as we may, the collective righteousness of many Saints will not strip Satan of all power—there must be divine intervention by the Lord at His coming. Remember from chapter 1 that Christ holds "the keys of hell and of death" (Rev. 1:18). At His coming, He will revoke the keys. The scriptures teach that Satan will be stripped of his power: "And in that day Satan shall not have power to tempt any man" (D&C 101:28). Once his power is gone, the Saints will live in blessed righteousness as described by Nephi: "And because of the righteousness of his people, Satan has no power; wherefore, he cannot be loosed for the space of many years; for he hath no power over the hearts of the people, for they dwell in righteousness, and the Holy One of Israel reigneth" (1 Ne. 22:26).

During this extended term of imprisonment of the wicked, not only will Satan, the master of evil, be rendered powerless, but so will his servants. There will be no more wicked successors waiting in the wings to fill the leadership void. We learn that the unrighteous "lived not again until the thousand years were finished" (Rev. 20:4–5). They are securely locked away and can do us no harm.

After the Millennium there will be one ultimate battle. John describes this final conquest of the Lamb over Satan: "And when the thousand years are expired, Satan shall be loosed out of his prison, And shall go out to deceive the nations which are in the four quarters of the earth, Gog and Magog, to gather them together to battle: the number of whom is as the sand of the sea. And they went up on the breadth of the earth, and compassed the camp of the saints about, and the beloved city: and fire came down from God out of heaven, and devoured them. And the devil that deceived them was cast into the lake of fire and brimstone, where the beast and the false prophet are, and shall be tormented day and night for ever and ever" (Rev. 20:7–10).

The term *Gog and Magog* appears in only two places in the scriptures. The first is in the prophecy of Ezekiel and has apparent reference to a pre-millennial event preceding the Second Coming of Christ: "The battle of Gog and Magog against Israel shall usher in the Second Coming—The Lord will come amid war and pestilence, and all men shall shake at his presence" (Ezek. 38, heading). "Set thy face against Gog, the land of Magog" (Ezek. 38, heading, 38:2). The second reference is the one just cited in the Revelation of John and has reference to the final battle after the end of the Millennium during which Satan will be cast out forever.

As these final battles are waged, those who have chosen to wear the mark of the beast on their forehead and who have pledged their allegiance to Satan will be conquered and cast out with their vile master. John saw, "And whosoever was not found written in the book of life was cast into the lake of fire" (Rev. 20:15).

Modern-day revelation is very instructive regarding these final battles: "And so on, until the seventh angel shall sound his trump; and he shall stand forth upon the land and upon the sea, and swear in the name of him who sitteth upon the throne, that there shall be time no longer; and Satan shall be bound, that old serpent, who is called the devil, and shall not be loosed for the space of a thousand years. And then he shall be loosed for a little season, that he may gather together his armies. And Michael, the seventh angel, even the archangel, shall gather together his armies, even the hosts of heaven. And the devil shall gather together his armies; even the hosts of hell, and shall come up to battle against Michael and his armies. And then cometh the battle of the great God; and the devil and his armies shall be cast away into their own place, that they shall not have power over the saints any more at all. For Michael shall fight their battles, and shall overcome him who seeketh the throne of him who sitteth upon the throne, even the Lamb. This is the glory of God, and the sanctified; and they shall not any more see death" (D&C 88:110–116).

We may have great hope and encouragement in knowing that there will come a day when the "sanctified . . . shall not any more see death." Death and hell are to be gone forever. Those who have kept their covenants and followed the course of righteousness will be joyous and jubilant at this time of finality and conquest over the powers of darkness. Never more will Satan torment God's children.

## LIVE WITH CHRIST A THOUSAND YEARS

*What do we value most? How may we know what a person really values?* Words may tell us—or they may not. If we want to know for sure, we must look at actions. As mentioned previously, to answer the question *What does this person value?* we must ask, *How does this person spend his or her time?* We all spend our time, one way or another, on what we value. If we value service to our country and community, then we spend time in this service. If we value spiritual growth and knowledge, then we spend time seeking these gifts. If we value our family relationships, then we spend time nurturing such relationships. If we truly value eternal life, then we spend the days of our mortal probation doing the things that will grant us such a life.

John sees the reward of the righteous who have shown by their actions that eternal life has been their true quest: "And I saw thrones, and they sat upon them, and judgment was given unto them: and I saw the souls of them that were beheaded for the witness of Jesus, and for the word of God, and which had not worshipped the beast, neither his image, neither had received his mark upon their foreheads, or in their hands; and they lived and reigned with Christ a thousand years. . . . This is the first resurrection. Blessed and holy is he that hath part in the first resurrection: on such the second death hath no power, but they shall be priests of God and of Christ, and shall reign with him a thousand years" (Rev. 20:4–6).

*How do we imagine a millennial life with Christ?* Personally, I imagine such a life as being involved in what I enjoy most about life now—less all of the evil that now plagues our fallen world. In our ward, a man and his wife were recently in need of a new deck. Their home once had a deck, but it had deteriorated and had to be demolished. Lacking this second-story, wraparound deck presented a serious fire-escape hazard for the home. The couple had neither the health nor the means to reconstruct the deck. My bishop had been particularly anxious about how we as a ward could help these people. As he expressed his concern, I offered my help along with the help of my son and my soon-to-be son-in-law. We planned the project, ordered materials, and, over the course of a week, constructed the deck. Projects like this excite me and provide me an opportunity to do some of the things I love most about life—working with my mind and hands, training and teaching my loved ones, providing meaningful and necessary service, and experiencing *spiritual* and *physical* creation.

My experience with this and other enjoyable life projects and activities has given me a fair glimpse—albeit just a glimpse—of both millennial and eternal life. I believe that we will always have meaningful work to do. I believe that we will work in joy and unity as families. I believe that we will be able to forever use our talents to bless our own lives and the lives of others. I believe that we will enjoy a fullness of knowledge and a fullness of joy—and we will do all of this in a world forever free of the damning grasp of the hand of Satan.

I find confirmation of this perception of millennial and eternal life from the teachings of President Lorenzo Snow. On one occasion, shortly before his death, he was touring the Brigham Young Academy with President Brimhall. They passed through a kindergarten room where the children were making clay spheres. President Snow asked to stop and watch for a while, and then he took one of the clay spheres in his hand and said, "President Brimhall, these children are now at play, making mud worlds, the time will come when some of these boys, through their faithfulness to the gospel, will progress and develop in knowledge, intelligence and power, in future eternities, until they shall be able to go out into space where there is unorganized matter and call together the necessary elements, and through their knowledge of and control over the laws and powers of nature, to organize matter into worlds on which their posterity may dwell, and over which they shall rule as gods."[21]

In mortality, even though we are surrounded by greed, evil, and war, we have the great privilege and opportunity of "building decks" for people. In millennial life, we will have the privilege and opportunity to build decks—and homes and Zion communities and temples and forever families—without the presence and influence of Satan and his hosts. In eternal life, we will have the great privilege and opportunity to have all of the growth and experience of our mortal existence combined into a grand eternal whole wherein we will forever and ever build eternal families with all of the attendant joy and fulfillment and none of the sorrow and disappointment of our fallen world. Oh, what joy, peace, and triumph—evermore!

## SMALL AND GREAT STANDING BEFORE GOD

*How is our book of life being written—What are we becoming?* I once heard the account of a famous violinist who was confronted after a concert by a lady who said to him, "I would give my life to play like you." The violinist replied, "That I did." It seems human nature to tend to jump to conclusions about the small view we may have of a person's life from the minor glimpses we see in the brief crossing of our paths—particularly in our public performances. But little do we know about the depth of a person's effort, sacrifice, and circumstance unless we pay the price to truly get to know that person. The five wise virgins did not share of the oil of their lamps not because they were stingy—they did not share because they could not share. Just as the violinist could not, even if he wanted to, endow his talent to another—so a person cannot impart what he has become to another. Gratefully, the Lord looks on our individual hearts and casts His judgments individually to us.

We must be especially careful to not set ourselves up as the judge of another's sins. We, following the example of our Savior, "cannot look upon sin with the least degree of allowance," but we must always remember the wonderful truth and comforting and saving doctrine that "he that repents and does the commandments of the Lord shall be forgiven" (D&C 1:31–32). How reassuring it will be someday when we come to fully recognize the truth that the Lord suits "his mercies according to the conditions of the children of men" (D&C 46:15). He knows the true intent of our hearts and will righteously judge us according to our choices and circumstances. He can truly and accurately read our book of life.

John records, "And I saw the dead, small and great, stand before God; and the books were opened: and another book was opened, which is the book of life: and the dead were judged out of those things which were written in the books, according to their works. And the sea gave up the dead which were in it; and death and hell delivered up the dead which were in them: and they were judged every man according to their works" (Rev. 20:12–13).

We must not confuse our personal book of life with the mortal books *about* our lives—even if they are autobiographies—for we do not fully see ourselves as the Lord sees us.

We may find hope in the knowledge that as God and Christ judge our lives they will not take any good thing away from us. They do not intend to enable and assist us over the span of our mortal lives, only to allow us to be blindsided by some great cataclysmic judgment that will negate all of our good preparation for eternal life. Just as we cannot give the oil of our personal lamps to another, neither can we spill and waste it all in a moment of thoughtless panic or commotion. It will never be wasted. It will remain forever with us. We have the sure promise that if we will allow our "bowels also be full of charity towards all men, and to the household of faith, and let virtue garnish thy thoughts unceasingly: then shall thy confidence wax strong in the presence of God; and the doctrine of the priesthood shall distill upon thy soul as the dews from heaven. The Holy Ghost shall be thy constant companion, and thy scepter an unchanging scepter of righteousness and truth; and thy dominion shall be an everlasting dominion, and without compulsory means it shall flow unto thee forever and ever" (D&C 121:45–46).

We may go forward with faith and courage. If we are righteous, we need not fear the battles of Gog and Magog—neither the Armageddon prior to Christ's Second Coming, nor the final post-millennial battle that brings the old serpent to his dark and final destination. If we use the days of our mortal probation to diligently "prepare to meet God" and to "not procrastinate the day" (Alma 34:32–33) of our repentance, then we will safely endure these events and joyously go forward to our promised rest.

# Chapter Twenty-One

# A New Heaven
# and a New Earth

*HOW WILLING ARE WE TO allow a remodeling of our lives by the Master Builder?* Many years ago, my wife and I bought our first home and excitedly moved into it with our newborn son. Although it was in a great location and on a large lot, the home was very small, having been built as a retirement dwelling for a senior couple. As our family grew, we could see that we would soon outgrow the home and be faced with the decision of whether to sell and move or build an addition. We choose to build an addition—and to make it affordable, we decided we would build it ourselves. Had we known at the beginning what a challenging project this would be, we may have lost courage and not made the attempt.

For the next few years, we lived amidst the chaos of excavated dirt, falling insulation, rough framing, hanging electrical wires, sawdust, uncovered floors, and every inconvenience that such a project entails. However, we eventually made it livable—and then comfortable—and then beautiful. For me personally, the construction of this home became one of the great growth experiences of my life.

As we were building what would be a physical and spiritual refuge for our growing family, I had an epiphany that what we were doing was actually a glimpse of what eternal life would be like as parents working to provide physical and spiritual homes for their children. This was one of the happiest times of my life. Whenever I smell the fragrance of a wild rosebush today, I am taken back in memory to the beautiful summer days I spent framing the home within a few feet of a fence full of sweet wild roses.

What I did not realize then was that the house and my life, along with it, would yet go through many significant and painful changes—that the Master Builder had much work yet to accomplish. I could not have possibly imagined then what I now see in retrospect. The trials and heartaches of life have worked on my soul just as the elements of nature have worked on the home—yet we are both still standing. I have come to realize—not by mere imagining but by personal experience—that our loving Heavenly Father has designed a plan for us wherein He would build us an earthly home, place us in it, and then allow us to struggle, learn, and grow through our own experience. In due time, our physical home would progress to a new destiny. In due time, our personal lives would also progress to a new destiny of our own choosing through the exercise of our agency. What a high adventure is this state called mortality!

## A NEW HEAVEN AND A NEW EARTH

*How well do we understand the change needed to transform our old earth and old ways into a new heaven and a new earth?* In these concluding chapters of the Revelation of John, we have a growing crescendo of praise, glory, and adoration to our God and Christ for the triumph of the plan of salvation and of the perfect Atonement. These verses of praise are interrupted by only a few passing references to the final fate and state of the wicked. The construction mess of our mortality is coming to a close. The ushering in of a new heaven and a new earth is at hand.

John "saw a new heaven and a new earth; for the first heaven and the first earth were passed away; and there was no more sea" (Rev. 21:1). Our earth—just like our personal lives—is growing, changing, and developing. The earth fell and became telestial and will someday be renewed to its paradisiacal state. Ultimately it will become a celestialized abode for celestialized Saints. Thus are our lives—growing, changing, and developing. The transformation of heaven and earth parallels the transformation of our hearts and souls. If we are humble and contrite, we will attain a finished, celestial state.

In reflection of our potential for exaltation and of our need for humility amidst change, I have long appreciated these words from the respected scholar and teacher, C. S. Lewis: "Imagine yourself as a living house. God comes in to rebuild that house. At first, perhaps, you can understand what He is doing. He is getting the drains right and stopping the leaks in the roof and so on: you knew that those jobs needed doing and so you are not surprised. But presently he starts knocking the house about in a way that hurts abominably and does not seem to make sense. What on earth is He up to? The explanation is that He is building quite a different house from the one you thought of—throwing out a new wing here, putting on an extra floor there, running up towers, making courtyards. You thought you were going to be made into a decent little cottage: but He is building a palace. He intends to come and live in it Himself."[22]

John then "saw the holy city, new Jerusalem, coming down from God out of heaven, prepared as a bride adorned for her husband" (Rev. 21:2). This return to the marriage metaphor now speaks of the glorious day of the uniting of things of heaven and earth. All of the righteous Saints of all ages and dispensations are now married, or united, with the Creator of heaven and earth. The righteous will experience joy and wonder beyond mortal comprehension. The long quest to establish Zion will now find fulfillment. In preparation for the day when Christ will rule and reign throughout the earth, old Jerusalem will be rebuilt and will stand in glory and righteousness. New Jerusalem will be built on the American continent to stand as a beautiful beacon of light and truth to the entire world. Enoch and the people of his ancient city will unite with this New Jerusalem.

We learn more of this splendid time from the Pearl of Great Price: "And righteousness will I send down out of heaven; and truth will I send forth out of the earth, to bear testimony of mine Only Begotten; his resurrection from the dead; yea, and also the resurrection of all men; and righteousness and truth will I cause to sweep the earth as with a flood, to gather out mine elect from the four quarters of the earth, unto a place which I shall prepare, an Holy City, that my people may gird up their loins, and be looking forth for the time of my coming; for there shall be my tabernacle, and it shall be called Zion, a New Jerusalem" (Moses 7:62). Joseph Smith commented on this verse and taught that men and angels would work together to build Zion and New Jerusalem (see *Teachings of the Prophet Joseph Smith*, 84).

At long last, the time of trial and mortal probation is past. The time of joy, happiness, and eternal peace is at hand. If we have had the faith to withstand the reconstruction of our souls by the Father of our salvation, we will have the great and eternal privilege of living *with* Him and living *like* Him for eternity.

## THE FORMER THINGS ARE PASSED AWAY

*What terrible heartache would we like to have healed by our Savior?* In Chapter 7, we discussed how God would wipe away all tears from the eyes of all of His children through the ages. John now revisits this comforting doctrine: "And I heard a great voice out of heaven saying, Behold, the tabernacle of God is with men, and he will dwell with them, and they shall be his people, and God himself shall be with them, and be their God. And God shall wipe away all tears from their eyes; and there shall be no more death, neither sorrow, nor crying, neither shall there be any more pain: for the former things are passed away. And he that sat upon the throne said, Behold, I make all things new. And he said unto me, Write: for these words are true and faithful" (Rev. 21:3–5).

To further illustrate this principle, I decided to conduct a random experiment by examining the news at the precise moment of this writing to see if I could find an example of how the saving and healing doctrine of Christ applies in the lives of individuals. As I expected, the headline story of the Internet news site I visited was one that has undoubtedly caused tears for many people—the criminal trial of a man who is charged with the kidnapping, raping, and killing of a nine-year-old girl. What a horrible and frightening experience this must have been for this innocent child as she was held captive by this vile man for three days. Who can even imagine the anguished sobbing of the parents and loved ones of this sweet angel through the dark nights of the many months since the commission of the crime? What sorrow and anguish have been at play in the hearts and souls of the cadre of the legal system who have dealt with this case! Have they wondered about their own innocent children and been caused to mourn the reality that in our fallen world, such a crime could happen to those they love?

Although this thought may be particularly difficult to entertain, especially by those mourning the victim, what about the tears shed by those who know and love the perpetrator? And in the eternal perspective of God's plan and Christ's eternal grace and mercy, we must also consider the tears and heartaches of the perpetrator himself. How does he feel—or how will he someday feel—about what he has done? Will even he come under the transforming umbrella of the Lord's tender mercy? As difficult and disturbing as this example is, it seems so typical of the daily events of the fallen and wicked world in which we live. Such terrible happenings and conditions simply add more awe to the healing power of the Atonement and the capacity of our Savior to heal all heartaches, ease all pain, and dry all tears.

I confess that one of the greatest doctrinal struggles of my life has been striving to understand why the totally innocent—such as this little girl—must be called to suffer the terrible misuse of agency by the vile and the wicked. *Why can't they be granted exemption?* has long been the question of my soul. Although I have not fully found my answer, I have come to know that there *is* an answer and that it lies in the perfect Atonement of Jesus Christ. All souls are in His hand and fall under His perfect blend of justice and mercy.

I take more comfort than I can ever express in the pure knowledge imparted us by John that "there shall be no more death, neither sorrow, nor crying, neither shall there be any more pain" (Rev. 21:4). We maintain our *hope* in Christ. Through Him, all will be *healed*. In Him, we will attain lasting *peace*. He will *triumph* over all things—including all of our personal misery, loss, and heartache. We have the repeated promise from the prophets that what we have lost will be restored in the Lord's due time.

What a day of celebration and thanksgiving we will have when we arrive at the point when the former things—death, sorrow, mourning, and pain—are finally and forever passed away! At the conclusion of Christ's suffering on the cross, He proclaimed, "It is finished: and he bowed his head, and gave up the ghost" (John 19:30). With this proclamation, He signified the end of *His* suffering and the completion of *His* atoning sacrifice. In his Revelation, John continues, "And he said unto me, It is done. I am Alpha and Omega, the beginning and the end. I will give unto him that is athirst of the fountain of the water of life freely" (Rev. 21:6). With this proclamation of "It is done," Christ signifies the end of *our* suffering and trial. The time of our mortal probation has concluded. The time of our eternal peace and joy, free from all pain and sorrow for evermore, has just begun. What a glorious commencement!

## INHERIT ALL THINGS

*How does the wealth of this world compare to the riches of eternal life?* The news at the time of this writing has included a most fascinating and instructive account of the world's richest people. First, the world's richest man announced that he is resigning from the day-to-day duties of his corporation so that he and his wife can devote the majority of their time and energy to the work of their charitable foundation, established to improve the education and health of people across the globe. Soon thereafter, the world's second-richest man announced that he was giving away the bulk of his multibillion-dollar empire to the richest man's foundation to help further that cause. Their efforts to make a difference in the world and to lighten the burdens of mankind are impressive.

The great instruction of these events comes as we contemplate the core desires of these, the world's richest. Likely all people at one time or another have fantasized of what they would do if they had unlimited resources. In these examples we have people who actually *do* have virtually unlimited resources and who could buy anything the world has to offer. Having arrived at this point, they have an apparent longing for something more—to help relieve the suffering and improve the station of God's children. A genuine caring and concern for others transcends the wealth of the earth and demonstrates that there are things of much more value than money.

As we relate this example to the building of the kingdom of God in the earth, we find many parallels. Through our great welfare and humanitarian efforts, the Church is trying to better the plight of the inhabitants of the earth. Generally as people become more temporally self-sufficient, they more fully reach their potential in spiritual matters and have more time, energy, and resources to devote to the building of the kingdom. God desires to provide for His Saints. He desires to bless His children with all of the good things of the earth that their faith can stand. He desires to bless us with His own style of wealth and riches.

John sees that "he that overcometh shall inherit all things; and I will be his God, and he shall be my son" (Rev. 21:7). Those who know the potential of what we may become through the eternal plan of God would recognize that even the world's richest have comparatively nothing when you consider their mere bank accounts. The only true wealth that any of us can hope to attain is the wealth of eternal life, which far surpasses and transcends our temporal world.

In the portion of our scripture we refer to as the "Oath and Covenant of the Priesthood," the Lord instructs us, "And he that receiveth my Father receiveth my Father's kingdom; therefore all that my Father hath shall be given unto him" (D&C 84:38). What, we might ask, does our Father have? He has all things—all knowledge, all power, all joy, all peace, all truth, and all of everything to live an eternal and perfectly happy life.

The beauty of the gospel is that we may actually become like our Father in Heaven and gain a life like His. It is of little wonder that Satan, the enemy of God, gets so jealously angry at this doctrine and that he expends so much effort trying to get his servants to refute and contradict this message of eternal hope. No wonder John calls them "fearful, and unbelieving, and the abominable" (Rev. 21:8). Nevertheless, refute as they will, the doctrine stands as truth eternal. We are the literal offspring of God. We are to address Him as *Father.*

As we continually strive to overcome the things of the flesh, we will live out our lives and eventually come to the end of our mortal probation. When we arrive at that end, we will know the truth. I recently saw displayed on the marquee of a church near my home: "Death separates what we *have* from what we *are!*"

## THE HOLY CITY: STREETS OF GOLD AND GATES OF PEARLS
*How do we imagine the beauty and grandeur of celestial glory?* I recall from my youth a television advertisement touting a particular snack item as being "indescribably delicious!" The implication was, "This product is so good that we cannot even find the words to express to you how wonderful it is. You will just have to buy it and find out for yourself." We could apply the same description to the celestial kingdom of God. Our Savior would have no problem expressing to us the glory of eternal life—the challenge would be that we, with our veiled mortal minds, could not nearly comprehend the glory and splendor that await those who qualify for exaltation. The best thing

we can do with our lives is live to qualify to go there and experience it for ourselves.

John received a firsthand look at eternal glory as he was "carried . . . away in the spirit to a great and high mountain, and shewed . . . that great city, the holy Jerusalem, descending out of heaven from God" (Rev. 21:10). The beauty and glory of eternal life will far transcend the beauty and glory of even the most precious gems and metals of the earth. Nonetheless, these precious gems and metals can serve as helpful object lessons in giving us a comparative feel of eternal glory.

Let's consider just a few examples from John's view and suggest a few possible illustrations of what they might represent. Remember, we need not worry too much about what is literal and what is figurative. We are not sure if the streets of the celestial kingdom are literally paved with gold—I doubt it. Joseph Smith simply said that they "had the appearance of being paved with gold" (D&C 137:4; gold pavement may well just be a mortal attempt to describe a celestial condition of light and glory).

In John's vision of the holy city as described in chapter 21, he sees:

- "[H]er light was like unto a stone most precious, even like a jasper stone, clear as crystal" (Rev. 21:11). To exalted beings in the celestial kingdom, all things are made crystal clear. All doctrinal questions are fully answered. For example, my struggle to understand why innocent children must suffer in this life will be made clear. If we qualify for eternal life, we will have a full and complete understanding of all suffering and will see the fullness of the redeeming power of God in the lives of all of His children. Of those who live *with* and *like* God, we are told, "But they reside in the presence of God, on a globe like a sea of glass and fire, where all things for their glory are manifest, past, present, and future, and are continually before the Lord" (D&C 130:7).
- "[A] wall great and high, and had twelve gates, and at the gates twelve angels, and names written thereon, which are the names of the twelve tribes of the children of Israel" (Rev. 21:12). Later in this chapter, we are told that "there shall in no wise enter into it any thing that defileth, neither

whatsoever worketh abomination, or maketh a lie; but they which are written in the Lamb's book of life"(Rev. 21:27). As an illustration, I think of the wall around Temple Square in Salt Lake City. Along the outer perimeter of the wall are sometimes those who spew forth false accusations and condemnations at our leaders and at our doctrines. It is refreshing to take just a few steps within the wall and to feel the Spirit and beauty of the sacred setting and the truth taught therein. Gates are symbolic of the ordinances of the priesthood. Nephi taught us that "the gate by which ye should enter is repentance and baptism by water" (2 Ne. 31:17). Our pass for entrance into the gate of the celestial kingdom is the receiving and keeping of our temple endowment. President Brigham Young taught, "Your *endowment* is, to receive all those ordinances in the House of the Lord, which are necessary for you, after you have departed this life, to enable you to walk back to the presence of the Father, passing the angels who stand as sentinels, being enabled to give them the key words, the signs and tokens, pertaining to the Holy Priesthood, and gain your eternal exaltation in spite of earth and hell."[23]

- "And the wall of the city had twelve foundations, and in them the names of the twelve apostles of the Lamb" (Rev. 21:14). Nearly every substantial community in America has some type of a memorial wall or monument in honor of those who have served our country and given their lives in battle for the cause of our freedom. One of the most notable of such shrines is the Vietnam Memorial in our nation's capital. It is fitting and proper that we honor and remember the brave men and women who have earned and protected our freedom. We have learned much from the Revelation of John about the role and mission of the special witnesses of Christ who have stood through the ages as true messengers to guide us safely through our mortal probation. It is significant that their names are written in the foundations of the wall, for the true Church is "built upon the foundation of the apostles and prophets" (Eph. 2:20). They, along with all who heed and follow them, will be held in humble remembrance throughout eternity.

- "[A]nd the city was pure gold, like unto clear glass" (Rev. 21:18). Pure gold is symbolic of the untarnished, enduring nature of eternal life in the celestial kingdom. Those who go there have been refined as gold—"For, behold, I have refined thee, I have chosen thee in the furnace of affliction" (1 Ne. 20:10). Clear glass symbolizes the purity and clarity of truth and doctrine always present with celestial beings. Joseph and Oliver recounted that in the Kirtland Temple "the veil was taken from our minds, and the eyes of our understanding were opened. We saw the Lord standing upon the breastwork of the pulpit, before us; and under his feet was a paved work of pure gold, in color like amber" (D&C 110:1–2). Those who gain eternal life will have the veil permanently removed so that all things will always be present before them.

- "And the foundations of the wall of the city were garnished with all manner of precious stones" (Rev. 21:19). Much insight is gained about the redeeming power of the Atonement from the introductory lines of a modern revelation wherein the Lord says, "Verily I say unto you, concerning your brethren who have been afflicted, and persecuted, and cast out from the land of their inheritance—I, the Lord, have suffered the affliction to come upon them, wherewith they have been afflicted, in consequence of their transgressions; Yet I will own them, and they shall be mine in that day when I shall come to make up my jewels" (D&C 101:1–3). All people of all nations of the earth are invited to come unto Christ and become His "jewels." The diversity and variety of the jewels seen by John represent well all nationalities, colors, hues, and backgrounds of God's children. All share a common lot—we transgress, and are thus afflicted. But through the miracle of the Atonement, we can become precious jewels bright and true. Just as jewels are specially shaped and polished to more brilliantly reflect light, so we, by our life experiences, are shaped and polished to more fully reflect the light and glory of eternal life. Once the gift of eternal life is bestowed and we become God's jewels, we will no longer be subject to tarnish or decay.

- "And the twelve gates were twelve pearls" (Rev. 21:21). How appropriate it is that the gates of the kingdom of God are symbolized by pearls. Just as a pearl is painstakingly produced in the oyster through a long process of irritation, pain, nourishment, and growth—so are we as God's children subjected to pain, affliction, and growth throughout our lives. As we faithfully endure, we gain spiritual maturity, luster, and brilliance. How profound is the instruction of our Savior when He taught that "again, the kingdom of heaven is like unto a merchant man, seeking goodly pearls. Who, when he had found one pearl of great price, went and sold all that he had, and bought it" (Matt. 13:45–46). If the richest men of the earth could come to know the true nature of God and of His promise to us of eternal life, they would recognize that their portfolios pale in comparison to the pearl of great price we call eternal life.

## GOD AND THE LAMB—THE TEMPLE AND THE LIGHT

In further description of celestial glory, John now explains that he "saw no temple therein: for the Lord God Almighty and the Lamb are the temple of it. And the city had no need of the sun, neither of the moon, to shine in it: for the glory of God did lighten it, and the Lamb is the light thereof. And the nations of them which are saved shall walk in the light of it: and the kings of the earth do bring their glory and honour into it. And the gates of it shall not be shut at all by day: for there shall be no night there. And they shall bring the glory and honour of the nations into it" (Rev. 21:22–26).

Let's consider why John saw no temple in the celestial kingdom. The purpose of the gathering of Israel is to bring us to the temple. The purpose of the temple is to bring us to Christ. John teaches that God and Christ are the temple. As we attain eternal life, we have, in the fullest sense possible, come unto Christ in His kingdom. Thus, the earthly temples have completed their purpose—we have come into the presence of God and henceforth and forever live in the temple of His glory.

The Prophet Joseph Smith taught, "What was the object of gathering . . . the people of God in any age of the world? . . . The main object was to build unto the Lord a house whereby He could reveal unto His people the ordinances of His house and the glories of His kingdom, and teach the people the way of salvation . . . It is for the same purpose that God gathers together His people in the last days, to build unto the Lord a house to prepare them for the ordinances and endowments, washings and annointings."[24] As previously stated by Brigham Young, the purpose of the endowment is to bring us into the celestial kingdom of God.

Let's consider why John saw that the celestial city had no need of the sun nor of the moon. The sun and the moon receive their light from the Son of God. He said, "Behold, I am the law, and the light. Look unto me, and endure to the end, and ye shall live; for unto him that endureth to the end will I give eternal life" (3 Ne. 15:9). The Light of Christ is the light that permeates the world from the power of Christ. This light bestows inspiration, enlightenment, and grace to all mankind. As we gain eternal life, we live in His presence and in His light forever. We will have no need of the secondary light sources of the sun and the moon—they will have served their purpose.

Our Heavenly Father delights in providing a celestial abode for His children. If we are true and faithful in all things and honorably meet the test of our earthly probation, we will most assuredly gain residence in the new heaven and new earth God provides for us. Once we gain the deed to this abode, we will never, ever lose the title. It will never fall into disrepair. It will remain forever clean, bright, and pure and serve forever as a peaceful and glorious refuge wherein we, with our families, will enjoy peace and happiness more than we can now even imagine.

# Chapter Twenty-Two
# Come, Lord Jesus

THERE IS AN ANNOYING BURDEN that weighs on and afflicts every mortal—the burden of pride. Although some are afflicted more than others, no one escapes the challenge and struggle of fighting against pride. The burden of pride clings tenaciously to us as it distracts us from our worship, persuades us to foolishness, mocks us, laughs at us, damages our relationships, and beckons us to evil. If we are not repentant and humble, pride grows and leads us into dangerous and terrible circumstances.

A classic talk I often hear quoted was given by President Ezra Taft Benson; he taught that the sin of pride is *universal* to all of us. We all carry this burden to one degree or another, and each day of our lives, we battle the vice of pride.

## THE PURE RIVER AND THE TREE OF LIFE
*How are we combating the evil of pride in our lives?* As we enter the last chapter of the Revelation of John, we come full circle in our study. We began our introduction of John's vision by reviewing the great vision of the tree of life given to Lehi and later to Nephi. In Lehi's vision, some caught hold of the iron rod, followed the path to the tree of life, and partook of the fruit thereof. Lehi then tells us that something tragic happened—they became ashamed of being among the righteous who were partaking of the fruit. What could possibly turn their eyes and hearts from something as glorious and sweet as the fruit of eternal life? They became afflicted by the great vice of pride.

Lehi tells us, as recorded by Nephi, "And I also cast my eyes round about, and beheld, on the other side of the river of water, a great and spacious building; and it stood as it were in the air, high above the earth. And it was filled with people, both old and young, both male and female; and their manner of dress was exceedingly fine; and they were in the attitude of mocking and pointing their fingers towards those who had come at and were partaking of the fruit. And after they had tasted of the fruit they were ashamed, because of those that were scoffing at them; and they fell away into forbidden paths and were lost" (1 Ne. 8:26–28). As Nephi is later shown his father's vision, he records, "And the large and spacious building, which thy father saw, is vain imaginations and the pride of the children of men. And a great and terrible gulf divideth them" (1 Ne. 12:18).

*Have we grown weary of living in the shadow of the great and spacious building?* I certainly have. I am weary of the constant daily grind of needing to sort out the true path we are to follow from all of the subtle—and often not so subtle—distractions thrown in our way by the laughing and mocking throng across the river. I have been saddened to see some give in to the voice of destructive popularity and social trend. My heart has been broken as I have witnessed hurt and sorrow come to some who have let go of the iron rod and have charted a new path toward the great and spacious building. On the other hand, my heart has been healed to see a return of precious souls to the rod of iron as they realize their need to be guided safely through the dark mists.

*Do we long for the day when the great and spacious building will be demolished and its foundation will be rooted up to make way for something good and glorious?* Although our current task is to faithfully endure the lifelong battle against pride, I certainly do look forward to the demolition of the great and spacious building.

John now gives us a glorious message of hope as he continues his description of celestial splendor in the day when the great and spacious building will be gone. He says, "And he shewed me a pure river of water of life, clear as crystal, proceeding out of the throne of God and of the Lamb. In the midst of the street of it, and on either side of the river, was there the tree of life, which bare twelve manner of fruits, and yielded her fruit every month: and the leaves of the tree were for the healing of the nations" (Rev. 22:1–2). It is instructive to recognize what John *does not* include here. The day of mortal probation has passed. Where are the mists of darkness, or temptations of the devil, that blind our way? They have, along with their purveyor, vanished into the dark pit. Where is the filthy river? It has dried up and no longer frightens or threatens us. Where is the great and spacious building? It is gone! What now stands in its place? The tree of life now stands on "either side of the river" with "water of life" or "living water" flowing from it to ever nourish the inhabitants of Zion. We may now turn in full circle and have no more view of the laughing and mocking crowd of the prideful world. They have had a change of address.

Out in the hinterlands of the Church Educational System area I supervise lives one of our early-morning seminary teachers. She and her husband and children are in the business of growing cranberries. I have toured this fascinating operation on a few occasions. One day as we were riding around the cranberry beds, to my surprise we came upon a large wolf standing up on the bank of one of the bogs. As we got closer, I realized that the joke was on me: the wolf was not real, but a decoy—it was the husband's little prank on his visitors. He then told me—not in jest—that they *do* have a very active wolf pack in the area. He informed me that when their children were small, they had to cautiously protect them from the wolves.

So it is in our world—we must help protect our loved ones from the "wolf pack" congregated in the great and spacious building. We must help them learn and feel the divine truth that if they get on the path and firmly grasp the rod of iron, they will be protected and safely guided to the tree of life. We must try to help them understand that if they gain access to the fruit of the tree—and then stay there—the day will come when they will no longer need to contend with those of the great and spacious building. If we are willing, humble, and diligent, we most assuredly will dwell where we have no more fear nor worry about the pride of the world.

## No More Curse

*How do we imagine the abundance of the celestial kingdom?* I have heard my mother, who as I've mentioned before was a child of the Great Depression, tell of Christmastime, when each child received a unique and precious gift—a single orange. Such scarcity may be hard for many of us to imagine because we can purchase oranges and a multitude of other fruits and foodstuffs from around the world year round in our grocery stores.

The celestial world is a world of abundance. John saw that the tree of life bore "twelve manner of fruits, and yielded her fruit every month: and the leaves of the tree were for the healing of the nations. And there shall be no more curse: but the throne of God and of the Lamb shall be in it; and his servants shall serve him" (Rev. 22:2–3).

The exciting knowledge that there "shall be no more curse" certainly has multiple physical and spiritual applications. We may accurately imagine the celestial sphere by imagining the elimination of all manmade pollution and desecration of our planet. There will be no more toxic waste, ravaged aquifers, smog-filled skies, polluted waters, or rusting and disintegrating infrastructure. We may also imagine everything that is good and of God being transformed and glorified. Undoubtedly we will experience brighter colors, sweeter and more fragrant smells, fresher air, more beautiful sounds—with all things accentuated to the positive beyond our most noble imagination. The millennial event of the Dead Sea being healed by the pure water flowing from the house of the Lord will be just a sneak preview of the expansive transformation that will bring our earth into its celestial state of glory. We will enjoy our oranges—and every other delicious blessing from God—always and forever in great and eternal abundance.

Spiritually, let us imagine the world *without* Satan and his abode—the great and spacious building. John's vision that the "leaves of the tree were for the healing of the nations" speaks of peace and of brotherhood beyond comparison to anything we now know. We may look at the millennial condition that occurs by the changing of "swords into plowshares, and . . . spears into pruninghooks: nation shall not lift up sword against nation, neither shall they learn war any more" (Isa. 2:4) as a preview of the wholesale transformation of the souls of those who attain celestial glory. Not only will there be no more war, but war will not even be in our realm of desire or possibility. Since there is no more pride of the world, we would not have anything to even consider fighting about. All friendships and bonds we have cultivated throughout our premortal, mortal, and millennial lifetimes will now blossom and perpetuate into eternal union. We are taught that "that same sociality which exists among us here will exist among us there, only it will be coupled with eternal glory" (D&C 130:2).

We began this book by reviewing the knowledge that to come unto the tree of life is actually to come unto Christ. The eternal, glorious expanse of the celestial kingdom is made possible by the provision of the eternal and perfect Atonement of Christ. His Atonement effects the healing of the nations. Whatever he touches with the power of His Atonement *lives*. If we allow Him to touch our broken and troubled hearts, they will live. If we allow Him to touch our families, they will live. Through Christ, the Father of Our salvation, we will live in celestial glory and splendor forever. We will have eternal communion with our Lord and Savior and access to all of the wonderful blessings He has created and provided for those who love and serve Him.

## DIVINE INVESTITURE OF AUTHORITY

As John's vision continues, we have an illustration of the principle of divine investiture of authority. Simply stated, our Heavenly Father delegates or invests His divine authority to His Son, Jesus Christ, who in turn speaks and acts for the Father as though He *were* the Father. Christ, in turn, invests authority in special witnesses to speak and act for Him.

In the Revelation, John is told, "Behold, I come quickly: blessed is he that keepeth the sayings of the prophecy of this book" (Rev. 22:7). Clearly, this is a statement of Christ referring to His own Second Coming. However, it is not being delivered by Christ—but rather by His angel, who is speaking and acting in first person as though he *were* Christ. The angel does this because of the divine investiture of authority he has been granted by Christ. The angel has spoken so well and delivered such a powerful message that John mistakes him for Christ and begins to fall down and worship him: "And I John saw these things, and heard them. And when I had heard and seen, I fell down to worship before the feet of the angel which shewed me these things" (Rev. 22:8).

My guess is that John well understood this principle but temporarily got caught up in the power of the moment in acting on his feelings of awe for the Savior. The angel now takes time to correct John's misperception that he is the Savior: "Then saith he unto me, See thou do it not: for I am thy fellowservant, and of thy brethren the prophets, and of them which keep the sayings of this book: worship God" (Rev. 22:9). Once the principle is reviewed and John remembers, then the angel continues representing Christ in first person: "And behold, I come quickly; and my reward is with me, to give every man according as his work shall be. I am Alpha and Omega, the beginning and the end, the first and the last" (Rev. 22:12–13).

## RIGHTEOUS STILL

*Are we committed to a lifetime of keeping our gospel covenants? Do we have as our goal to be righteous still in ten or one hundred or one thousand years from now?* My wife and I met—not by chance but by arrangement—in the Chicago Illinois Temple. At the time of our meeting, she lived in the Midwest and I lived in the West. We dated twice—we each flew one time to the other's turf. We then became engaged to be married. We met in mid-December and were married four months later in mid-April in the temple where we met.

Some have marveled at our daring. It is really not so difficult to understand—we simply had each lived enough of life that we had discovered what we were looking for. As we enjoyed our two dates, we discovered in our conversation and association that we were each looking for a companion who would be "steadfast, and immovable in keeping the commandments of God" (1 Ne. 2:10). *Steadfast and immovable* became our watchwords. We certainly recognize our mortality and potential for sin, but our daily prayer is that we may continue to keep our covenants throughout the time of our mortal probation. Our intent is to *still* be keeping our covenants throughout the balance of our lives.

John sees in his vision the final conclusion of the judgment of God: "He that is unjust, let him be unjust *still*: and he which is filthy, let him be filthy *still*: and he that is righteous, let him be righteous *still*: and he that is holy, let him be holy *still*. . . . Blessed are they that do his commandments, that they may have right to the tree of life, and may enter in through the gates into the city" (Rev. 22:11, 14; emphasis added).

Consider the key word *still*—implying, for example, "they are *still* righteous, after all of this time" or "they *still* trust God and live

His gospel after all of their trials." This doctrine is so beautiful and so consistent with the major theme taught throughout the Revelation of John: entrance into the celestial kingdom of God is not dependent on monetary wealth or social status or leadership position. Attaining exaltation depends on being steadfast and immovable in keeping the commandments of God.

It's inspiring how Nephi concluded his ministry after living a long and faithful life. He didn't expound some deep and mysterious thing. Instead, he reviewed the first principles and ordinances of the gospel: faith in Jesus Christ, repentance, baptism, and receiving the Holy Ghost. He then gave us the sure formula to guarantee our exaltation: "Wherefore, ye must press forward with a steadfastness in Christ, having a perfect brightness of hope, and a love of God and of all men. Wherefore, if ye shall press forward, feasting upon the word of Christ, and endure to the end, behold, thus saith the Father: *Ye shall have eternal life*" (2 Ne. 31:20; emphasis added).

We don't have to become perfect in mortality to gain eternal life. We do need to embrace the principles and ordinances of salvation and chart our course to celestial glory. Once we have charted such a course, we need to be steadfast and immovable in pressing forward on that path. We will have the joy and excitement of learning more and more as we depart this life. In our next estate, we will not have to worry about losing our way—if we have made sure our way here. If we have walked the true path, our salvation is made sure.

Life is not so complicated. We just need to become righteous and worthy. We need to *still* be righteous and worthy next week and next year and every week and every year until the end of our mortal probation. If we are *still* righteous when we die, we will have eternal life—guaranteed! That is sweet and delicious doctrine!

## ADD UNTO—TAKE AWAY FROM

At the conclusion of the Revelation, the Lord adds some words of warning about those who would tamper with the revealed word of God. He says, "For I testify unto every man that heareth the words of the prophecy of this book, If any man shall add unto these things, God shall add unto him the plagues that are written in this book: And if any man shall take away from the words of the book of this prophecy, God shall take away his part out of the book of life, and out of the holy city, and from the things which are written in this book" (Rev. 22:18–19).

Much misunderstanding has arisen from this verse. Some have gone so far as to suggest that this verse at the end of the Bible places a seal—not only on the Bible, but on scriptural canon. Unfortunately, this misperception has been a stumbling block to many in accepting continuing revelation and the continually expanding canon of the Lord.

A few points should be considered in addressing the thought that this verse places a closing seal on the Bible. First of all, when John wrote these words, there *was* no Bible—it had not yet been compiled. Second, just because the book of Revelation was placed at the end of the New Testament when the New Testament was compiled offers no proof that it was the last book written. Many scholars, for example, believe that John wrote the Gospel of John *after* he wrote what we know as the book of Revelation.

Moses made a similar comment to the verse just quoted from the Revelation: "Ye shall not add unto the word which I command you, neither shall ye diminish ought from it, that ye may keep the commandments of the Lord your God which I command you" (Deut. 4:2). He later said, "What thing soever I command you, observe to do it: thou shalt not add thereto, nor diminish from it" (Deut. 12:32). If we were to apply the same misinterpretation to these verses from Moses that people sometimes apply to the Revelation verse, there would be no Bible or printed scripture after the time of Moses. The only logical and sane interpretation of this matter is that John had great reverence and respect for the glorious vision he was receiving, so he placed a protective warning on it.

The fact that the Lord would warn of those who would take away from the words of the book is in itself evidence that some tampering was already occurring or that it would shortly occur. We learn from the vision of Nephi that tampering with the Bible would occur. Prophesying of the writings of the Bible, he says, "And after they go forth by the hand of the twelve apostles of the Lamb, from the Jews unto the Gentiles, thou seest the formation of that great and abominable church, which is most abominable above all other churches; for behold, they have taken away from the gospel of the Lamb many parts which are plain and most precious; and also many covenants of the Lord have they taken away" (1 Ne. 13:26).

Nephi, in his vision, is then given the reassuring and welcome knowledge that the plain and precious truths taken from the Bible will not be gone forever but will be restored: "I beheld other books, which came forth by the power of the Lamb . . . these . . . shall establish the truth of the first, which are of the twelve apostles of the Lamb, and shall make known the plain and precious things which have been taken away from them" (1 Ne. 13:39–40).

Gratefully, we have the Book of Mormon, the Joseph Smith Translation of the Bible, the Doctrine and Covenants, the Pearl of Great Price, and the continuing words of our living prophets to guide and direct us throughout the entire span of the earth's temporal existence. What great blessings would be denied mankind had the word of the Lord ceased at the conclusion of the Revelation of John.

## COME, LORD JESUS!

*Are we receptive to the Savior's gracious invitation to come unto Him?* Consider the word *come*. It's not a word of coercion but one of gracious invitation. John records, "And the Spirit and the bride say, *Come*. And let him that heareth say, *Come*. And let him that is athirst *come*. And whosoever will, let him take the water of life freely. . . . He which testifieth these things saith, Surely, I *come* quickly. Amen. Even so, *come*, Lord Jesus" (Rev. 22:17, 20; emphasis added).

The sweet invitation of our Savior unto us is, "Come unto me, all ye that labour and are heavy laden, and I will give you rest" (Matt. 11:28). His love for us is so profound and His commitment to us so deep and abiding that He stands with His merciful arms always open to receive all who will humble themselves and come unto Him and receive of His gift. He reminds us that His redemption is available, with no prerequisite of worldly status—"let him take the water of life *freely*."

The price of salvation is not measured in the accounts and ledgers of our fallen world but in the commitment and conversion "written not with ink, but with the Spirit of the living God; not in tables of stone, but in fleshy tables of the heart" (2 Cor. 3:3). Those who accept of His invitation to prepare their hearts for conversion and ultimate eternal life anxiously await the day of His coming. Such is the joyful anticipation of those prepared for the coming of the Savior—the five wise virgins who have spent their lifetimes filling and trimming their lamps are now ready for marriage to the Savior of the world. The consuming desire of their hearts is, *Come, Lord Jesus.*

It is awe-inspiring to ponder these few verses in which John concludes his mighty vision. He has sacrificed and served for his extended lifetime as a special witness of Christ. He has had the great privilege of seeing this comprehensive vision of the span of the earth's existence—particularly of the second advent of Christ and of His millennial reign and His ultimate role in granting eternal life to His children. Christ has just reminded John once again that He is on His way—"Surely, I come quickly." The concise yet profound and consuming wish of John's righteous heart at this announcement is, *Come, Lord Jesus.*

In our mortal world where the downward spiral of evil will continue to expand and gather speed, the wicked will fear the day of judgment and wish that even "the mountains and rocks, Fall on us, and hide us from the face of him that sitteth on the throne" (Rev. 6:16). As they so tremble and quake, the vast multitude of righteous and faithful Saints will echo the wish of their righteous hearts: *Come, Lord Jesus.*

This invitation—Come, Lord Jesus—is as sweet music to the ears and souls of the righteous. It is a message very deeply rooted in our theology and in our worship service. It is the prayer of the righteous that our Savior will come. As the Lord said to Emma Smith, "For my soul delighteth in the song of the heart; yea, the song of the righteous is a prayer unto me, and it shall be answered with a blessing upon their heads" (D&C 25:12).

## Grace Be with You

*How much understanding of and appreciation for the Lord's grace do we possess?* As members of the Church, we are privileged to receive apostolic blessings. Although most do not receive these blessings individually, the strength and power of such blessings is no less personal and individual. Our Heavenly Father has the power and capacity to multiply the harvest of an apostolic blessing into the lives and hearts of individuals. These blessings often begin when an Apostle or prophet says something like, "As a special witness of Jesus Christ, I desire to invoke His blessing upon you." Such sweet introductions to apostolic blessings are then followed by pronouncements of peace, healing, and comfort. We are often blessed that we will have the strength and courage to endure our heartaches and trials. One of the great benefits of being a member of this Church is to fall under the healing umbrella of the Apostles' blessing of us. This healing is open to all.

John now beautifully frames his vision in matching bookends of the profound and comforting doctrine of grace. At the beginning he said, "Grace be unto you, and peace, from him which is, and which was, and which is to come" (Rev. 1:4). As John now closes this hopeful vision, he places his second bookend as his *apostolic blessing* for us. It is short and direct—and very profound. He simply says, "The grace of our Lord Jesus Christ be with you all. Amen" (Rev. 22:21).

This enabling grace allows us to move forward through the hardships and heartaches of our lives. This gift of grace helps us to achieve what we could not do on our own. That is the message of our Lord and Savior to us through John the Revelator and through all of His special witnesses of all dispensations—that if we do our very best, He will do the rest. Through His enabling grace and tender mercy, we may lay claim upon eternal life.

What a beautiful and appropriate way for John to conclude his vision—with his apostolic blessing and promise for the Lord's grace to be with us!

# Epilogue

THE DESIRE OF MY HEART is simple as I now conclude my writing about the Revelation of John. I began by suggesting the themes of hope, healing, peace, and triumph. I have attempted to identify these themes throughout the Revelation of John. It is my desire that as you have read these pages, you have found these inspiring themes interwoven amidst the battles, plagues, promises, and blessings bestowed upon the earth.

My greater desire, however, is that you *personally*—whoever you are and wherever you may be called to wander in your earthly sojourn—may have these blessings of hope, healing, peace, and triumph as your constant and eternal traveling companions.

May you always be blessed with "the *hope* of a glorious resurrection, through the grace of God the Father and his Only Begotten Son, Jesus Christ" (D&C 138:14; emphasis added).

May all of the aches of your heart, whatever their cause, be healed, and may the promise be yours that "unto you that fear my name, shall the Son of Righteousness arise with *healing* in his wings; and ye shall go forth and grow up as calves in the stall" (3 Ne. 25:2; emphasis added).

May you have fulfillment in your life of the Savior's promise that "*peace* I leave with you, my *peace* I give unto you: not as the world giveth, give I unto you. Let not your heart be troubled, neither let it be afraid" (John 14:27; emphasis added).

May you have daily and ultimate victory over the enemies of righteousness with which you may be confronted. May you realize the same blessings promised the Prophet Joseph: "My son, peace be unto thy soul; thine adversity and thine afflictions shall be but a small moment; And then, if thou endure it well, God shall exalt thee on high; thou shalt *triumph* over all thy foes" (D&C 121:7–8; emphasis added).

May the "grace of our Lord Jesus Christ be with you all. Amen" (Rev. 22:21).

# Endnotes

1 *The American Heritage Dictionary of the English Language, 4th ed.* (Houghton Mifflin Company, 2004) http://dictionary.reference. com/browse/orchestrate.

2 David B. Guralnik, *Webster's New World Dictionary of the American Language* (Englewood Cliffs, New Jersey: World-Publishing, 1970), 1000.

3 Joseph Smith, Jr., *History of the Church of Jesus Christ of Latter-day Saints,* B.H. Roberts, ed. (Salt Lake City: The Church of Jesus Christ of Latter-day Saints, 1909), 5:401.

4 Stuart Hample and Eric Marshall, *Children's Letters to God* (New York: Workman Publishing, 1991).

5 *History of the Church,* 4:209.

6 The First Presidency of the Church, "The Origin of Man," *Improvement Era,* Nov. 1909, 81.

7 *History of the Church,* 2:71.

8 Ronald D. John, "A Sparrow in the Tabernacle," *Ensign,* June 1989, 24.

9 David B. Guralnik, *Webster's New World Dictionary of the American Language* (Englewood Cliffs, New Jersey: World-Publishing, 1970), 1464.

10 Church Educational System, The Church of Jesus Christ of Latter-day Saints, *New Testament Teacher Outline,* 1984. Cited from *Messiah* inside album cover, notes by Jay Welch; reprinted from album M2S 607 by permission of CBS Masterworks.

11 James L. Ferrell, *The Peacegiver* (Salt Lake City: Deseret Book Company, 2004), 33.

12 Carl Sagan, *Pale Blue Dot: A Vision of the Human Future in Space*

(New York: Random House,1994), 50.

13 *History of the Church,* 1:176.

14 *History of the Church,* 2:123.

15 Clive Staples Lewis, *The Problem of Pain* (San Francisco: HarperSanFrancisco, 2001), 126.

16 *History of the Church,* 6:566.

17 "The Second Coming: Gardener," media presentation prepared by the Church Educational System (Salt Lake City: The Church of Jesus Christ of Latter-day Saints, 2003).

18 Philip Smucker, "Iraq builds 'Mother of all Battles' mosque in praise of Saddam," *Telegraph News, UK,* July 29, 2001.

19 Lorenzo Snow, Address presented at the 71st Semi-Annual General Conference of The Church of Jesus Christ of Latter-Day Saints from the Tabernacle on Temple Square, Salt Lake City, Utah, October 5, 1900.

20 James E. Faust, "The Light in Their Eyes," *Ensign,* Nov. 2005, 5.

21 Leroi C. Snow, "Devotion to Divine Inspiration,"*Improvement Era,* June 1919, 658–59.

22 Clive Staples Lewis, *Mere Christianity* (New York: Macmillan, 1960), 174.

23 *Journal of Discourses,* 2:31.

24 *History of the Church,* 5:423–24.

# About the Author

Reg Christensen and his wife, Carol, live in Waunakee, Wisconsin. They are the parents of seven and grandparents of eight. Reg serves as the Church Educational System coordinator for the Green Bay, Madison, and Wausau Wisconsin stakes and as director of the Institute of Religion adjacent to the University of Wisconsin in Madison. He began his CES career in Lehi, Utah, where he taught released-time seminary for twenty-three years. Reg has enjoyed a lifetime of Church service as a missionary, Young Men president, bishopric counselor, high councilor, stake executive secretary, branch president, bishop, high priest group leader, ward clerk, and ward seminary teacher. He enjoys reading, gardening, traveling, exploring nature, bird watching, and being with family and friends.